THE REVENUE IMPERATIVE: THE UNION'S FINANCIAL POLICIES DURING THE AMERICAN CIVIL WAR

FINANCIAL HISTORY

Series Editor: Robert E. Wright

THE REVENUE IMPERATIVE: THE UNION'S FINANCIAL POLICIES DURING THE AMERICAN CIVIL WAR

BY

Jane Flaherty

Routledge
Taylor & Francis Group

LONDON AND NEW YORK

First published 2009 by Pickering & Chatto (Publishers) Limited

Published 2016 by Routledge
2 Park Square, Milton Park, Abingdon, Oxfordshire OX14 4RN
711 Third Avenue, New York, NY 10017, USA

First issued in paperback 2015

Routledge is an imprint of the Taylor & Francis Group, an informa business

BRITISH LIBRARY CATALOGUING IN PUBLICATION DATA
Flaherty, Jane
The revenue imperative: the Union's financial policies during the American Civil War. – (Financial history)
1. Finance, Public – United States – History – 1861–1875 2. United States – History – Civil War, 1861–1865 – Economic aspects 3. United States – History – Civil War,
1861–1865 – Finance
I. Title
336.7'3'09034

ISBN-13: 978-1-138-66352-7 (pbk)
ISBN-13: 978-1-8519-6898-5 (hbk)

Typeset by Pickering & Chatto (Publishers) Limited

CONTENTS

LIST OF TABLES AND GRAPHS

ACKNOWLEDGEMENTS

I would like to thank Michael Middeke and Mirabelle Boateng at Pickering and Chatto for their patience. Robert E. Wright has been a continued source encouragement – I appreciate all the assistance he has given me. This project began as a dissertation completed under the supervision of Harold C. Livesay, and the members of my committee, Thomas R. Dunlap, Henry C. Schmidt, and Pamela Matthews. All provided helpful comments and suggestions, and I appreciate their guidance and enthusiasm for this project. I wish to give special thanks to Harold Livesay whose insights and editorial skills helped me tremendously. He is as fine a friend as he is a scholar. Other individuals who commented on parts of this work include: Joseph G. Dawson, April Hatfield, Troy Bickham, of Texas A&M University, and James L. Huston of Oklahoma State University. I also thank the four unanimous reviewers who have commented on different portions of this manuscript. All these scholars have generously shared their expertise, posed challenging questions, and helped me refine my argument. *Civil War History* and Kent State University Press have given me permission to publish a version of a "The Exhausted Condition of the Treasury on the Eve of the Civil War," which appears in *Civil War History*, March 2009, as Chapter Two in this volume.

The Department of History at Texas A&M University has generously supported my research. I would also like to thank the Glasscock Center for Humanities Research and the College of Liberal Arts at Texas A&M University for the fellowships and travel support they have given me. James Rosenheim, director of the Glasscock Center, has created a vigorous intellectual environment that contributed greatly to this project. I thank Juwairia Zubair, William Lynch, and Clare Lynch for their research assistance and help in preparing this manuscript. I appreciate the assistance from librarians at the National Archives and Library of Congress. I have also been very fortunate to work with the librarians at the Sterling C. Evans library at Texas A&M University, whose warm greetings and vigilance has been a great asset to me. In particular, I'd like to thank Joel Kitchens and Bill Page for their assistance. I would also like to thank the citizens of the state of Texas who have supported my work through their contributions to Texas A&M University.

Many thanks to my friends, both near and far, who have been a source of great comfort during this phase of my life. In particular, I appreciate support and good cheer from Bill and Nancy Connell. Finally, I wish to express my gratitude to my parents who have done so much for me - their love and encouragement has sustained me. Finally, I thank my children Clare, Finn, and Patrick whom I love dearly.

To William and Kathleen Flaherty and Clare, Finn
and Patrick Lynch with love and gratitude

INTRODUCTION

This book provides an overview of the Union financial policies during the American Civil War. While other notable works have analysed aspects of the Union finances this volume addresses the Union government's wartime fiscal policies as a whole. The title of this book indicates my primary thesis. I propose that the revenue imperative, the attempt to keep pace with the burgeoning expenses of the war, governed the Union's financial strategy more than their pre-war ideology or attempts to appease special interests, as other historians have argued.[1] Preserving the nation placed insurmountable strains on the antebellum organization of the government, resulting in a fundamental restructuring of the American financial system. Although this change came about incidentally, rather than by design, I believe this financial transformation does constitute a critical 'watershed' in American economic history.[2] The fiscal policies developed to keep the Union forces fed, clothed and armed became the 'father of what followed', and laid the groundwork for the intensive financial dislocations that manifested later in the nineteenth century.[3]

A close examination of the internal revenue measures inaugurated during the war clarifies my proposition. Throughout the antebellum period, the national government relied overwhelmingly on indirect taxes as its primary source of revenue. These 'duties, imposts, and excises', were collected as tariff revenue at ports throughout the United States. Because of this reliance on indirect taxes, the federal government became a less tangible force in the economic lives of most Americans. Conversely, direct taxes on real and personal property, the rates of which were determined by assessment, became a revenue method employed primarily by state and local governments. Only during the Quasi-War of the late eighteenth century, or the war against Great Britain that began in 1812, did Congress resort to collecting direct taxes. This financial structure fit neatly into the 'fiscal federalism' that evolved during the decades before the Civil War.

When historians of the United States contemplate federalism, they generally focus on how this governing structure allowed the 'peculiar institution' of slavery to develop, and inevitably, rend the nation. In this book, I argue that this fiscal federalism played an important role in the determining Union financial policy.

For over a century, and most recently by Robin Einhorn, scholars have focused on the 'centrality of slavery to taxation'.[4] Slavery became the backbone of the American economy in the antebellum era; it represented the most important 'economic interest' in the country until the passage of the Thirteenth Amendment. This weight alone made slavery a key aspect in the government's economic policy. While not denying that slavery affected the development of national fiscal structure, I suggest instead that balancing the reach between state and national authority played a more important role in shaping national tax policy until the advent of Civil War. Policies enacted during the war sought to overcome the constraints of fiscal federalism, not to fulfill a Republican desire to nationalize the American economy. Regarding fiscal policy, Republicans sought to generate enough funds to restore the nation. The dire need for revenue during the American Civil War compelled an expansion of the 'power of the purse' beyond the constraints imposed by this antebellum structure. Because Congress had depended on customs receipts as its primary source of revenue for four decades, lawmakers had few ready options for meeting the tremendous costs of civil war.

In developing these revenue measures, the Republicans borrowed from the past rather than developing innovative new policies. The resulting legislation relied heavily on precedent. However, because the nation had never endured such a trauma, and the needs of the Lincoln administration far outpaced those of its predecessors, the remedies of the past could not cure the ills of a nation spending hundreds of millions of dollars fighting a war against itself. These realities led to many of the changes in policy that have since become a fundamental part of the American economic life: paying income and excise taxes, national control over bank policy, and a standard, periodically reliable, United States currency. These changes did not occur because of the Whiggish intentions of the dominant Republican Party, but rather as a desperate attempt to keep pace with the burgeoning expenses of a war.

Finally, in erecting this new revenue system for the nation, the Republicans did not impose a regressive internal revenue system on citizens. Instead, the duties on manufacturers emerged as the primary source of wartime internal taxes. Because manufacturers bore the initial burden of these taxes, they successfully lobbied Congress for increased protection from foreign competition. This protectionism continued through the late nineteenth century.

By examining these revenue measures, one can see that the fiscal policies adopted by the new Republican administration represented an attempt to cope with a financial crisis, rather than impart a particular preconceived agenda. The lawmakers reacted with more speed than deliberation, and often sacrificed their principles to provide the means to prosecute the war and reunite the nation. Once peace returned, the question of how to restructure this hastily-created tax structure, and whether to 'sink' the debt or cut revenues, vexed lawmakers. The traditional abhorrence to government debt conflicted with calls to relieve Americans, both from the Union and former Confederate states, from the tax burden that arose during the conflict. However, the expansion of the fiscal powers of the national government grew beyond the established bounds of the antebellum tradition and would never return to the established limits. While the national government again relied primarily on customs duties as its primary source of revenue after the war, the introduction of permanent, internal taxation rendered obsolete the traditional revenue boundaries. This resulted in a more regressive and protectionist government revenue system than ever promoted before the war. I argue that this occurred more from the contingencies of war than the designs of men.

Pragmatism played a significant role in shaping economic policy. In matters of political economy, American leaders of different political leanings repeatedly displayed an extraordinary pragmatism. Historians Carolyn Webber and Aaron Wildvaskyin observed, 'Americans are the most unideological people' who 'practice more than they preach.'[5] The development of American fiscal policy remained a fine balance between high ideals and grounded practicality. This began in the colonial era, when everything from playing cards, scraps of paper and wampum passed as currency. The fiscal system created in the early Republic demonstrates this pragmatism. A 'sharp dichotomy between theory and practice' existed in American economic policy, Daniel Elazar noted. When faced with difficult choices, lawmakers resorted to practical solutions. I do not dispute the commanding literature that shows ideology played a significant role in the development of the American government, however this study does suggest that in the realm of fiscal policy, the 'dominance of pragmatism', often overwhelmed the ideological goals of political leaders.[6]

The Republican leaders who drafted the fiscal legislation that financed the war were forced to make a series of capitulations as they crafted their measures. While governor of Ohio, Salmon P. Chase, the first Secretary of the Treasury during the war, modified his well-publicized enthusiasm for hard currency and free trade. Both times he described his change of heart as a 'practical' acceptance of a situation that would endure for 'an indefinite period'.[7] During the war, Chase oversaw the adoption of Greenbacks as a legal paper currency, earning him the nickname 'Old Greenbacks', although throughout his political life, he had distained 'soft currency' 'Chase had resorted to greenback currency ... as a matter of necessity in a unique situation [although] he had always been a hard-money man', concluded John Niven, his recent biographer. He turned to greenbacks solely as a 'wartime expedient'. Similarly, Hugh McCulloch first visited Washington DC in 1862 in his capacity as a bank president to lobby against the National Bank bill introduced by Chase. A year later, he accepted the nomination for the position of comptroller of the currency, with administrative duties over the very system he journeyed to Washington to oppose. 'My opinion in regard to the establishment of a national banking system underwent a change', he admitted later.[8]

In both instances, these Civil War leaders faced enormous challenges and ceded their principles to the circumstances. The economic policies crafted during this period were dictated less by Republican determinism or ideology than by the exogenous forces of war. These demands compelled the Republican lawmakers to pass legislation that they would never have considered previously. And they had to do so hastily. The historical literature places too much emphasis on how Republicans directed the course of the war with deliberation and preconceived ideals. Instead, the war directed the policies. The crisis that rent the nation soon after the Republicans took office played a far more significant role in the development of their fiscal policy than the predisposition of the party leaders.

The tax policy crafted during the war must also be appreciated as a series of capitulations, rather than the fulfilment of a party's economic determinism. Gavin Wright once observed that, '... in many areas, Republicans were pressured by events into accepting policies they would otherwise not have dreamed of adopting'.[9] The Republicans enacted legislation to cope with the fiscal pressures created by the war, not to fulfill their antebellum economic agenda. They acted less like captains charting a new economic course than sailors clinging to the ships' steering wheel hoping to survive the storm. To endure this storm, the Republicans turned to precedent rather than create innovative new policies.

Historiographical Overview

Whenever scholars speak of 'revolutionary' changes that occurred during the Civil War era, the spectres of Charles and Mary Beard arise. The Beards have left a legacy in the historical profession that few can match, and most (including me) respect. They believed that economic considerations provided the primary motivation in shaping American history. As part of their continued explorations of the influence wielded by economic interests, the Beards declared that the Civil War represented a 'Second American Revolution' in which the 'capitalists, laborers, and farmers of the North and West drove from power in the national government the planting aristocracy of the South'.[10] Louis Hacker refined the Beards' ideas in 1940. The resulting 'Beard–Hacker' thesis identified the economic determinism of the industrial North as the force that drove the Civil War legislative agenda and the subsequent post-war settlement. The Republican Party, established in 1854 and triumphant in the presidential election of 1860, represented the interests of this rising order. Republicans 'captured the state' and used it as an instrument to secure the 'progress of industrial capitalism', Hacker declared[11]

Identifying the economic determinism of northern 'interests' as the source for the profound changes the nation underwent during the war distinguishes the Beardian interpretation.[12] The Beard–Hacker thesis has permeated the literature on economic change in the Civil War era. So thoroughly, in fact, that subsequent writers who find this argument 'colorful, but theoretically unsatisfying', nevertheless mimic much of the language and theses presented by the Beards and Hacker. Richard Bensel noted that, 'The American state was captured by the Republican Party'.[13] Thus, the 'antebellum northern agenda for the political economy was impressed upon the American state with little compromise or mediation'. This resulted in the South becoming 'systematically impoverished' while the 'clientele' of the Republican Party, the 'finance capitalists' triumphed.[14]

Although the concept of the Civil War as a revolution is linked most closely to the Beards, defining the era as a 'revolutionary' period predates their scholarship. As James McPherson has demonstrated, the men in blue and grey, soldiers, legislators and presidents, understood that they struggled to redefine the meaning of republicanism and liberty in American society. The main actors themselves, particularly the Radical Republicans, referred to the Civil War era as a 'revolution'.[15] Since the advent of the new social history, writers focusing on the Civil War period concur with Eric Foner that the emancipation of four million slaves represents the 'most revolutionary aspect of the period'.[16] Here lies the crux of the problem many scholars have with the Beards – they underestimated the impact of slavery, and the subsequent struggles of the freedmen, in their examination of the era. They claimed the origins of the war came 'merely by the accidents of climate, soil, and geography', reflecting their Progressive-era inattentiveness to the importance of race in American history.[17] The Beards, and later Hacker, also erred in focusing on northern expansion, rather than the southern economic diminution. As Stanley Engerman and J. Matthew Gallman recently noted, 'The most dramatic changes occurred within the southern states, and the post-bellum southern economy differed more dramatically from that of the antebellum years than did the Northern.'[18] The Beards suggested that northern intrigues, rather than the war and emancipation, spurred this declension. Thus, to concur with the Beards, as I do, that a revolution occurred in the United States between 1860 and 1877, does not necessarily wed one to the 'Beardian interpretation'. However, embracing economic determinism as the key to understanding this 'social cataclysm' does.

In rejecting the premise that northern industry benefited directly from the war, economic historians, beginning in 1961, launched a sustained challenge to the belief that the Civil War sparked an industrial revolution and economic transformation.[19] These scholars have demonstrated instead that a 'tremendous thrust' in manufacturing production occurred before the war.[20] Rather than an impetus to industrialization, the war represented a 'costly and bitter interruption' to the dynamic economic expansion that occurred during the antebellum era.[21] 'Manufacturing output' in Philadelphia, for example, fell by 15 per cent during the war.[22] The significance of emancipation as an economic event has led to a renewed interest in the Beardian concept of the 'revolutionary' aspects of the era; however one may consider this scholarship more an embrace of a 'Stevensian' than 'Beardian' interpretation of the Civil War, since it was Thaddeus Stevens (R., PA) who never lost sight of the social and economic importance of slavery in American society.[23]

In another challenge to the Beards' take on the period, recent scholarship has shown that the divergence between North and South in antebellum economic development had more to do with the investment in slaves and attitudes toward slavery than southern hostility to industry.[24] Closer examinations of economic activity during the war have led to another challenge to the Beardian interpretation. Stuart D. Brandes and Mark Wilson demonstrated that the industrialists might not have nefariously influenced the political leaders as much as the Beardian interpretation suggests. In *Warhogs*, a comprehensive history of war profiteering in the United States, Brandes shows that northern suppliers of the Union army did not engage in 'unmitigated greed'. Instead the war represented 'a mixed record of waste and efficiency, of profit and loss, of fraud and sacrifice'. Similarly, Wilson revealed that, 'elected Republican Party officials ended up having surprising little direct control over the North's military economy during the Civil War. Instead veteran military officers managed the national war economy that emerged by early 1862'.[25] With regard to economic policy, Elizabeth Lee Thompson's penetrating study of the Bankruptcy Act of 1867 found that piece of Republican legislation actually 'buttressed the economic security of white southern men', and allowed this elite to 'resuscitate themselves economically' after the war. Rather than spawning the 'revolution', this overtly Republican economic legislation facilitated the counter-revolution.[26]

While this literature has weakened the bite of the Beards' analysis, admirable scholars such as Marc Egnal, still conclude the Beards were 'more right than their critics'.[27] Why? Because the social, political, and (I argue here) financial landscape of the country did change during the course of the war. Although scholars have backtracked from the primacy of the influence of economic interests on the impact of the war, many continue to accept the predominance of determinism, or the implicit belief that the changes wrought by the war originated in the motives or ideology of the Republican Party (particularly the dominant Whig element within the party). The Beards described the fighting itself as a 'fleeting incident … the physical combat that punctuated the conflict merely hastened the inevitable'. Predestined by the victory of the Republican Party in the 1860 election, this 'inevitable' subjugation of the South would have occurred even without the war.[28]

Scholars intrigued by the resonance of the Republican Party's pre-war ideology have discounted the economic motivations at the heart of the Beard–Hacker approach, but instead embraced an ideological determinism. Where the Beards depicted economic motivations as the impetus for change, others see the free labour ideology as the primary determinant in shaping wartime legislation. 'Party members' faith in individual labor *made* them pass sweeping laws to enable workers to prosper and develop the nation, but the same faith *made* Republicans oblivious to the actual conditions they were creating for those workers', concluded Heather Cox Richardson.[29] Similarly, Michael Green asserted that Republican policy flowed from 'their shared beliefs'.[30] Egnal argued that the tilt in power towards the 'representatives from the [Great Lakes] region made clear the priorities that ... came to dominate the Republican party' and direct the enactment of war policy.[31] Political determinism courses through these works.

These interpretations in part explain the uniformity of criticism directed at the Republican Party's policies during the Civil War. The Lincoln administration's effort to manage war costs has drawn sharp criticism from a broad field of historians and economic historians. By relying 'mainly on loans', the administration increased the cost of the war.[32] Treasury secretary Salmon P. Chase's obstinate adherence to the Independent Treasury System caused the suspension of specie payments in December 1861, creating an unnecessary fiscal crisis.[33] Treasury Secretary Chase should have used banks as government depositories, rather than clinging to the Independent Treasury system.[34] However, once he finally shed this anachronistic structure, he replaced it with a National Banking system that stifled the innovative and market responsive aspects that worked in the old order.[35] Congress approved issuing a national fiat currency, the Greenbacks, which caused 'a great disturbance of established economic relations' and historic levels of inflation.[36] Neither Chase nor his associates 'realized that bold [tax] measures were needed'.[37] Instead, they relied on protective tariffs, a policy that the party embraced even before the war, with the passage of the Morrill tariff.[38] The delay in the development of an effective internal revenue system proved 'a major blunder'.[39] When the Republican legislators finally introduced national tax legislation, they 'failed to provide adequate taxation'.[40] Instead, they recommended 'regressive taxes'[41] that demonstrated 'the party state's' support for the creation of a 'new class of finance capitalists during the war'.[42] Indeed 'Mr. Chase's failure was inevitable'.[43] Because Republicans clung to their 'naïve' economic policies, 'they unwittingly laid the groundwork for the turmoil of the late nineteenth century'.[44]

In this book, I argue instead that events outside of the Republican leaders' control played a significant part in the fiscal revolution that occurred in this era. I do not suggest that these earlier interpretations are 'wrong', but instead that they are too narrowly focused. The Republicans did not orchestrate these changes but reacted to the circumstances they inherited and the escalating demands of the war. I do not dispute that a 'revolution' in the fiscal policy of the nation occurred, only that contingency, rather than economic motivation or political determinism, played the pivotal role in shaping these changes. The effort to manipulate and transform American economic policy during the Civil War era, either for ideological reasons or to reward specific economic interests, has been overemphasized. The 'revolution' identified by the Beards did not occur because a 'capitalist class was marching onward in seven league boots' intent on rewarding their patrons. Nor did the 'Republicans' belief in the ultimate power of individual labor' play a dominant role in shaping wartime fiscal policy.[45] Instead, overcoming the limitations of the antebellum fiscal system directed the course of wartime financial policies. In reaction to the unprecedented expense and carnage that accompanied the American Civil War, lawmakers created a new financial system for the country. This system did not destroy the antebellum structure, but instead modified it in a way that would have implications throughout the remainder of the century. The struggle to find enough funds to 'give daily bread to the armies of the Union and provide munitions of war' compelled the Republicans to adopt policies that created a new financial system for the United States.[46] This process began during the Buchanan administration as an attempt to compensate for the limitations of the past.

1 FISCAL FEDERALISM

To understand the financial polices enacted by Republican leaders during the American Civil War, one needs to appreciate the limitations created by the system of fiscal federalism that developed during the antebellum era.[1] Throughout this period in American history, the fiscal powers of the national government remained constrained. State governments had more flexibility in raising revenue and more control over banking policy. The national government sustained itself primarily through import duties. Collecting tariffs emerged as the most efficient and cost-effective means of providing revenue for the central authority. Internal taxes remained the revenue device used primarily by state and local governments; the federal government levied these taxes only in times of war or the threat of war.

Taxing citizens through imports complemented the federalist structure of government. States assumed responsibility for 'lives, liberties, and property' of citizens, maintaining control of the laws and activities within their boundaries. Concurrently, the national government depended on indirect taxes on consumption through tariff duties. Since the tax became incorporated into the price of the good, the consumer paid the levy in small increments (through each purchase), and remained insensible of the actual amount contributed to the Treasury. The tax gatherer did not touch citizens individually. Collected through an intermediary, such as a customs officer at a distant port or a merchant, indirect taxes provided steady revenue when trade was good and the economy functioning properly. However, when any economic disruptions occurred and trade slowed, this diminished the revenue stream to the government. In matters of financial policy, this emerged as the governing paradigm of the pre-Civil War era. States, rather than the federal government, held primary responsibility for regulating banks, investing in internal improvements, and collecting taxes from citizens. This became a fundamental challenge in early American finance during recessions or wars.

This system reflected the vision of government James Madison articulated at the Philadelphia Constitutional Convention. During the proceedings, Madison told the delegates that the national government needed 'vast' powers within its sphere; however this authority would not be exercised on the citizens of the country 'individually'.[2] Instead, states would remain the primary governing influence in the lives of Americans. He expanded on this theme later in *Federalist 45*. The powers granted to the national government, he wrote, were 'few and defined'. Its influence would grow only in times of 'war and danger'. Otherwise, the central government would exert little 'personal influence' over the citizens of the country. State governments would remain the guarantors of the 'lives, liberties, and properties of the people', while securing 'internal order, improvement, and prosperity'.[3] These thoughts reflected Madison's understanding 'that a national government would be too distant to perform all the functions traditionally performed by the states'.[4] They also foretold the national system of taxation that emerged from the Convention.

The early revenue system of the United States supported this federalist system. Indirect taxes became the basis of national revenue. Direct taxes, on the other hand, secured the states' finances, through assessments of real and personal property. These taxes provided the most tangible form of revenue collection a government could undertake. Citizens knew exactly how much they contributed, and paid these taxes 'directly' to their local government officials, in visible sums, rather than piecemeal when purchasing goods. These taxes supported local projects, where citizens saw the results of their investments. States did not rely solely on direct taxes, as the national government relied on indirect taxes. Instead, they used a variety of revenue schemes to meet their expenses. 'There were few limits on what states could do to raise revenues,' noted John Joseph Wallis.[5] This becomes an important aspect of fiscal policy at the outbreak of the Civil War; while states had a variety of options for meeting war expenses, the national government's immediate options for addressing the initial costs of the war were far more circumscribed. Because the Union government could not harness the wealth of the nation quickly, it had to resort to a number of alternative methods to finance the costs of the American Civil War.

Life and Soul of Government

The roots of this system can be traced to the colonial era. The tax policies within the separate British North American colonies varied. 'By 1763, no two colonies had exactly the same revenue laws', observed Robert A. Becker.[6] The Articles of Confederation created a decentralized government. States controlled the purse during the Revolutionary War. The Continental Congress could not levy taxes; instead, the states contributed to a 'common Treasury' that paid the war costs and other 'national expenses'. The Congress had to petition states for compliance with wartime requisitions.[7] Often this meant that the supplies needed to feed, clothe and arm the Continental forces did not materialize. 'For some days, there has been little less than famine' in the camp, General George Washington wrote from Valley Forge during the disastrous winter of 1777. In one of the many letters he penned begging state officials to provide wartime supplies, Washington's aide-de-camp, Alexander Hamilton pleaded, 'For god's sake, our distress is infinite'.[8]

The ultimate success of the Revolutionary War did not ensure national survival. America entered a 'critical period' in which the debt from the war, continued fear of foreign powers, competing ideologies, and a collapsing Continental currency threatened the future of the Revolution.[9] This economic tumult created the desire in citizens for a stronger central government. 'The movement to strengthen the Union', observed E. James Ferguson, evolved from the need to meet debt obligations and instigated the movement to grant Congress the 'power of the purse'.[10] Robert A. Becker argued that the Constitution stifled the more progressive tax policies emerging in the individual states.[11] Roger H. Brown counters that the failure of the states to meet their Revolutionary War financial obligations provoked the nationalists to draft a Constitution that gave the central government more fiscal muscle.[12] The states' failure to act as effective 'administrative agents' for the new nation diminished the fear of consolidating power in a stronger central government.[13] 'The fundamental defect', in the Articles of Confederation, Hamilton complained to George Washington, is that 'the power of the purse is too intirely [sic] to the state legislatures.'[14]

During the colonial era, Americans enjoyed a standard of living 'probably the highest achieved...in any country up to that time'.[15] But the economy of the fledgling country suffered in the early years. From 1775–90, 'something truly disastrous happened to the American economy'.[16] McCusker and Menard estimated that the economic performance during this period fell by 46 per cent (in comparison, at the onset of the Great Depression the gross national product fell 48 per cent).[17] States resorted to currency financing, printing paper money to pay their obligations, and contracting loans to cover the costs incurred during the war. Although the 'continentals' underwent tremendous devaluation during the war, recent work by economic historians has emphasized the virtues of the state-based currencies circulating during the immediate post-Revolutionary period. 'The movement to print more money [after the Revolution] was not a continuation of the wartime issues, but rather the return to prewar practices regarding paper money', Mary Schweitzer explains. 'Paper money was an accepted part of monetary policy both before and after the Revolution'. John J. McCusker has shown that these colonial monetary policies were an important element in the success of the colonial economy.[18] Strained for revenue throughout the Revolutionary War, Congress in the post-war period could not rectify its financial embarrassments. Americans abandoned their fear of centralizing power in the national government in order to stabilize the finances of the country. To ensure survival, they determined 'to experiment with a conservative formula of sound money and unrestrained private enterprise.'[19]

The Rich may be Extravagent, the Poor can be Frugal

'Taxation is the great means of protection, security and defence in a good government', remarked Robert Yates, in one of his many anti-federalist tracts under the pen name 'Brutus'. However, he continued, it can also produce 'the great engine of oppression and tyranny in a bad one'.[20] The delegates to the Convention faced the challenge of providing for the former, without unleashing the latter. Upon their arrival in Philadelphia, a majority of the delegates readily agreed to vest the 'power of the purse' in the national government. Peter L. Rousseau notes that while colonial policies regarding money 'functioned adequately' in meeting the needs of the local economies, 'when the system functioned badly, as it did at various times in New England and in the Carolinas, it caused serious difficulties for the individuals involved in market transactions'. For this reason, he interprets the movement to develop a more unified monetary policy as a positive development in moving the country forward economically. Creating a more unified tax policy also spurred the delegates.[21] Congress's fiscal impotency under the Articles of Confederation convinced the Philadelphia delegates to grant new taxing powers to the central government.

Despite the movement towards consolidating financial power in the national government, the Framers of the Constitution also understood that state governments needed to retain their viability. Because of the size of the nation, state governments needed to maintain internal order. This belief helped shape the early commitment to a federalist structure of government. 'A very extensive territory cannot be governed on the principles of freedom otherwise than by a confederation of republics', argued the Pennsylvania Ratification Convention's minority report. Therefore the states must maintain authority over their 'internal government'.[22] Local representatives and local governance best protect the interests of the people. Having rid themselves of one unresponsive, distant, authoritarian government, early republicans did not wish to establish another. The breadth of the country made self-supporting state governments necessary. The Framers faced the challenge of developing a tax system that would provide the flexibility for local, state and the national governments to collect enough revenue to sustain themselves, while not overburdening the individuals who would be paying these taxes.

The new Constitution granted the central government the power to 'lay and collect taxes, duties, imposts, and excises', independent of the states. States would no longer contribute to a 'common Treasury', as they had done under the Articles of Confederation. The national government would not depend solely on state 'requisitions' or need unanimous state approval to meet the nation's fiscal needs. Uniformity in the duties, imposts and excises obligated the same tax on goods throughout the country, and would keep the majority in the large states from indiscriminately taxing the smaller states. This system of taxation freed the national government from state fiscal control. No longer would it have to rely on requisitions from the states to pay its bills. 'Money is the nerve – the life and soul of government', Governor Randolph explained to the Virginia ratification convention in defence of taxing powers vested by the Constitution. The general government needs to have 'the power of providing its own safety and existence'.[23]

The Constitutional Convention delegates proceeded with the understanding that the United States would generate most of its revenue from indirect taxes. 'All hands', according to Madison, agreed that indirect taxes would form the basis of federal revenue. Imports such as wine, silk and other fineries represented 'luxuries' and taxing these 'extravagant' goods shielded the thrifty from paying these duties. 'The rich may be extravagant, the poor can be frugal; and private oppression may always be avoided by a judicious selection of objects proper for such impositions', explained Alexander Hamilton in *Federalist 21*. Well-selected import duties avoided the 'inequalities' in taxation.[24] They became a hidden tax, with the citizen's contribution to government masked by his or her consumerism. Revolts against state impositions continued throughout the 'critical period'. According to Roger Brown, those writing the Constitution wanted to avoid additional unrest, and import duties seemed ideal for the task.

Relying on indirect taxes, especially import or export duties, seemed the most practical means of meeting the Treasury's needs. 'A very considerable part of the revenue of the United States will arise from that source', James Wilson explained to the Pennsylvania ratification convention. He then reiterated the virtues of indirect taxation:

> It is the easiest, most just, and most productive mode of raising revenue. It is a safe one because is it voluntary. No man is obliged to consume more than he pleases, and each buys in proportion only to his consumption. The price of the commodity is blended with the tax, and the person is often not sensible of the payment.[25]

Collected at ports or individual businesses, indirect taxes did not involve systematic assessments of individual property. The 'infatuation with foreign commerce and luxury' led to an 'anti-luxury hysteria amongst many commentators who extolled the virtues of republican simplicity', Drew McCoy noted.[26] Consumption taxes also had the advantage of 'discouraging luxury', since fineries would become more costly.[27] For these reasons, indirect taxation re-enforced the ideals of establishing a republican nation. Since duties on imports tended to hit goods purchased by the wealthy, rather than the poor, lawmakers further consoled themselves with the belief that taxing imports constituted, at the time, a form of progressive taxation, because most imports equated with luxuries that good republicans did not have to buy. With a progressive tax, the average rates rise with the tax base; the wealthy pay a higher percentage of their income as taxes than those less fortunate. Regressive taxes take a higher percentage of the earnings of those with low incomes.[28]

The Philadelphia delegates never seriously considered excise taxes as a permanent source of national revenue. Collecting excise taxes required not only a merchant selling the good to cooperate, but an inspector to come into your home to find any pre-owned taxable goods. Since alcohol production and consumption was a home-based activity, the most productive of excise taxes opened the individual's home to inspection. Though the Constitution granted the power to collect these 'odious' taxes, they had the potential to incite the citizens' hostility by the invasive means of determining if you owned a taxable good. The power to lay excises, cautioned Luther Martin, 'authorizes officers to go into your houses, your kitchens, your cellars, and to examine into your private concerns'. Congress could tax 'every article of use or consumption, on the food that we eat, on the liquors that we drink, and the clothes we wear, or the hearths necessary for our warmth and comfort'.[29] Excise taxes had been 'in detestation in most countries and have always met with opposition', noted a petitioner to the first Congress.[30] 'The genius of the people will ill brook the inquisitive and peremptory spirit of excise laws', Alexander Hamilton predicted in *Federalist 12*.[31] Excise taxes also strained the structure of fiscal federalism. Many states collected excise taxes (particularly on liquor), and they did not wish to compete with the national government for this revenue. Collecting excise taxes would also mean expanding the role of the federal government, since the 'excise man' would move within the states collecting the taxes. Only with the beginning of the Civil War did the government commence using excise taxes extensively and permanently.

For these reasons, the tax policy of the new country quickly emerged as a method for buttressing the federalist system. Two separate forms of government, able to generate distinct revenue for their different spheres, could draw from the same taxpayers without provoking their wrath. 'Congress would take what was easiest to the people', Theodore Sedgwick reassured the Massachusetts ratification convention, 'the impost, next excise, [and] the direct tax would be last'.[32] Although this system of relying on indirect taxes for the national revenue emerged with little conflict, vesting the national government with the power to collect a direct tax raised more hackles, both in Philadelphia and during the ratification debates. Securing this secondary, 'back-up' form of income provoked great angst because it deviated from this federalist structure, and many believed this would threaten the ability of states to coexist with a more powerful central government.

The Direct Tax

The direct tax provisions in the Constitution unleashed bitterness and angst both at the Convention and in the debates prior to ratification, though all recognized that this would constitute a minor form of national revenue. American historians have lost interest in the important nineteenth-century difference between direct and indirect taxes since the passage of the Sixteenth Amendment made that distinction obsolete. But this became a critical issue during the Civil War revenue debates, and the crux of the battle over the income tax in the late nineteenth century.

An indirect tax falls on consumption; for this reason, many understood it as an avoidable tax. 'An import duty', Benjamin Franklin explained, 'is added to the first cost ... if the people don't like it at the price, they refuse it and are not obliged to pay' the tax.[33] If the government sets the tax too high, people will not purchase the article, or they will smuggle it past the customs agent. This response keeps indirect taxes within their 'proper bounds'.[34] Further, the consumer pays the tax to a merchant through the purchase of a good, and not 'directly' to the government. This keeps the national authority from 'individually' taxing Americans and reinforces the ideal of allowing the local, rather than the national government, to interact with citizens. In contrast, a direct tax bears on the value of what you own, as determined by an assessment. You can avoid indirect taxes by not purchasing a good; however you could not avoid paying a direct tax, except through evasion.[35]

Article I, section II states 'representatives and direct taxes shall be apportioned among the several states', and Article I, section IX reaffirms that 'no capitation or other direct tax shall be laid unless in proportion to the census'. These clauses inflamed the populace because they addressed three issues that smouldered throughout the ratification debates: the division of power between the state and federal government, how the state and central government would share the limited tax revenue extracted from Americans, and finally, how slaves should (or should not) be counted when determining representation.

The confusion over how Americans interpreted a 'direct tax' began at the Convention. Madison recorded that on 22 August Rufus King (MA) asked for a 'precise meaning' of the term 'direct taxation, but no one answered'.[36] However, King later showed a clear understanding of the concept when he distinguished the types of property that assessors would evaluate.[37] Each state could determine what to tax, but all understood that direct taxes fell on property: real and personal, both the value and productive capacity of that property, as well as on individuals as capitation or poll taxes.[38] After independence, direct taxes provided the primary source of revenue for the state and local governments. Because of the difficulty of assessing income before the nineteenth century, governments ordinarily did not apply direct taxes to wages, but on the 'faculty', or potential productivity, of a farm. Levied by the British Parliament in 1799, the first modern income tax was classified as a direct tax. Other nations in Europe would follow that practice. Only in the United States would the income tax be classified as an indirect tax. Historians have added to the confusion by misusing the terms indirect and direct in reference to taxes. Americans now pay many different taxes 'directly' to the national government, so the important historical distinction has become garbled.[39]

Slavery played a significant role in developing the direct tax powers in the Constitution. Offered as a means for breaking the stalemate over representation and slavery, the direct tax incorporated the infamous 'three-fifths clause' that counted three-fifths of the number of slaves in a state for calculating representation to Congress. Delegates from states with small slave populations objected to this proposal, arguing that it would over-represent slave owners in the legislative branches.[40] James Madison suggested that the delegates needed to check one 'vice and interest' with 'another vice and interest' and proposed 'representation and taxation ought to go together'.[41] The next day, 12 July, Gouverneur Morris (PA) suggested a 'proviso that taxation shall be in proportion to Representation'. He admitted that some objections to this motion would surface, but this idea would be favourable by 'restraining the rule to direct taxation'.[42] He offered this compromise to assuage those who resented including slaves in the enumeration. His motion passed quickly. Later he regretted his compromise, and his paternity for a tax he came to loathe. He meant it as a 'bridge to assist over a certain gulph', he lamented, not a permanent feature.[43] Roger Sherman (CT) criticized any attempt to tie slaves to taxation. 'It made the matter worse', he complained, because it implied 'they were *property*' and denied their humanity.[44] However, the compromise worked and became incorporated into the Constitution.

Madison explained to the Virginia Ratification Convention the advantage southerners reaped from this arrangement. This 'mode of representation and taxation', he informed his fellow Virginians, meant that Congress could never 'lay such a tax on slaves as will amount to manumission'.[45] A majority in the non-slaveholding states could levy a high excise tax on slaves knowing their constituents would skirt the burden. An excise tax on slaves could have resulted in slaveholders facing a disproportionate payment for their chattel, and subsequently become an instrument in removing the curse of slavery from the nation. Under the direct tax provision, the same poll tax on slaves would apply to free labourers and 'five negro children of South Carolina are to pay as much tax as the three governors of New Hampshire, Massachusetts, and Connecticut'.[46] Southerners received further security for their 'peculiar' property, knowing that 'Congress could no longer tax slaves arbitrarily', Charles Bullock noted.[47]

Nationalists argued that the direct tax protected the federal government in case of a disruption in trade during a war. 'Should our tranquility be exposed to the assaults of foreign enemies, or violence among ourselves,' James Wilson argued at the Pennsylvania Ratification Convention, 'the objects of commerce may not furnish a sufficient revenue. Certainly, Congress should possess the power of raising revenue from their constituents to provide for the common defence and general welfare of the United States'.[48] Alexander Hamilton, remembering his 'infinite distress' during the Valley Forge winter, defended retaining the direct tax power in the Constitution as a means for the central government to ensure it had enough revenue. In *Federalist 36* he stated, 'I acknowledge my aversion to every project that is calculated to disarm the government of a single weapon which might be usefully employed for general defense and security'.[49] The direct tax would act as a supplement to the indirect taxes, in case of war, blockades, or other declines in commerce.

> Southerners welcomed the direct tax as a means of protecting their slave property from excessive taxation. Since all agreed that import duties would generate the most revenue for the federal government, the additional tax they would have to pay for their chattel proved a small concession for the opportunity to expand their representation in Congress. When it became clear that southern leaders would not accept the Constitution without 'security' for slavery, the direct tax provided a reasonable compromise, and remained one of many 'bridges' cobbled together to ratify the Constitution that only Civil War could remove.

To Annihilate Totally the State Governments

A Federalist system of government relies on authority being exercised concurrently but not oppressively. Anti-Federalists believed that granting national power of direct taxation would undermine the ability of the state governments to collect the revenue they needed to survive, since state and local governments depended on land, poll, and faculty taxes for their revenue. All these constituted direct taxes. 'Land was the major base of taxation in colonial America' and provided the primary means of support for the state governments.[50] Granting the national government the power to collect these same taxes would endanger the revenue base of the states. George Mason summarized this concern during the Virginia Ratification convention. This power 'is calculated to annihilate totally the state governments', he fumed. 'Will the people submit to be individually taxed by two different and distinct powers'?[51] The direct tax power provided further evidence to the Anti-Federalists that the Constitution created a 'national, consolidated government, not a federal or confederated one', according to Cecilia M. Kenyon.[52] Brutus echoed this sentiment. 'There is no way of avoiding the destruction of the state governments' if this provision was not changed, he predicted.[53] Melancton Smith equated the state governments under this provision to 'an animal without blood or subsistence'.[54] John Williams elaborated on this point:

> 'States have concurrent jurisdiction with Congress in taxation ... it is evident as the laws of Congress are the Supreme Laws of the land that their taxes whenever they interfere with taxes laid by states, must and will claim a priority ... they may abolish state taxes; they may constitutionally monopolize every source of revenue and thus directly overturn the state governments. Either the people will be doubly taxed or the state governments will be destroyed'.[55]

Destroying state government would extinguish the liberty the nation fought and suffered for during the Revolution. 'Central to the defense of liberty were popularly controlled institutions', explained Max Edling. Only the local and state governments, the most responsive and representative assemblies, 'could secure this liberty'.[56] For this reason, although the Constitution vests the national government with the authority to levy direct taxes, Congress invoked this power rarely. This became another important element of fiscal federalism during the early nineteenth century.

The anti-federalist's vitriol against this provision had precedent. When the British Parliament enacted the Stamp Act in 1765, they stumbled across a barrier that the colonists considered sacrosanct. 'Americans', explained one member of Parliament to his colleagues, 'think that the imposition of internal taxes ought to be confined to their own assemblies'. The colonists accepted external taxes, such as duties levied on goods imported to the colonies and exported from them, as legitimate sources of revenue for a distant monarch. However, internal taxes, including poll taxes, excises, stamp duties and taxes on land, remained the sole purview of local colonial assemblies, according to Thomas Slaughter. English rulers in London had no right to share 'concurrent jurisdiction' in internal taxes. Local representatives best understood their situation and could determine the proper means and amount to tax. Therefore, Parliament had no right to dip into this well of revenue.[57] This distinction between external and internal taxes of the colonial era re-emerged during the debates over the new republic's Constitution; however, the focus changed to indirect and direct taxes. 'All hands' agreed that the national government could collect duties on imports, just as England had collected external taxes. However, many believed direct taxes, like colonial internal taxes, should remain the sole purview of the state and local governments.

Allowing the national government to levy direct taxes mimicked Parliament's attempt to collect internal taxes in the colonies. State and local governments alone understood local problems and conditions of citizens and therefore levied fair and equitable direct taxes. A distant government (in Philadelphia, New York or London) imposing a direct tax would apply the burden unfairly, especially if apportioned to the states by population without other distinctions.[58] Every state collected direct taxes, both in the colonial and early republican eras. Both the colonies and early states printed paper money, necessitated, in part, to provide a mechanism for paying these local taxes. These burdens increased after the Revolutionary War. 'Crackdowns' on delinquent taxpayers 'detonated rural violence' that rocked many state governments and increased the frustrations with the confederation's fiscal structure.[59] Shay's Rebellion remains the most prominent of these uprisings, but not the only one. The direct taxing powers in the Constitution exacerbated these tensions.

Anti-Federalists believed that the direct tax clauses granted the national government taxing powers that would overwhelm the state governments' ability to raise their own revenues. 'The idea of confederation is lost', lamented Brutus.[60] This authority, according to Luther Martin, proved the 'aim and desire' of the supporters of the Constitution, to 'encrease the power of the general government as far as possible', thereby 'destroying the powers and influence of the states'.[61] The Pennsylvania ratification convention's minority report predicted, 'Congress may monopolise every source of revenue and thus indirectly demolish the state governments'.[62] Massachusetts, South Carolina, New Hampshire, Virginia, New York and North Carolina shared this sentiment. The report from the ratification conventions of these states proposed amending the Constitution to deny Congress the authority to levy a direct tax, or at least require the government to collect it through the state tax apparatus, rather than sending federal officers into local communities.[63]

As part of an empire, state governments received significant revenue from the British government. Parliament granted the colonial assemblies 'substantial reimbursements' for military campaigns. Between 1740 and 1775, the British government spent an estimated £450,000 (roughly $89.8 million in 2007) annually on the American colonies. Local officials distributed these funds judiciously, Edwin J. Perkins argued, and they quickly became absorbed into the economy.[64] This loss of revenue, coupled with the new taxing powers granted to the national government, would reduce states to poverty, localist leaders believed. The deterioration of the American economy during the Revolutionary era exacerbated these concerns. This economic tumult helps explain the vitriolic response to granting the national government the power to levy direct taxes. Historians have overlooked the importance of this reaction against direct taxation for two reasons. Research on the direct tax has focused instead on its contribution to the early decisions regarding slavery in the colonies, concentrating on the implications of the three-fifths clause. Second, most studies have also concentrated on the development of the direct tax and its relation to the income tax. These studies jump from the Constitutional Convention to the Supreme Court decision in *Hylton* v. *United States* (1796). Both strategies miss the deep concerns of politicians of the period regarding the role of maintaining sovereign states in the federalist system.

In clouding the literature further, historians have accepted the anti-federalists' charge that the Constitution grants 'unlimited' power to levy taxes 'in any mode they please'.[65] E. James Ferguson and Thomas P. Slaughter repeat the anti-federalists' statements, each referring to Congress's taxing power as 'unlimited'.[66] Dall Forsythe and Max Edling equivocate; Forsythe stating that they were 'almost entirely successful' in placing 'no limitations on the kind of taxes' the government could levy. Edling noted that Congress had 'almost unlimited power to tax'.[67]

Contrary to these perceptions, the Constitution constrains the central government's taxing power. First, the House of Representatives, the legislative chamber most representative and beholden to voters because the members stand for election every two years, levies all taxes. No monarch or executive can arbitrarily demand revenue from the American citizens. Once enacted by the House, the Senate, representing the states, has to concur. 'No taxes [may] be imposed upon [Americans] without their consent by representatives of their own choosing, who will participate with them in the public burthens and benefits', Roger Sherman argued.[68] Money cannot leave the Treasury 'but in consequence of appropriations made by law'. Further, Congress must publish 'public accounts of the receipts and expenditures of all public money' from time to time (Article I, Section IX).

Apportioning the direct taxes by population stripped the national government of its ability to levy taxes 'discriminatingly' on property.[69] One section could not overburden another (in principle at least). This restriction would later be cited to question the constitutionality of the income tax. Third, the Constitution permits the central government to collect excises, imposts and duties, but requires uniform taxes throughout the country. Individual states could not be taxed selectively, despite their wealth or population. Also, because 'there is no material difference' in what individuals in states purchase, the uniform duties, the Founders believed, fell evenly across the country.[70] Finally, Article I, section IX bans any taxes on exports; in 1787, this greatly limited the revenue-gathering opportunities of the government, since export duties had been collected during both the colonial and early national period. This restriction on taxing exports becomes important again in 1865, when Congress yearned to place a duty on cotton leaving the reunited country to help generate a sinking fund to pay down the war debt.

The Constitution did not establish a government with 'unlimited' taxing powers. Tariffs would generate most revenue. Although Congress could levy direct taxes, collecting this revenue was considered a threat to the sovereignty of the states. Popular sentiment against the excise made this a tax of last resort except in times of war or when trade fluctuated. Limiting the taxing authority any further would strip the government of its ability to secure the United States against foreign aggression, any disruption in trade, or whenever government ran a deficit. Thus, the taxing authority granted to the national government by the Constitution became a perceived power: one that citizens sensed, and knew, but remained less tangible than anticipated. National direct taxes would strain the federalist structure, and therefore were not used. Loosed from seaports and customs houses, national tax collectors would cross the boundary of the state and national 'sphere' and cut into revenue designated for the local governments. States wanted to keep these taxing options available to protect their viability. State and local governments helped preserve and protect national sovereignty and individual liberty across a broad and expanding nation. Although the anti-federalist efforts to limit the direct tax clauses of the Constitution did not work, their reaction helped shape the tax policy during the antebellum era.

As anticipated, the federal government resorted to direct taxation only during three crises: the Quasi-War scare in 1798, the War of 1812 and the American Civil War. The expense and difficulty in collecting these taxes limited their appeal as a regular source of national revenue. The model of fiscal federalism prevailed: the national government would remain within its 'due limits', collecting revenue only indirectly from citizens. During war or disruptions in trade, it could invoke greater taxing powers in order to protect the nation. Limited only by the ban on collecting import or export duties, states had more flexibility in their taxing powers: they did not face the same uniformity or apportionment restrictions under the Constitution. They needed this flexibility not only to protect the 'lives, liberties and properties' of their citizens, but also to help maintain a republic stretched over a large territory. Throughout the antebellum era, the states, not the national government, flexed this fiscal muscle.

Early Tax Policy

Congress enacted the nation's first revenue measure on 4 July 1789. The resulting tariff provided a modicum of protection, but remained primarily a revenue measure. The legislation imposed specific duties on thirty-six commodities and applied *ad valorem* rates to selected, enumerated imports. The duties averaged approximately 15 per cent.[71]

Because the federal government assumed and consolidated the Revolutionary War debts amassed by the states, in 1791 the revenue needs of the government overwhelmed import duties. At the behest of Treasury Secretary Alexander Hamilton, Congress levied the first internal taxes. Historically, duties on alcohol had proven one of the most dependable forms of taxation. Many states, including Pennsylvania, collected alcohol excises. These taxes targeted distilled liquors, the production of which remained a household affair. Duties on 'ardent spirits', Hamilton argued in *Federalist 12*, favored agriculture, the economy, the morals and health of society'.[72] Besides these virtues, Hamilton had another motive for invoking a liquor excise as an early tax. He had assured opponents of the Constitution that states would possess 'independent and uncontrollable authority to their own revenue for the supply of their own wants'.[73] However, he admitted early in his tenure at the Treasury that he hoped to 'leave the states under as little necessity as possible of exercising the power of taxation'.[74] He pushed for the enactment of the whiskey excise to claim 'so valuable a resource of revenue before ... reoccupied by the state governments'. Hamilton wanted to 'starve the states of revenue', Chernow theorized, in order to 'shore up the federal government'.[75] He wanted to use the taxing powers conferred in the Constitution as an instrument for strengthening the central government's power.

The resulting excise taxed whiskey at the still, not through sales. This provision drew into the taxman's net the small scale, rural distiller who produced liquor for home consumption or barter. This legislation sparked the 'Whiskey Rebellion' in western Pennsylvania. These folk had experience protesting liquor taxes. As noted above, excise taxes generated a special sort of venom because they required inspection of the premises to determine if a person owned any of the objects taxed. Local assessments, made by individuals familiar with the area and its people remained more preferable. However, western Pennsylvanians harassed colonial then state revenue officers as early as 1684 with the same zeal they exhibited in 1794 while tarring and feathering the federal taxman. These demonstrations constituted more than an effort to shirk taxes. Instead, Thomas P. Slaughter suggests, the whiskey uprising demonstrated the conflict between 'center and periphery, cosmopolitans and localists, East and West, those who feared strong central government and those who demanded local autonomy'.[76] The distant national government had not responded to the rural citizens' need for roads and protection from attacks from Native Americans. They only showed up when they needed money. This angered the residents of rural counties throughout the Republic, Slaughter posited. Peter Rousseau opines that a shortage of currency needed to pay the tax also helped spark the rebellion.[77]

Since the proceeds from the whiskey excise fell short of expectations, Congress levied additional taxes. To quell criticism that the whiskey excise fell hardest on those least able to pay, the Revenue Act of 1794 attempted to fix more progressive taxes, by imposing duties on pleasure carriages, the manufacture of snuff and fine sugar, the proceeds from sales at auctions and stamp duties.[78] Assuming state debts, fortifying the nation's credit, and creating a revenue system that would support these initiatives would help ensure the vitality of the national government. This revenue measure also became part of the Federalist Party's programme of consolidating power within the new central government.

Slavery also tainted the opposition reaction against the 1794 revenue measure. The carriage duty troubled James Madison, who served in the early Congresses as a representative from Virginia. Classified as an indirect tax, the carriage duty posed a particular threat to southern interests. Virginians owned more carriages per capita than any other Americans, so the tax fell disproportionately on those he represented. Also, Madison had assured the delegates to the Virginia Ratification Convention that the direct tax clauses protected slave owners from forced manumissions because indirect taxes could not be levied on individuals. However, the carriage tax challenged this supposition. This duty fell on a specific form of property. Rather than collecting the tax on the sale of carriages, the assessors would look for prior ownership of carriages, taxing property rather than consumption, the primary difference between direct and indirect taxation. The owner paid the tax directly to the government agent without an intermediary. Classifying slaves as property rather than persons, as southern delegates to the Constitutional Convention had done repeatedly, opened slaves to the same tax that Hamilton proposed for carriages. The attack on the carriage duty did not just aim to thwart the Federalists' 'nationalizing pretensions',[79] but also provided an early attempt to keep the national government from interfering with the ownership rights in slavery.

The Supreme Court case of *Hylton* v. *United States* (1796) created important precedents for later fiscal policy. First, the justices used the prerogative of judicial review (before *Marbury v. Madison*), where the Supreme Court determined the validity of congressional legislation.[80] Second, the Court determined that a tax on carriages did not represent a direct tax and therefore did not violate the constitution's restriction on apportionment. More specifically, the Court defined a tax on expenditures as an indirect tax. The justices did not enumerate specific items that qualified for a direct tax, only stating that 'capitation or poll taxes' plus those 'apportioned' could be considered under this category. To tax 'any specific article by the rule of apportionment would ... create great inequality and injustice', Justice Chase observed.[81] Direct taxes, then, could not be laid on any 'specific article'.

This decision created the standard for internal revenue legislation throughout the nineteenth century. After the Civil War, it became the basis for the court battles over the income tax. Throughout the antebellum era, when the national government needed to supplement customs duties, southerners pushed for direct taxes, primarily on property in the form of land or slaves. Since states with heavy slave populations would pay more under this scheme (again because of the representation/taxation formula in the three-fifths clause), this seems curious. However, direct taxes, done properly, afforded southerners two measures of comfort: local control of assessments and eliminating the possibility of an excise tax laid on their particular form of property. The constraints of generating revenue under fiscal federalism became apparent early. These limitations became clear during times of distress and war.

War Finance

Throughout the period of United States history from the Revolutionary to the Civil War, the ability of the federal government to raise income quickly was curtailed. Tariff revenue remained a fickle source. Internal taxes crossed the lines of fiscal federalism, were difficult to collect in such a large country and provoked citizen protests. Yet, on three occasions during this period, the federal government needed funds quickly for national defence: at the onset of the Quasi-War in 1798, for the War of 1812 and during the Mexican–American War. In these situations, the United States embraced the system of 'Dutch Finance', whereby a government borrows for the 'extraordinary' costs of war and taxes for the 'ordinary' costs of administration, including the payments on the interest of the loans. This suited the system of fiscal federalism because the burden of war expenses could be handled without a significant increase in taxes.[82]

Because the financial power of the government remained restrained under this system, borrowing money quickly during wars proved a great challenge to the Treasury. During this period a distinctive pattern emerged that would have significant ramifications for the financing of the Civil War: the private capital of a few wealthy individuals would be tapped to help bolster public credit. A handful of men would provide the initial capital to meet the government's needs in exchange for securities. They would then market these securities to banks, states, companies and other foreign and domestic investors. By controlling the market on these securities, these men made a handsome profit for themselves on commissions, favourable interest rates, and by purchasing the bonds below the market price that they subsequently would establish. Robert Morris, the first Superintendent of Finance for the emerging United States, pledged his personal wealth to raise the capital for the Revolutionary War, and profited from his transactions. This type of arrangement remained the common practice throughout the antebellum era when the government needed credit.[83]

During the Quasi-War, President John Adams's administration recommended the first direct tax in July 1798 to help raise money to strengthen the national defences. The administration feared an imminent attack from the French and wanted to develop the navy to stymie the invasion. The plan apportioned the burden of $1.3 million amongst the states according to population. In collecting the tax, officials could assess 'dwelling houses' and land, and fix a per capita tax on slaves. Federal officers assessed the property and collected the taxes; local authorities only outlined the rules for assessment.[84] This plan ignored the proposals made by the state ratification conventions, anti-federalists during the debates over the Constitution, and Democratic-Republicans in Congress. The national government, not local governments, controlled the assessment and collection process, limiting the state governments' role in implementing this law.

The direct tax passed the same day as the Alien and Sedition Laws. These acts particularly inflamed the residents of Bucks and surrounding counties in southern Pennsylvania, because many of these residents claimed recent German ancestry. John Fries, one of the three leaders of the rebellion, had fought in the Revolutionary War and led a militia company against the whiskey insurgents in 1794. He considered himself both a loyal American and a Federalist. However, the Alien and Sedition Acts angered the veteran. Compounding the problem, most of the residents did not know the federal assessors and collectors as they knew their local officials. The collectors did not speak German, as did many residents of the area. Soon after the assessors arrived, a rumour spread that they differentiated between German and non-German speaking property owners, and assessed the 'foreigners' homes differently (by counting windows). Crowds resisting the tax assessors dissipated as quickly as they formed, and there were no injuries.[85]

Like the Whiskey Rebellion, the Fries uprising registered the public's anger at the direction taken by the new government. The participants in Fries Rebellion 'believed they had acted in accord with the Constitution, not against it'. The opposition centred less on the money requisitioned by the government than the means they used to collect it. This represented a reaction against the expansion of federal power through the passage of an 'unconstitutional law'. Anthony Joseph stressed that the Fries Rebellion represented an attack on the Alien and Sedition acts, rather than a 'tax revolt'. However, like later direct tax measures, the return from the tax disappointed. Only 83 per cent of the anticipated revenue landed in the Treasury. This long lapse between enacting the legislation and collecting the cash became the norm rather than the exception with the direct tax. The government borrowed little during for this event, but paid a high interest rate of 8 per cent.[86]

These popular uprisings gave a political opportunity to Thomas Jefferson and the emerging Democratic-Republican Party. John Fries, for example, after being convicted of treason, then pardoned by President Adams, never again voted for a Federalist candidate. President Jefferson opposed all internal revenue schemes and the Federalist administrations' methods of collecting them. The election of 1800 signalled the public's desire for a more limited national government 'with clearly defined and enumerated powers'.[87] After his election, Jefferson asked a willing Congress to repeal all internal taxes. Thereafter, the Treasury relied on import duties and land sales until the War of 1812.

President Jefferson's Treasury secretary, Albert Gallatin, advocated limiting internal taxes. Taxes, Gallatin warned, led to 'encroaching government, temptations to [start] offensive wars ... nothing can be more effectual' to maintaining a republican government, 'than a repeal of all internal taxes'.[88] Gallatin held federal expenditures below $10 million, raised tariff rates, and then reaped a windfall as US trade expanded. Gallatin's frugality and the increasing customs revenue helped generate a surplus each year from 1801–11, excluding the 1809 deficit created by the Embargo Act. The average tariff rate rose from 8.5 per cent in 1789 to 16 per cent during Jefferson's tenure. Concurrently, the public debt declined from $86.4 to $45.2 million.[89] Soon, though, war forced another round of internal taxation.

A resurgence of hostilities with Great Britain culminated in the War of 1812. The 'financial disasters and absurd treasury management' of this conflict portended many of the problems that arose during the American Civil War.[90] Congress renewed internal taxation reluctantly. Secretary Gallatin strongly recommended inaugurating a schedule of internal duties and reviving the collection apparatus before the war started. In his 1812 report, *Increase of Revenue*, Gallatin proposed doubling selected customs duties, as well as imposing an internal tax scheme that resembled the Federalist programme.[91]

These internal taxes produced $14.2 million between 1812–17 but loans, rather than taxes, sustained the government during the war. The Madison administration contracted over $61 million in loans to finance the war, realizing only $45 million of that amount because they could not market the bonds at par. Four individuals, Stephen Girard, David Parish, John Jacob Astor and Jacob Banker, provided the capital for approximately $21 million of the total loans. These men profited handsomely from these investments. Stephen Girard used the influence he purchased with his credit to pressure lawmakers into allowing him to receive a charter for his private bank, which greatly enhanced his personal fortune. In marketing the bonds to the broader public, the Treasury accepted bank notes as payment for the bonds; the Treasury lost millions when these notes depreciated.[92] These lessons were not lost on Salmon P. Chase, the Treasury secretary at the onset of the Civil War.

In addition to the excise taxes, the Madison administration also levied a series of national direct taxes. Apportioned according to the 1810 census, these added another $10.5 million to the war chest. The Madison administration rejected using Washington revenue officers to collect these taxes; instead they gave states a greater role in this tax programme. State agents assessed the property then collected the tax. This gave local control to the national taxes. The Direct Tax of 1813 apportioned the tax not only among the states, but also to the different counties within the states. It gave each state the option of paying their tab upfront and receiving a 15 per cent discount on their quota. Rather than creating a new, and costly, federal bureaucracy as the Federalists did, Gallatin's proposal used state officers to assess and collect the taxes, in the manner recommended during the ratification debates.

Congress enacted one more direct tax during the course of the War of 1812. State governments determined how best to distribute the burden amongst the counties. Under the Federalist plan, the Treasury determined the amount each county throughout the nation would pay. Also, a state could receive a 15 per cent discount on its bill if it paid the entire amount within a year. Eleven states took advantage of this opportunity. Finally, the Madison Treasury discarded the complicated valuation system devised by Wolcott, instead basing the tax on the value of lands, houses and slaves 'at the rate each is worth in money' rather than a predetermined fixed rate. This resembled the requisition system used under the Article of Confederation. While vested with expanded powers under the Constitution, the national government still had trouble getting the states to pay in full. Despite the incentive for paying the tax promptly, the direct tax returns disappointed again and revenue trickled into the Treasury as late as 1825.[93]

Throughout the War of 1812, Congress expanded the tax schedule in an effort to keep pace with the interest payments on the burgeoning debt. Candles, nails, iron, hats, umbrellas, saddles, bridles, shoes and playing cards all carried new duties. The Democratic-Republicans, who had vehemently protested Hamilton's economic policies, soon found themselves adopting a similar programme. They chartered a Second Bank of the United States, revived the most contentious taxes, and increased custom duties, culminating in the Tariff of 1816, the most protective tariff enacted in the United States until that time. Necessity overwhelmed earlier concerns about the invidious nature of national taxation.[94] Although Gallatin's successor, Alexander J. Dallas, recommended retaining internal taxes as a permanent part of the government's fiscal policy after 1817, Congress did not comply. After 1817, Congress levied no internal taxes until 1861. Tariffs, collected 'with more ease to Government and less inconvenience to the People', remained the primary source of revenue for most of the nineteenth century.[95]

The Mexican–American War was the only other Treasury experience with war financing before 1861. A short conflict, with little outlay, it nevertheless provided an important lesson for Civil War legislators. The war was financed through borrowing via the issue of treasury notes and government bonds. Most of these securities sold above par, and for specie, rather than bank notes. The Second Bank of the United States had been dismantled, so private firms handled the sales of securities: E. W. Clark and Co. and Corcoran and Riggs were the leaders in this effort. Cummings noted the 'favoritism' by [Treasury secretary] Robert J. Walker towards Corcoran's firm. The partners in this firm earned roughly half as much as Jay Cooke's firm earned during the Civil War, while generating far less in loans than did Cooke's firm. This helped the private establishment to make a windfall on the sale of bonds. The prosperity of the country at this time facilitated the rapid sale of the bonds, and the subsequent ease with the payment of the interest. Jay Cooke, who worked for E.W. Clark and Co., observed and learned from these developments. Although characterized (correctly) as someone who profited greatly from Civil War finance, the profits made by Corcoran and Riggs and E.W. Clark and Co. on the Mexican American War were proportionately far greater, and the evidence of improper collusion between the Treasury and these firms far better substantiated.[96]

Other Revenue Options

Until the Civil War, customs duties regularly provided 95 per cent of federal revenue. Although 'all hands' agreed early they would provide the best source of revenue for the government, lawmakers considered other options. Throughout the late eighteenth and early nineteenth centuries, Congress debated the extent to which public lands could help bolster the government's revenue. Both the early Federalist and Republican administrations hoped to use public land sales as a reliable source of funds. The original thirteen colonies comprised over 300,000 square miles; the Louisiana Purchase added another 400,000 miles to the public domain. Land remained the single greatest asset controlled by the federal government through the nineteenth century. Naturally, many saw this asset as a potential source of wealth and stability for the emerging government.

However, two competing interests soon emerged. Speculators wanted land sold in large tracts, with prices attached to the entire parcel, not per acre. This would favour wealthier purchasers with ready capital for investment, and provide a relatively quick and easy means of getting money into the Treasury, and allow a relaxation of tariff rates. However, speculators would then control the land, and the prices set for selling it to future migrants. Settlers, however, preferred small allotments sold at per acre prices. This strategy encouraged more westward migration and provided a greater benefit for farmers hoping to develop the vast domain. Should the government encourage settlement or use the land primarily for revenue? Selling land in small segments to individuals provided less revenue and created greater bureaucratic challenges in administering the sales, but facilitated the growth of the overall economy.[97]

The Land Ordinance of 1785 allowed anyone to purchase 640 acres for one dollar per acre. The policy changed in 1800 to selling 340 acres for two dollars per acre. These policies favoured those with large sums of money, and discouraged the small farmer from moving west and establishing his homestead. In 1820, the tide changed to opening the land for settlement, rather than using it as a source of revenue. Land sold in lots as small as 80 acres, for $1.25 per acre. This policy continued until the Homestead Act of 1862 granted land to settlers for free and relinquished the use of public lands for revenue.[98]

Settling, rather than selling, the land became the government's primary objective. The presence of squatters, whose farms began to dot the vacant tracts, made relying on income from land sales impractical. 'The settlers did not have the money, were destined not to have it, but settle the land they would. And back of every demand for revenue ... was the stronger desire to make the government secure and great through the spread of people over millions of acres'.[99] Relinquishing this bountiful source of future income also tied the government to tariff financing and indirect taxation. The movement to lower the rates of these duties prompted many to call for land sales to help pay the government's bills. However, public land sales had proven an inefficient and unreliable source of federal revenue.

Selling national public lands spread over millions of acres, and located over a thousand miles from Washington proved difficult to administer. (States enjoyed greater success because they controlled a small portion of land to sell and distribute.) Thus public land sales proved an inefficient and unreliable source of federal revenue. Most land sold on credit or with dubious paper currency, resulting in forfeiture. In 1820, for example, land purchasers owed the government $21 million for their property whereas the entire federal budget that year totaled $17.8 million.[100] When President Andrew Jackson made these transactions payable only in specie, rather than credit or paper currency, the revenues from public land sales plummeted from $24.8 million in 1836 to $6.7 million in 1837.[101] Although abundant, and potentially productive sources of revenue, land sales did not provide a practical source of reliable funds for the national government.

Throughout the antebellum era, politicians faced this choice: either use the public domain for generating revenue (by selling to the highest bidder, generally speculators), and subsequently lowering tariff rates, or distribute the land for a minimal fee to those who wished to settle in the west. The latter choice would wed the country to relying on customs duties as the primary source of revenue. This debate lay at the heart of the controversy over the Homestead policy, and partially explains the vehement opposition to providing cheap land for farmers.

Reviving the direct tax became another financing option for the government during the 1850s. Calling to 'change the existing system of taxation', advocates of free trade wanted to revive the national direct tax.[102] The Southern Commercial Convention in Savannah, meeting in December 1856, called for the elimination of all customs duties and adoption of a national direct. 'Each man would pay according to his ability ... [and] Congress would be more economical of the public money as the rich and influential would be averse to taxing themselves'.[103] John C. Calhoun, Jr argued further that 'the South had been prosperous in defiance of a most unjust and oppressive system of taxation'. Repealing the tariff would allow southern commerce to 'flourish like the green bay tree'.[104] Collecting direct taxes through the states would relieve the dependence on tariff income, which would allow for an easing of the rates. However, the difficulty of collecting direct taxes made this idea unpopular outside of the southern commercial interests. Keeping the government dependent on tariffs also freed states to experiment with their own financing options.

State Policies

While the central government resorted to tariff financing, state and local governments developed an imaginative array of fiscal schemes. 'Tax free finance' became the objective of most states, according to Peter Wallenstein.[105] Hamilton's plan for assuming and centralizing the Revolutionary War debts not only strengthened the national government, but allowed states to begin their federal life with a clean fiscal slate.

A series of three ordinances passed between 1784–90 that established the policy of the federal government allocating public lands to states for education and development. Grants of the public domain benefited 'directly or indirectly' virtually 'every function of state and local governments', Daniel Elazar explained.[106] Allocations of public lands allowed states to support education, commence internal improvements and, through land sales to settlers, provide revenue for state budgets. Local administration made state land sales a more stable and reliable source of revenue than national land sales. States acquired land from federal allotment, but also 'the seizure and redistribution of Indian land'. Grabbing 'western lands' from Native Americans gave states 'revenue far exceeding the costs of administering the land program'.[107]

States also invested in 'quasi-public corporations'.[108] These activities produced revenue that paid for social welfare and education initiatives. Banks emerged as one of the favourite ventures for state investment. States purchased bank bonds and stocks, and also taxed the capital, dividends, deposits, notes and profits banks generated. Throughout the antebellum era Massachusetts, for example, collected over half of its revenue from a 1 per cent tax on bank capital. 'New York and Virginia were the only states to derive less than 20 percent of their revenue' from banks in any five year period, Sylla, Legler and Wallis found.[109]

The purchase of stock or investment in bonds of corporations helped underwrite internal improvements in states. The interest from these investments provided another source of 'tax-free' revenue. States helped foster private initiatives. Between 1807 and 1867, France chartered 647 corporations, whereas the six New England states alone chartered over 6,700 corporations from 1800–62.[110] Road, canal and railroad companies all received state support and in turn helped support social spending through interest and dividend payments as well as toll collections. New York's sponsorship of the Erie Canal remains the most famous and successful example of state support for a 'quasi-private' venture. The state reaped a great windfall from the canal's success, and this example encouraged other states to provide support for internal improvement projects. Not all these projects succeeded. John Majewski reported on the 'disastrous' investment made by Pennsylvania on the Mainline canal system. In total, the Pennsylvania commonwealth spent approximately $42 million on internal improvements during the antebellum era. Yet, the 'mainline' transportation system in which they invested became a boondoggle. This misadventure, coupled with the Erie's success, helped propel New York City past Philadelphia as the nation's leading commercial metropolis.[111] Although the federal government withdrew from supporting internal improvements after the election of President Andrew Jackson in 1828, states quickly filled the void. Between 1790 and 1860, state and local governments spent over $425 million on transportation, while the federal government spent only $54 million.[112] In Pennsylvania, for example, the Legislature enacted 132 laws in 1815, and 725 in 1860, and 'perhaps 90 percent of these' involved private business concerns.[113]

Where did the states get this money, if not from general taxation? States demonstrated flexibility and ingenuity in their revenue schemes. Many states employed specialty taxes, such as licenses, fees, taxes on corporate profits and poll taxes. Maryland passed a tax on the notes used by the Bank of the United States which led to the famous Supreme Court decision *McCulloch* v. *Maryland* (1819), which asserted the supremacy of the national government over the states when the two collide. Mississippi used her tax policy to advocate social and economic policy. The state's first constitution exempted banks and railroads from taxation to encourage development. To discourage free blacks from settling in the state, the Mississippi legislature in 1822, the state levied a $3.00 capitation tax on each 'free male of color', while male slaves and free white males paid only 75 cents.[114]

These various taxes contributed a small portion to state finances. For the real money used to fund the purchase of banks and corporate shares and support the development of internal improvements, states borrowed money. Capitalists near and far invested in state bonds and the private securities that received the backing of state governments. Foreign investors poured over $500 million into the United States before the Civil War, underwriting national and state debts. Foreigners liked these state-supported bonds because 'faith in the nation's resources were so great', and Americans 'were so frugal'.[115] Also, the investors believed they would receive steady interest payments from taxation if the states' other financing schemes fell short.

This expectation received its first great trial after the Depression in 1837. 'One after another' of the state budgets collapsed under the weight of their indebtedness. The states carried a debt of $230 million at the time and could not keep up with the interest payments. Florida and Mississippi completely repudiated their obligations. Arkansas, Indiana, Illinois, Maryland, Michigan, Pennsylvania and Louisiana all defaulted on interest payments. This defalcation created a great backlash, both within the states and abroad. Jefferson Davis, the governor of Mississippi when the state defaulted, would later regret his indifference to the 'crocodile tears' shed by English investors who lost thousands on the bonds issued by his state. During the American Civil War, English investors who remembered Davis's role in the default hesitated to lend money to the Confederate States of America.[116] The enthusiasm foreign capitalists had for all types of 'American things' soured. When questioned on why American railroad securities sold poorly on the British market in 1859, an Englishman replied 'the record of that experience [states defaulting] now operates as a bugbear to Englishmen to this day'.[117] Although national bonds continued to attract foreign investment any sign of trouble made these investors cautious. Bond sales during the Civil War relied heavily on Union army victories.

Movements to revise state constitutions swept the country. Before 1840, no state constitution limited the amount of debt a state could carry, but within fifteen years, nineteen states added these restraining amendments.[118] Until the early 1840s, states succeeded in bolstering their budgets without extensive taxation. Once they could no longer depend on deficit financing, states relied on direct taxes to provide for the basic services of governing. 'They provided minimum revenue but remained cumbersome and unpopular', Sylla noted. Alexis de Tocqueville described the process for collecting these taxes:

> The state usually employs the officers of the township or the county to deal with the citizens. Thus, for instance, in New England the town assessor fixes the rate of taxes; the town collector receives them; the town treasurer transmits the amount to the public treasury; and the disputes that may arise are brought before the ordinary courts of justice. This method of collecting taxes is slow as well as inconvenient.[119]

Poll and property taxes, tailored to local conditions, predominated. In response to the fiscal collapse of states under their debt obligation, tax revenue had to increase. Most states adopted a general property tax, to provide more secure revenue, and to keep officials from encumbering the state with unsustainable debt. Sixteen states adopted uniformity clauses that applied the same rate to both real and personal property.[120] States also experimented with income taxes (Pennsylvania, Maryland, Virginia, North Carolina, Alabama and Florida), and inheritance taxes (Pennsylvania, Louisiana, North Carolina, Massachusetts, Virginia and Maryland). Though Americans paid taxes to the national government only through tariffs, they experienced taxation through their state and local governments. In 1860, states collected $93.6 million in direct and indirect taxes from their residents, whereas the national government collected $56 million.[121]

When all else failed, states turned to lotteries. Approximately 130 separate lotteries were authorized for 'government functions' between 1790 and 1860. Virginia used lottery proceeds to build a toll bridge whose revenue supported 'needy children'. In 1811, Maryland promoted a lottery to erect a monument to George Washington.[122] In 1832, lottery sales throughout the country generated $66.4 million in revenue; the national government's receipts for that year totaled only $31.8 million.[123] Aid to education, poor relief and internal improvements fell to the states, as the national government assumed Madison's 'due limits'.

Conclusion

Throughout the antebellum era, states emerged as the sources of finance for internal improvements as well as social welfare and education spending. They accomplished this through direct taxation of citizens and a number of innovative financing strategies. Through these initiatives, the ideal of states meeting the needs of citizens 'individually' strengthened. Financially, the national government remained removed, both in collecting taxes and in investing in construction, social welfare or education. In 1860, the nation stumbled toward war, incapacitated by a financial system that impaired its ability to address the pressing needs for economic mobilization. In the past, when the need arose for funds to meet extraordinary expenses, the Treasury relied on the private capital of a few wealthy individuals, who fronted the money and marketed the government securities, reaping handsome profits for their patriotism. The system of fiscal federalism, developed and strengthened over the course of six decades, challenged the leaders who had to find the funds to fight the Civil War.

2 THE 'EXHAUSTED CONDITION OF THE TREASURY'

The Civil War fiscal crisis began before 12 April 1861. The United States Treasury tottered in a state of 'utmost confusion' months before Edmund Ruffin shot at the troops holed up in Fort Sumter.[1] The Treasury had been the country's traditional 'dynamic center' of government, yet now it faced bankruptcy.[2] Congress was notified on 11 February 1861 that 'little more' than $500,000 remained in the central depository in Washington. Demands for $2 million in 'unanswered' requisitions had accumulated in the department, with $6 million more due to public creditors in early March.[3] Staff in most executive departments could not draw their salary that January. Members of Congress had gone unpaid since the start of the session the previous December.[4] Worse yet for a nation stumbling into battle, 'The War and Navy departments', reported the Treasury department's secretary, John A. Dix, 'have calls for large requisitions [that] have been delayed on account of the exhausted condition of the Treasury.'[5]

'To understand the measures submitted to Congress', John Sherman wrote in reference to the fiscal legislation introduced in the Thirty-seventh Congress, 'it is necessary to have a clear conception of the condition of the Treasury at that time, and of the established financial policy of the government immediately before the war.'[6] Yet historians rarely include the state of the pre-war Treasury in their review of the Civil War legislation.[7] Studies of finances during the war usually offer only a brief mention of the 'unsatisfactory condition of the Treasury in 1860', then move on to the wartime policy.[8]

Analyses of the economic impact of the Civil War era often begin with a litany of Union strengths: in manpower, industrial output, capital resources, railroad miles and the value of real property. These factors gave the Union 'an overwhelming preponderance in most sources of economic power', according to Richard N. Current.[9] However, in April 1861, the economic power of the Union seemed more tenuous. Merchants and planters in the future Confederate states owed northern businesses approximately $200 million in unpaid receipts at the start of 1861; as more southern states seceded, repayment seemed unlikely.[10] Throughout 1861, 5935 northern businesses failed, with over $193 million in liabilities.[11] When Civil War erupted, trade revolving around cotton represented the 'major feature in American commerce'.[12] 'King Cotton' held many northern businesses in his grasp. The secession crisis foretold a great financial loss, rather than a potential war boom. The economic dominance of the Union seems obvious in hindsight, but those engaged in managing the Union's finances perceived economic weakness and uncertainty.

On the eve of the war, the Union finances 'humiliating', John Sherman worried, 'The problem was not whether we could muster men, but whether we could raise the money'.[13] The lawmakers charged with organizing the divided nation's finances had to balance their great faith in the future with the limitations inherent in the nation's fiscal system. Victory seemed less likely the longer the war continued. One can trace this uncertainty, in part, to the fiscal federalism erected during the Constitutional Convention and solidified throughout the antebellum era. Contrary to the perception that the national government possessed 'unlimited' taxing authority, a tight fiscal leash inhibited the options available for addressing the 'financial embarrassments' faced by Congress in 1861.[14] Americans created a government that taxed its citizens minimally and indirectly. Throughout the antebellum era, state and national leaders reinforced this structure. America did not need standing armies, Alexis de Tocqueville explained, because, 'no discontented minority has as yet been reduced to declare open war'. Should this occur, he continued, the American fiscal system 'would prove a perpetual hindrance to a government whose pecuniary demands were large'.[15] The antebellum determination to curtail the national government's role in managing the economy created obstacles for the lawmakers who needed to generate enough revenue for fighting the Civil War. Mark Wilson's recent work suggests that 'elected Republican Party officials ended up having surprising little direct control over the North's military economy during the Civil War. Instead veteran military officers managed the national war economy that emerged by early 1862'.[16]

The 'hindrances' in fiscal authority played a significant role in directing the Union's financial options as the Civil War began. The men who redesigned this system did so with more urgency than deliberation or conviction. The need to overcome the antiquated fiscal system fostered during the antebellum era played the predominant role in influencing the financial decisions of the administration.

I do not deny that constituent interests influenced Republican legislators as well.[17] Nor do I question the ideological commitment made by politicians or soldiers to preserving the Union.[18] Instead, I suggest that the condition and structure of the government in 1861 greatly influenced the subsequent wartime fiscal policy. The Republicans assumed control of a government separated from the economy during the antebellum era. The limitations inherent in the federalist system created many 'hindrances', as de Tocqueville noted. Because the states controlled policies regarding banks and currency, the national government could not readily harness the wealth of the nation when the Civil War erupted.

The first 'modern war in American history' compelled many changes in the economy, particularly the fiscal system.[19] These developments did constitute 'revolutionary' changes, as suggested by Charles and Mary Beard.[20] However, the effort to manipulate these transformations, either for ideological reasons or to reward specific economic interests, has been overstated. Rather, the exigencies of war overwhelmed the limits that constrained the government during the antebellum era. The 'revolution' identified by the Beards did not occur because a 'capitalist class was marching onward in seven league boots', intent on rewarding their patrons.[21] Nor did the 'Republicans' belief in the ultimate power of individual labor' play a dominate role in shaping wartime fiscal policy.[22] Instead, preserving the nation placed insurmountable strains on the antebellum organization of government finance. Exacerbated by the 'exhausted condition of the Treasury' before the war began, the struggle to find enough funds to 'give daily bread to the armies of the Union and provide munitions of war' compelled the Republicans to adopt policies that created a new financial system for the United States.[23] 'When I left [Washington]', Dix wrote to retired president James Buchanan on 28 March 1861, 'I do not think the [Lincoln] administration had any settled policy. It was merely drifting with the current, at a loss to know whether it were better to come to an anchor, or set sail'.[24] This statement, I believe, reflects the true nature of the 'party-state', and the nation, on the eve of the Civil War.

The Growing Debt

President James Buchanan's administration mismanaged the nation's finances. At the time of Buchanan's inauguration in 1857, the Treasury recorded a $1.3 million surplus, and a moderate $28.7 million debt. By the start of Abraham Lincoln's first term, the Treasury sagged under the weight of a $25.2 million deficit and a $76.4 million debt, the largest peacetime obligation in the nation's history.[25]

Bad luck, fiscal imprudence and political stalemate fostered this derangement. Soon after President Buchanan settled into the White House, the Panic of 1857 swept the country. The Ohio Life Insurance and Trust Company failed in August 1857. The largest bank in Ohio and purveyor of eastern loans and specie to the western states collapsed after embezzlement and easy credit emptied its reserves. Banks in New York responded by calling in many of their loans, triggering a ripple effect. Businesses and banks nationwide, unable to respond to the demands of their paymasters, declared bankruptcy. One by one, New York, Boston and Philadelphia banks reacted defensively, hoarding their reserves and tightening their credit. As a result, an epidemic of business and bank failures occurred.[26] *Harper's Weekly* reported in December 1857 that, 'the people are suffering from a revulsion almost unprecedented in severity'.[27]

Iron furnaces throughout Pennsylvania, the president's home state, closed, and production fell from 883,000 tons in 1856 to 705,000 in 1858. The value of wheat exports dropped from $22.2 million to $9 million between 1857 and 1859. Wheat comprised the largest export commodity produced by the northern states. Contrasting this despair, foreign and domestic cotton sales continued apace. Cotton exports rose in value to $161.4 million in 1859 from $131.56 million in 1857. The economy of the free labourers languished, while the 'King Cotton' economy, built upon the scarred backs of slaves, flourished. The economic effects of the Panic further exacerbated this sectional tension. This disjunction convinced many southerners of the 'superiority' of the slave-labour based economy.[28] Calomiris and Schweikart have argued persuasively that the Panic resulted from the uncertainty caused by the political tumult regarding the future of the western territories. This would help to explain much of the unease in the US securities market that arose during the Buchanan administration.[29]

Although the Panic ended quickly, the downturn in northern and western states, coupled with the growing prosperity of the South, increased sectional tensions. The Panic also initiated a financial crisis. Customs receipts, the primary source of revenue for the national government, lagged throughout the Buchanan administration. Federal revenues never matched the income collected during any year of President Franklin Pierce's term. Import duties fell from $64.2 million in 1856 to $41.7 million in 1858 with only a slight rebound to $49.5 million in 1859.[30] While the Buchanan administration had the misfortune of coming to office at the onset of the Panic, they exacerbated their troubles by not adjusting their wants to fit this new economic climate.

Table 2.1: Receipts and Expenditures, 1854–61 (in millions)

Year	Customs Revenue	Total Revenue	Expenditures	Surplus/ Deficit
1854	$64.2	$73.8	$55.0	$18.8
1855	$53.0	$65.3	$58.6	$ 6.7
1856	$64.0	$74.0	$68.7	$ 5.3
1857	$63.8	$68.9	$67.6	$ 1.3
1858	$41.7	$46.6	$73.9	−$27.3
1859	$49.5	$52.7	$68.9	−$16.2
1860	$53.1	$56.0	$63.2	−$ 7.2
1861	$39.5	$41.4	$66.6	−$25.2

Source: Davis, *Financial History of the United States*, p. 267.

Reduced revenue did not curtail the administration's spending. Expenditures from 1857–61 topped those of any previous peacetime administration's, despite the drop in income. Buchanan initiated a 'flood of innovations', according to Philip Klein.[31] His attempt to acquire Cuba, the attack against the Mormons, using the Navy to 'protect' American vessels engaged in the illicit slave trade, and expansion of the postal service all extended the scope of government spending and increased the deficit.[32]

Corruption also sapped the federal budget. Historian Mark W. Summers described the administration's malfeasance as 'the most devastating proof of government abuse of power since the founding of the Republic'. President Buchanan built his cabinet from political friends and supporters. This 'compatible group' shared a common sympathy with the objectives of the tenacious southern wing of the Democratic party. President Buchanan gave autonomy to his secretaries, dubbed the 'Buchaneers', and rarely questioned their appointments or budgets. Corruption and profiteering beset the War and Navy departments. Republicans in Congress convened the Covode Committee to investigate the charges. Although they could not find any hard evidence for an impeachment proceeding, they uncovered many dubious and suspicious activities conducted by the president and his 'Buchaneers'. 'Considerable evidence' exists, according to Jean H. Baker, 'that the president's efforts to bulldoze the Lecompton Constitution' through Congress 'involved several forms of bribery'.[33]

On top of these extravagances, the government had legitimate bills to pay. To meet all these obligations, President Buchanan's administration resorted to deficit financing, as indicated in the table below.

Table 2.2: Loans Contracted by the Buchanan Administration

Date approved	Notes or bonds	Authorized amount (in millions)	Amount sold (in millions)	Rate	Sold at par or discount
23 Dec. 1857	Notes	$20	$52.70	6%	Par
14 June 1858	10–20 yr. bonds	$20	$20	5%	2–7% premium
22 June 1860	10–20 yr. bonds	$21	$7	6%	1.45% below par
17 Dec. 1860	Notes	$10	$10	6%	Interest rates from 6–12% accepted; bids as high as 36%
8 Feb. 1861	10–20 yr. bonds	$25	$18.4	6%	11% below par
2 Mar. 1861	Notes	$10	$35.30	6%	par

Source: 'National Loans of the United States', *Tenth Census*, pp. 368–71.

During their four years in office, the Buchanan administration enacted six different 'emergency' loans to pay ordinary government expenses. This represented the first time an administration used deficit financing to meet regular administrative costs. Short-term Treasury notes and long-term bonds were marketed to meet the administration's accumulating expenses. As the financial and political crisis mounted, each loan became harder to secure, and the terms of the loans more disadvantageous to the Treasury

When borrowing money, the national government incurred two obligations to the lenders: first, to pay the interest on the loans regularly and in gold; second, to repay the principal at full value when the loan matured. Once investors lose faith in the government's ability to meet either of these prequisites, borrowing becomes more expensive. The ability to sell the security at par, or for its face value, diminishes. Lenders can demand higher interest rates or purchase securities below par to offset the risk of a default on the interest or principal.[34] Selling securities below par effectively raises the yield, or ultimate amount of interest or principal received by the lender. Thus, lenders can earn substantial returns on their investment when they lend money to a government in distress, as long as that government survives the crisis.

Until the credit crisis of 2008, the United States had been, historically, one of the great success stories in 'emerging financial markets'. Richard Sylla notes that within a decade of the founding, Americans enjoyed a 'vibrant securities market [that gave] liquidity to governmental and private security issues'.[35] Throughout the antebellum era, different administrations, state governments, canal and railroad companies borrowed money with relative ease by issuing bonds. This ability to borrow remains one of the remarkable aspects of early American history. For this reason, the inability of the Treasury to sell bonds on good terms after June 1858 caused great concern.

Treasury notes and longer-term bonds paid the expenses accumulated by the Buchanan administration. Issued in smaller denominations, and for shorter terms, Treasury notes gave lenders greater flexibility. Accepted for all [state] taxes, public land sales and federal bond purchases, Treasury notes 'were as liquid as specie', so investors could reclaim their money quickly if necessary, or if they lost faith in the government. Treasury notes also allow investors to 'ride the tide of interest rates and keep their assets as liquid as possible'.[36] As sectional tensions mounted, investors became increasingly cautious when loaning money to the United States government. They would not commit to long-term securities, instead opting for Treasury notes. This dependence on Treasury notes to meet ordinary government expenses began a policy of short-term borrowing that the Republican administration could not reverse at the onset of the war. Many historians have chastised the Republicans for adopting 'the policy of depending on short-term issues' that would eventually increase the costs of the war.[37] However, this reliance on Treasury notes began during President Buchanan's term because the market would not support longer-term debt. The compounding effect of the Buchanan administration's failure to either cut expenses or raise revenue subsequently impaired the ability of the Republican administration to raise funds for the 'extraordinary' expenses of war. 'It would be ruinous practice in the days of peace and prosperity to go on increasing the national debt to meet the ordinary expenses of government', Buchanan acknowledged in 1859. However, he never stopped the borrowing binge. Buchanan authorized the last loan of his administration on 2 March 1861, two days before the inauguration of Abraham Lincoln.[38]

The United States had managed its debt well, despite early republican concerns about the perils of indebtedness. Rafael Bayley, who completed a history of US debt for the Census Bureau, remarked, 'The United States have been wonderful in their rapid accumulation of debt and their equally rapid reduction'.[39] Only during times of great uncertainty, such as the months before the War of 1812, did the government sell securities at interest rates higher than 8 per cent. Between 1810–20, on a decennial average, the long-term interest rates of the United States never went higher than 6.39 per cent.[40] The United States carried a debt throughout its history, except briefly in 1835.[41]

Throughout the antebellum era, investors had poured money into the United States. The reliability of the federal interest payments enticed many Europeans to invest in US securities, especially railroad bonds. After the collapse of the state bonds in the 1840s, foreigners surveyed the debt in the United States more cautiously. Foreign investing declined, but did not stop. Jay Sexton notes that foreign interest in US securities 'waned' in the late 1850s, but foreign investment in the US amounted to $444 million by 1861.[42] 'We are heavily in debt to Europe,' the *New York Tribune* noted on 4 April 1857.[43] Despite the experience with the states, the national debt remained a good investment for Europeans because scheduled interest payments arrived on time and in gold. However, skittish concern for these securities resurfaced. Between 1857 and 1861, investors expressed their distrust in the stability of the Union by demanding some of the highest interest rates and steepest discounts in US history.

The Secession Crisis and the Treasury

In December 1860, the Buchanan administration began to disintegrate. Four cabinet officers resigned in support of the secessionist movement. Howell Cobb left his post as Treasury secretary on 8 December 1860. To fill Cobb's seat, the president turned to Philip F. Thomas, commissioner of Patents and former governor of Maryland. Thomas openly sympathized with the secessionist movement; later his only son served in the Confederate army. Soon after his appointment was announced, Thomas confided in his memoirs that, 'New York capitalists had gone to Mr. Buchanan and said they would not subscribe for the loan as long as a southern man remained at the Treasury'. Buchanan sacked Thomas after the new secretary had served less than a month.[44]

Immediately thereafter a meeting of 'bank officers and directors of moneyed institutions' held at the Bank of Commerce recommended John A. Dix as the next secretary. He was confirmed on 11 January 1861. Dix had served in the Army for sixteen years and fought in the War of 1812. Admitted to the bar in Washington, DC in 1824, Dix returned to New York, and quickly emerged as a leader in his state's Democratic Party. He held a number of public positions in the 1830s and 40s, including Secretary of State for New York. Between 1845 and 1853, he served in the US Senate, completing the term of the Silas Wright, who became New York's governor. Dix ran unsuccessfully for governor of New York in 1848. Later, President Franklin Pierce asked Dix to serve as his Secretary of State. A 'cabal' of southern politicians, who abhorred Dix's sympathy for the Free Soil Movement, thwarted his nomination. Dix's son later reported that 'great indignation was felt by this breach'. This fostered Dix's long animosity for the Democracy's 'slave interests'. It also invoked great sympathy and support amongst the northern Democrats, particularly in New York. Dix returned to private law practice and launched a literary magazine called the *Northern Light*. Regarded as a cultured and well-read man of great integrity, he traveled frequently in Europe and his travelogues enjoyed popularity in the US. When 'great frauds' besmirched the New York post office in 1860, President Buchanan, a long-time friend of Dix's, asked him to take over the position of Postmaster. He established order in the New York postal service, which endeared him to the political and business leaders of the city. They turned to Dix again to rescue the Treasury early in 1861.[45]

When Dix arrived at the Treasury, he found that 'Public business had been neglected, letters from merchants and capitalists remained unanswered, and complaints from all parts of the country had been unheeded'.[46] The secretary soon faced new difficulties. As the southern states seceded, local authorities claimed the federal revenue stored in their local customhouse vaults. On 30 January 1861, for example, Joseph E. Brown, governor of Georgia, ordered the collector in Savannah to pay 'no more money from the customs house to any government or person without my order'.[47] Of the 152 ports of entry that collected tariffs in 1858, fifty-two of these lay in states that eventually joined the Confederate States of America.[48] These ports generated approximately 6 per cent of the federal customs revenue (New York alone accounted for 68 per cent) during the late antebellum years, but their detachment threatened to disrupt trade at a time when the government needed every cent.[49] More importantly, cotton would no longer travel north for export, which would curtail northern imports.

Dix received a flurry of dispatches, many from southern customs officers declaring their intention 'as good and loyal citizens to obey the authority of my state' and turn over the duties they collected to their state governments. Other officials who wished to remain loyal to the Union wrote to Dix, pleading for instructions.[50] Many captains of the revenue cutters stationed in southern ports surrendered their ships.[51] The captain of the *McClelland*, a cutter anchored in New Orleans, refused to obey the order to depart for a safe port. Dix instructed the lieutenant who reported the insubordination to arrest Captain Breshwood and sail for New York. 'If anyone attempts to haul down the American flag', Dix commanded, 'shoot him on the spot'.[52] (This occurred ten weeks before the assault on Fort Sumter.) Despite Dix's bravado, the *McClelland* fell into Confederate control until June 1862, when Major General Benjamin Butler reclaimed federal authority in New Orleans. As a token of respect and friendship, Butler sent Dix 'an identical flag' plus the 'Confederate flag which was hoisted by traitor hands in its place'.[53] Revenue cutters were not the only loss. When the Louisiana secession convention seized the port, they also took control of the Mint and Customs House. The vaults in the two buildings contained approximately $600,000 in specie, a further blow to the ailing Treasury.[54]

Losing New Orleans had long-term repercussions beyond that of coin, tariffs and revenue cutters. It imperiled the economic stability of the Union because, as a Treasury report warned, Confederate control of the port would strike 'a fatal blow at the free navigation of the Mississippi'. Seizing this key port gave the future Confederate States control of the 'commerce of the West ... Any importer sending his wares up the river to northern consumers would have to pay two tariffs — one to the [Confederate States] when he passed through New Orleans, and one at the final destination'. Over twenty Union inland ports would be affected, including Chicago, St Louis and Pittsburgh. Farmers exporting their commodities might face an export tariff, the report speculated, a scenario that eventuated when the Confederate Congress enacted an export duty in May 1861.[55]

General William T. Sherman, whose service in the army had taken him to many southern states, and therefore given him a keen perspective on southern politics and culture, outlined the magnitude of the problem to his brother John in a 1 February 1861 letter:

> If the South have free trade, how can you collect revenues in the eastern cities? Freight [from these cities] would be about the same as rail from New York, and importers at New Orleans [who] have no duties to pay undersell the east...the north [must adopt free trade] or blockade' because it could no longer control New Orleans.[56]

John Sherman, representative, and soon senator, from Ohio, found these events of special importance. As Chair of the House Ways and Means Committee he remained deeply concerned with the fiscal straits of the government. Further, his constituents relied on the export of farm commodities for their well-being and had elected Sherman to represent these interests.[57] He understood that the loss of New Orleans was a blow to the economic fortunes of his state as well as the

Union. The disruption in trade led to a fall in customs receipts for the first three months in 1861.[58]

The money grab extended to the capitol as well. According to the *New York Times* on 3 March, the day before Lincoln's inauguration, federal employees scrambled to pocket some loot before the change in administrations. Under the 'spoils system', a new administration meant a change not only at the helm, but also throughout the government, particularly with a new party in power. Federal workers expected to lose their sinecures to Republican partisans, and determined to take what they could.

> The rush upon the Treasury was greater than was ever before known, and before noon, every dollar in the public vaults had been paid out. [One man] ran from room to room endeavoring to get ahead of the crowd and secure the requisite officials' signatures before he could reach the Treasurer's counter ... When every eagle had taken flight, drafts were issued on the sub-Treasurer at New York.[59]

The Lincoln administration faced these challenges when sworn into office on 4 March. The Union carried the largest debt the government had ever accumulated without engaging in a war. The growing hostilities made large outlays inevitable, although the vaults stood empty. Note and bond holders expected their interest payments, on time and in gold, an inflexible demand if the government wanted to keep its credit from sinking any lower. Attempts to borrow additional funds met with scepticism. The loss of customhouses and the uncertainty of trade curtailed government revenue. The Union faced the prospect of war with an empty Treasury, no secure source of income, and the national credit hobbled. 'Financially, the federal government was more poorly prepared for war in the early months of 1861 than it had been since its establishment', stated economist Robert T. Patterson.[60] On the eve of the Civil War, the Treasury stood bereft of funds, facing a perilous future as new leadership assumed responsibility for the nation.

The Morrill Tariff

Throughout American fiscal history, when the federal government faced financial 'embarrassments', officials raised tariff rates to augment income. Because customs duties represented well over 90 per cent of national income until the Civil War, adjusting tariff rates remained the most practical means of increasing the flow of funds into the Treasury when necessary. Trade had slowed during the secessionist winter; this, coupled with the disruption in collecting customs duties, resulted in a drop in federal receipts between January and March 1861. Not only did this have a direct effect on increasing the deficit, it also reduced the amount of specie coming into the country, since importers paid all duties in coin. Because interest payments on federal loans were paid in gold, the decline in tariff revenue greatly increased the government's credit difficulties. Bond purchasers demanded steady interest payments in gold. Without sufficient customs receipts, investors remained sceptical about the government's ability to pay interest rates in gold and on time. This increased the stress on the federal budget, as the government scrambled to meet the interest payments. Rates rose as investors viewed the growing sectional tensions in the United States with deep wariness. In the past, Congress relieved these derangements by increasing revenue.

However, the political crisis of the late 1850s stymied efforts to adjust the tariff in order to raise more money for the ailing Treasury. Internal taxes had not been collected in the United States since the War of 1812, so adjusting tariff rates provided the most efficient means of correcting budget shortfalls. In 1859 Buchanan asked Congress to raise tariff rates, stating, 'I would recommend that the necessary revenue [for government expenses] be raised by an increase in the present duties on imports'.[61]

Both the Thirty-fifth and Thirty-sixth Congresses became bitter forums for the increasing sectional divide. These tumultuous congresses featured angry debates over the admission of Kansas and the Lecompton Constitution, the reaction to Dred Scott decision, the vitriol over the John Brown raid and the caning of Senator Charles Sumner. In addition to the political repercussions that ensued, a 'fiscal logjam' resulted.[62] No tariff measure could pass, although both Republicans and Democrats agreed that something needed to be done. 'Things look dark here', Secretary Dix lamented on 16 January 1861. 'The utter inactivity of Congress stupefied those who otherwise would have some hopes'.[63]

Not until 2 March 1861, when President Buchanan signed the Morrill Tariff into law, did Congress fulfill his request for increased revenue. As noted above, this measure did not only adjust tariff rates, but also provided the last emergency loan for the Buchanan administration. Obscured by the political cant of both contemporaries and historians, the bill's significance as a revenue measure has been underappreciated. Implemented as a direct response to the fiscal crisis created by the Buchanan administration, the Morrill Tariff represented an effort to augment federal revenue for the depleted Treasury. As Justin S. Morrill (R. VT) noted repeatedly during the course of the debates, the tariff aimed to reinstate the rates of the 'free trade' tariff of 1846, rather than implement a new system of protection. The administration needed funds to pay the interest on the accumulating debt. Without more revenue, the government's credit remained impaired. However, political acrimony overwhelmed repeated efforts to address the 'exhausted condition of the Treasury'.[64] This impasse and the resort to Treasury notes began the government's dependence on short-term borrowing that became an integral part of the Civil War financing. Sectional tensions hobbled all remedies to the fiscal emergency that rent Congress and the nation.

With the debt enlarged by $50 million during the four years of the Buchanan administration, faith in US securities now ebbed. The deterioration of the country's finances inspired the London *Economist* to observe in the early months of the war, 'It is out of the question, in our judgment, that the Americans can obtain, either at home or in Europe, anything like the extravagant sums they are asking – for Europe won't lend them; America cannot'.[65] Even before the large outlays for the war, lenders expressed scepticism about the debt carried by the United States. The fiscal problems of the country only grew worse as the Civil War approached.

The New Administration

Into this mess stepped an administration comprised of a political party that had existed for only seven years. The Republicans, a minority party with an unstable base, had won their first national election against a divided opponent and with fewer votes than the other candidates combined. They won 116 seats to the Thirty-sixth Congress, but did not reach that number of seats again until the Thirty-ninth Congress.[66] Roy Nichols noted 'in the spring, 1861 elections, the first public referendum since the Republican administration was assembled Lincoln faced defeat at the polls, particularly in Ohio and Connecticut.' The withdrawal of southern representatives gave them an overwhelming majority in Congress; however they knew the Democracy remained strong, and their majority could slip away. Throughout the Civil War, they had a tenuous political mandate and always had to look over their shoulders to gauge the voters' reaction.[67]

A rejection of the more aggressive policies of the southern slaveholders' demands had united a disparate group of Democrats, Whigs and American Party nativists under the banner of this new party. Politicians from these different parties abhorred the 'political heresy', which dictated that slavery could exist in 'any or all territories of the United States.' Although this opposition to the 'slave power' united Republicans, they did not agree on many other substantive issues.[68] Richard Hofstadter described the early Republican Party as a conglomeration of,

> abolitionists and Negrophobes, high and low tariff men, hard and soft money men, former Whigs and former Democrats embittered by old political fights, prohibitionists and tipplers, Know-Nothings and immigrants.[69]

More recently, Allen C. Guelzo found that Abraham Lincoln's support in Illinois came from a 'socially heterogeneous mix that included farmers, a carpenter, trunk manufacturer, butcher, bank teller...ironically the "rich men" [other historians] expected to find at the core of party organization' supported Stephen A. Douglas instead.[70]

Although they shared a common 'rising hostility to the aggressive slave power' and believed this threat endangered the future for free labour, other political concerns continued to cause rifts within the ranks.[71] Sharp disagreements over practical matters of governance plagued the Republicans as they assumed leadership. This dilemma surfaced quickly with regard to fiscal policy. Many former Democrats, most notably the new Treasury secretary, Salmon P. Chase, did not dance to the Whig fiddle.

Former Whigs dominated the Republican Party. The Whig party, which rose and fell between 1834 and 1856, coalesced in opposition to President Andrew Jackson's economic initiatives. A common philosophy towards handling the nation's finances lay at the core of their organization. Michael F. Holt summarized their approach to governance in stating, 'government at all levels of the federal system should be used positively to elevate people economically, socially, and morally through internal development of the nation's civil institutions and economic infrastructure'.[72]

This faith in an energetic government translated into defence of the Second Bank of the United States, 'a well-regulated currency, a tariff for revenue to defray the necessary expenses of the government, and discriminating in special reference to the protection of domestic labor', as they stated in their 1844 platform. The Constitution vested Congress with the power to 'make [internal] improvements [that] are necessary for the common defence', they reiterated in 1852.[73] President Jackson's attack against the Second Bank of the United States united Whigs; they continued to rail against the state bank system erected in its stead. Whigs justified protective tariffs to spur industry, provide wage security for workers, and generate additional revenue for federally funded internal improvement projects. The 'American System', articulated by Whig leader Henry Clay, epitomized the Whig economic philosophy.

Contrasting the Whigs, the Democratic Party espoused a limited national government and repeatedly extolled the virtues of a 'laissez-faire' doctrine. Their characteristic commitments', according to Jean H. Baker, 'included states rights, federal restraint, and an assertive Unionism ... they were for state rather than national government, for white rather than black, for freedom rather than control'.[74]

The Jackson administration's economic policies emphasized these philosophies. In 'killing' the Second Bank of the United States, the Jacksonians hoped to end the 'privilege' and 'monopoly' in the distribution of government funds. State banks became the main government depositories in an effort to provide them and their customers 'greater regularity and predictability' in finances.[75] 'Government should have no more concern with banking and brokerage than it has with baking and tailoring', lectured William M. Gouge, a Democrat who earlier headed the Treasury.[76] The complementary call to restrict government transactions to 'sound currency', with gold and silver coins the soundest of them all, emphasized the Jacksonian desire to retain 'economy' in government. Because specie had always been in limited supply in the United States (starting in the colonial era), advocating a government whose revenue derived solely from coin translated into a government with constrained financial muscle. The use of bank notes, cheques and other forms of 'paper money' led to extravagance, overspending and 'ruinous fluctuations arising from alternate expansions and contractions of bank issues'.[77] To further limit government expenditure, the Democratic Party in the post-Jackson era abhorred protectionism, which brought more specie into the Treasury coffers, and called repeatedly for tariffs for revenue only.

These approaches to fiscal policy differed sharply. 'The Constitution does not confer upon the general government the power to commence internal improvements', stated a series of antebellum Democratic platforms. The 'federal government is one of limited powers' that has no right to 'interfere or control the domestic institutions in the states'.[78] Democrats relied on 'hard' money, where Whigs looked to economic expansion through ready access to credit and the resulting 'soft' currencies. Democrats distributed many of the financial powers of the government to the states, whereas the Whigs fought for economic development through national programmes. Democrats consistently invoked the benefits of free trade, where Whigs used protectionist tariffs to help foster home industry. Democrats wanted state governments to fund internal improvements; Whigs believed in federally directed, large-scale improvement projects. Democrats advocated using direct taxation when necessitated by fiscal 'embarrassments', rather than loans or increased tariffs. Whigs preferred the ease, efficiency and benefits of raising import duties. Horatio Seymour, a New York leader in the Democratic Party, summarized the parties' differences when he characterized the Democrats as the 'let-alone party' and the Whigs as the 'meddling party'.[79]

Salmon P. Chase, President Lincoln's second choice to lead the Treasury, embodied this juxtaposition. One of the greatest ironies of the historiography detailing the 'Republican' economic measures passed during the war is that 'the first Republican Secretary of the Treasury was a Democrat'.[80] Chase arrived at the Treasury from a winding political road. He had worked on an anti-Mason presidential campaign, served on the Cincinnati city council as a Whig, tried to solidify the Liberty and Free Soil parties during the 1840s, and represented Ohio in the Senate beginning in 1849 as a Free Soil Democrat. In reaction to the Kansas-Nebraska Act, in 1854 he helped draft the 'Appeal to Independent Democrats' and create the new political organization that became the Republican Party. Ohio voters chose him as their first Republican governor in 1855, then senator in 1859.[81]

Chase's commitment to the abolitionist movement spurred this eclectic political journey. He emerged as one of the nation's leading anti-slavery politicians in the 1830s, before the movement gained popular support in the 'free states'. As an attorney in Cincinnati, Chase represented fugitive slaves fortunate enough to escape into Ohio, earning him a national reputation as the 'Attorney-General for runaway slaves'.[82] His well-publicized briefs in these cases, and frequent denunciations of the peculiar institution, gave Chase a national reputation as a leader in the effort to end slavery. 'It is difficult now for anyone unacquainted with the earlier days of the slavery struggle' to understand the intense animosity toward Chase because of these efforts, according to Jacob W. Schuckers, Chase's secretary and later biographer. Chase 'was the object of hate, bitter and unrelenting' because of his abolitionist views.[83] However, when the public sentiment turned, and support for abolitionism spread in the northern states during the 1850s, Chase received accolades for his many years of service to the anti-slavery cause. In moving between parties, Chase wanted to find the best political vehicle to abolish slavery. The Republican Party finally achieved this goal. On the eve of the 1860 Republican convention, Chase enjoyed a greater national reputation than Abraham Lincoln and thought, optimistically, that he might win the nomination. However, his well-known criticism of protective tariffs made him an impalpable candidate for the former Whigs in the party.

Despite his political vacillations, and early legal career representing the Bank of the United States in Ohio, Chase consistently retained his faith in the economic principles of the Democratic Party. In an 1851 letter, Chase restated his belief in the 'fundamental laws' that included:

> 'Limitation of state indebtedness, coupled with prompt and honorable discharge of existing obligations; equal taxation of all property, whether corporate or individual (direct taxes), restriction of legislative power to legitimate subjects...No Democrat', he continued, 'will dissent from those resolutions which administer a deserved rebuke to the Whig administration now controlling the actions of the general government, and reaffirm those Democratic doctrines in relation to the tariff, the Bank of the United States, and the Independent Treasury'.[84]

Later, in 1868, he confided to a friend, 'on the questions of finance, commerce, and administration generally the old democratic principles afford the best guidance'.[85] Chase distrusted banks and bankers, supported 'sound' rather than 'soft' money, remained uneasy with the large loans contracted during the Civil War, preferred direct rather than indirect taxes, and continually urged 'economy' in government administration. All these views expressed the core economic principles of the antebellum Democratic Party.

Although writers often speak of Chase's inexperience in finances, his qualifications matched, if not exceeded, those of his predecessors. Under fiscal federalism, a state governor had more direct experience with banking and revenue policy (outside of tariffs) than a Treasury secretary. Most importantly,

Chase tended to over rely on those he trusted.[86] Here one finds another great irony of the Beardian interpretation of the war policy: rather than developing or enriching a 'clientele' of industrial or finance capitalists, many of Chase's policies sought to circumvent the power a few bankers maintained over the government's borrowing practices. He wanted instead to 'extend the circle of contribution as wide as possible', rather than continue the antebellum practice of relying on a few wealthy individuals to keep the nation solvent.[87]

Ambition rather than inexperience remained Chase's weakness. Consumed by the 'cancer' of an intense desire to become president, his colleagues found him 'an ostentatiously correct Puritan', 'somewhat severe, ponderous', with an 'intense selfishness for official distinction and power' and considerably vain.[88] He migrated between parties not only to end slavery, but also to provide a vehicle for his presidential aspirations. As Stephen Maizlish observed, 'Chase could see no distinction between his pursuit of worldly recognition and his ideals, between his ambitions and his dreams of reform'. His niece recalled that

> He abominated cards and waltzes ... there was no going to the races or the theatre for any member of his family. He was very religious; and almost puritanical in his observ-ance of the Sunday. He would not even allow us to write letters on Sunday.[89]

Chase tried to soften his anti-protectionist position to earn the 1860 presiden-tial nomination, but his equivocating resulted in distrust rather than support. 'His philosophy is free trade', Justin S. Morrill noted soon after Chase took the position at the Treasury.[90] Many former Whigs in Lincoln's administration never warmed to Chase. Despite Chase's consistency in supporting the aboli-tionist cause, many suspected that his desire to become president often trumped his anti-slavery fervor.[91] 'He strove to attain an honor which was never his', Jay Cooke related.[92]

Former Whigs' suspicions regarding Chase seemed justified when, while Treasury secretary, he mounted a surreptitious campaign to take the 1864 Republican presidential nomination from President Lincoln. After this attempt failed, he courted Democrats to win their support for their party's nomination in 1868, while he served as Chief Justice of the Supreme Court. These misgiv-ings, coupled with Chase's fundamental differences with regard to the economic policy, created a great animosity toward the Treasury secretary. Chase main-tained a 'cold courtesy' with William H. Seward and other former Whigs in the party.[93] Deep differences on the core economic issues of the antebellum era still divided the Republicans when they assumed the leadership of a broken nation. Republican candidates had practised 'avoidance and compromise' in articulating their economic platform before and during the 1860 election.[94] Members of the party wrangled throughout the war years on the basic economic questions that had divided the political classes throughout the antebellum era. Hard money or soft, free trade or protective tariffs, expansive or limited government: these differences did not disappear once the Republicans came to office. These internal differences tainted the efforts of the administration to meet the fiscal challenges brought by the Civil War.

Selecting Chase as Treasury secretary 'nettled' the Whig establishment in the party. One 'Ohio Whig' who learned of Lincoln's plans to include Chase in his Cabinet in order to represent all elements of the new party mourned, 'in the name of God can it be that' you incorporate 'such incongruous and repulsive elements as Chase' into the first Republican administration.[95] The President-elect believed that all elements of the party needed representation in his Cabinet. 'It became apparent', observed John Niven, 'that Lincoln wanted a coalition Cabinet in which previous party affiliations, competing ideologies, and representatives of the distinct sections of the Union were balanced'.[96]

When Chase began his tenure at the Treasury, he and President-elect Lincoln had not developed any plan or strategy for addressing the nation's economic problems. Chase met with Lincoln in Springfield, Illinois for two days in January 1861, but left the meeting believing that 'he would be more useful in the Senate' than as Treasury secretary.[97] Lincoln told Chase during their discussions that, 'I sent for you to ask whether you will accept the appointment of secretary of Treasury without, however, being exactly prepared to offer it to you'.[98] Chase lobbied for the position, telling those who agreed with him regarding the 'proper financial and economical policy of the Administration' that they needed to 'visit Mr. Lincoln and discuss everything and unreservedly with him'.[99]

Over the winter, Chase began to reconsider. He preferred to represent Ohio in the Senate, he concluded. Chase knew he had strong support from many fellow Democratic-Republicans in the ranks of the party, but he also knew he faced strong opposition within the Cabinet. When Chase arrived in Washington, D.C. on 1 March 1861, he still believed he would serve the country by representing Ohio as its senator. Without informing Chase, Lincoln sent his name to the Senate for confirmation after the start of the session. The Cabinet divided along sectional and political lines. Their ideological commitment to limiting the expansion of slavery did not lead to any agreement over how to manage the crisis of disunion. Little cooperative discussion occurred before the inauguration. The Lincoln administration began its tenure without a firm plan of action in hand. The skirmishing between former Whigs and Democrats to secure factional influence in the new administration replaced meditative discussions over how best to address the nation's problems. Seward so opposed Chase's nomination that he offered his resignation even before the inauguration, an offer Lincoln declined. The dialogue that did occur, particularly between Chase and Seward, seethed with tension. At one cabinet meeting, while Chase discussed his 'financial views',

Gideon Welles, Secretary of the Navy, observed that the other secretaries 'were not prepared to have him [Chase] set up a standard of financial, political, or party orthodoxy for them'.[100] Chase had no time to work on the economic problems of the country before he took office.

Although known for his haughtiness and ravenous ambition, one may look at Chase's predicament upon assuming his new job with some sympathy. In his first official report to Congress in July 1861, Chase wrote that:

> He [Chase] has but reluctantly assumed the charge of the vast and complicated concerns of his department, and he is deeply conscious how imperfectly he is qualified by experience, by talents or by special acquirements for such a charge. He understands also, better perhaps than anyone outside can understand, the difficulties incident to the task...the criminal insurrection deranges commerce, accumulates expenditures, necessitates taxes, embarrasses industry, deprecates property, cripples enterprise, and frustrates progress. He has simply endeavored, under these perplexing circumstances to meet the case just as it is.[101]

Although the Republicans won a majority in the House of Representatives in 1858, they had no experience as a governing party. They did not share common beliefs regarding economic policy. This lack of cohesion, coupled with the 'exhausted condition of the Treasury', did not bode well for successful implementation of a strategy to correct the nation's economic distress. The disaffection within the ranks extended beyond the Whig–Democrat divides. Senator William Pitt Fessenden, an old line Whig, admitted two months before Lincoln's inauguration that 'I am getting fairly to detest him [Seward]'.[102]

Once the war began, a common purpose to reunite the nation emerged, both within the party and the nation. However, the challenges faced by the new administration continued. The government's finances rested upon an antiquated fiscal system. When the Civil War erupted, the new administration laboured under the constraints of a fiscal system designed to 'divorce' it from the economy. To address the challenges of financing the war, the Republicans had to dismantle this system. However, they did not initiate this fundamental change in the nation's financial structure: the war forced it.

The 'Stunted Government'

A systemic change in the American banking system occurred after President Andrew Jackson's 'Bank War' of 1832. The demise of the Second Bank of the United States, followed by the Panic of 1837, left the financial institutions of the nation in a state of disarray and subsequently depression. Peter Temin has argued persuasively that many exogenous factors, and not solely these domestic financial policies, led to the Panic.[103] Those who suffered during the downturn believed the actions of private bankers created the crisis. 'By casting doubt on the solvency of some banks', Harry Scheiber wrote, 'Jackson contributed to public distrust of all banks and increased the tendency of private persons to hoard specie'.[104] One congressman declared in 1838 that 'Hereafter I will doubt the solvency of all banks.'[105] The void created by the dissolution of the Second Bank of the United States, plus the public perception that bank policy had created the depression they endured, led to the fundamental reordering of the fiscal framework of the country. 'Whether caused by specific economic grievances or qualms about the perversion of the proper moral order', Michael Holt noted, 'anti-banking sentiment was a major political force until the 1840's'.[106]

Congress established the Independent Treasury in the wake of this financial upheaval. Inaugurated in 1840, at the end of Martin Van Buren's one term as president, the 'Constitutional Treasury', or 'Sub-treasury' as its advocates liked to call it, aimed to 'divorce' public funds from private banks. The Treasury alone should secure public funds, rather than placing the wealth of the nation in the hands of untrustworthy bankers. Bank failures took public as well as private funds. Banks recklessly issued notes without sufficient reserves, and this ended the nation's prosperity, according to the political rhetoric. Therefore the Independent Treasury, which kept government funds out of weak banks, best protected the public credit. David Kinley, who wrote the definitive history of this institution, summarized this sentiment when he noted that 'the severance of the government from the banks, as banks were then constituted ... was the means of removing a large element of uncertainty from the credit of the government, and of insuring to the currency the 'soundness' for which the people had struggled so long in vain'.[107]

The Independent Treasury Act, repealed in 1841 when the Whigs ascended to power, returned in 1846 during the administration of James K. Polk. The key provision of the revitalized law directed receivers of public funds to keep them 'safely without loaning, using, or depositing in banks or exchanging for other funds'. The government would not entrust its revenue to state or private banks, except to facilitate a transfer from receivers to a public depository. This measure aimed to 'divorce' public funds from capitalists who could use them for private gain. In addition, the 1846 act introduced the 'Specie Clause': the Treasury could use only or gold and silver coins, or Treasury notes, in all transactions. This law also left the regulation of the banking industry to the individual states. The national government became its own banker and securities broker and allowed states to frame the rules under which banks operated.[108]

Supporters of the Independent Treasury hailed the institution as the ballast that secured the government's credit. William Gouge, a former Treasury secretary in the Jackson administration who emerged in the 1850s as the Independent Treasury's ombudsman, captured the Democracy's enthusiasm for this system in 1855:

[the Constitutional Treasury] is all that now stands between us and paper money inflations similar to those of 1817 and 1835 to be followed by revulsions similar to those of 1819–21 and 1837–43. It is a system which ought to be strengthened and extended so that it may be faithfully carried out in all its provisions.[109]

The ease with which the government raised $49 million to finance Mexican–American War, and blunted the impact of the Panic of 1857, convinced Democratic officials that the Independent Treasury best secured the government's credit. 'I am well satisfied', Howell Cobb stated in his 1858 annual report, 'that the wholesome restraint which the collection of the government dues in specie exerts over the operation of our present banking system contributed in no small degree to mitigate the disasters of the late revulsion'.[110] President Buchanan, two months later, also cited the Independent Treasury as a great success.[111] 'Notwithstanding its many imperfections', Kinsley commented, 'the system seems to have been at this time in good working order, and was apparently accomplishing all that its advocates had claimed for it'. Howard Bodenhorn noted that after 1842, with the concurrent rise of free banking and the Independent Treasury, "bank failures became rare and loss rates were small".[112]

Some of the 'imperfections' of the less regulated banking system created problems for the management of the economy on the eve of the Civil War. Under the 1846 law, Treasurers and receivers could deposit their specie with banks only to facilitate transfers and exchanges. The banks often ignored this provision, as they did during the Mexican–American War (as noted in the previous chapter) and used the deposited specie for their purposes. This permitted select banks to reap handsome profits, a situation that undermined the spirit of the law. Because banks had a disincentive to transfer money quickly, these transactions moved slowly. Transferring funds from New York to Washington, for example, took as long as 135 days; in one case, 604 days passed before $25,000 arrived in New Orleans from Boston.[113] Mobilizing the nation's wealth under this system proved problematic.

Because of these delays, and the commissions charged by bankers, Gouge suggested that the proliferation of railroads and steamboats allowed for government agents to transfer specie from one depository to another 'with great dispatch and very small expense' and without using banks.[114] When implemented, this change resulted in the wealth of the nation moving about in steamboat holds, railroad cars, and in some instances, 'horse-pulled dray-carts'.[115] When the vaults in Washington, D.C. were emptied on 3 March 1861, officials were not sure when they would have money at their disposal in the central Treasury.

Another 'imperfection' related to how the Treasury held the funds. The depositories stored funds in an insecure manner in many facilities. When Gouge toured the different depositories in 1855, he found a lack of vaults or protection from fire or other natural calamities. The 1846 legislation had directed the Treasurers to hold the public funds in safes, but did not allocate the money for their purchase until after 1857. $10,000 had been stolen from the Pittsburgh depository when the night watchman ('a drunkard') accosted the Assistant Treasurer and took his keys. One depository in Indiana consisted of an apartment off the 'chief tavern in town' where 'hundreds of thousands of dollars of United States money' rested peacefully over the years in 'wooden boxes resembling in form a giant coffin'.[116] Small-scale transactions, such as those at the post offices across the country, could not be completed with specie; so those civil servants ignored the law and traded in local currency, postage stamps or other substitutes for money. After collecting the fees for postage, they turned to banks to convert the local currency into coin, and paid a fee for the service.

The limits of this archaic system did not impede the expanding economy of the late 1840s and pre-Panic 1850s. California gold, as well as an upsurge in cotton and wheat exports, doubled the amount of specie circulating throughout the country. The increase in commerce created 'little friction in the workings of the new fiscal machinery', Kinley opined.[117] Despite the withdrawal of public revenue from the monetary mix, the economy continued to chug. 'The specie from these sources [California and exports] so greatly increased the gross amount in the country that the spasmodic influence of Treasury receipts and disbursements upon the reserved and the lending power of banks became apparent only in crises', Bray Hammond noted.[118]

Treasury Secretary Cobb strengthened the Independent Treasury in a series of circulars issued between 1857 and 1858 that prohibited the deposit of public revenue in banks even for transfers. Instead, the Treasurers could issue drafts that could be cashed for specie at a depository. (Only postmasters were exempt from this rule.) He ordered the number of depositories increased to 'one or more for each state' to encourage collectors in rural areas to follow the rules and not use banks as intermediaries. He also allocated more funds for vaults and fireproof safes. Cobb's orders further strengthened the 'divorce' between the government and the banks by not depositing public funds into private or state banks for any purposes.[119] In interpreting these regulations as late as 1862, Salmon P. Chase advised his employees, 'It must be remembered that the law confined national payments and receipts to coin and notes of the United States. Officers of the Treasury, army or navy, all officers of all departments must obey and enforce this law'.[120] Bray Hammond quipped, 'Like a good lawyer, Chase was sticking to what he considered to be the law's demand'.[121] Rather than 'eas[ing] constitutional scruples about the government's role in economic activity', Chase's decision to adhere too firmly to the law set in motion the sequence of events that led to the suspension of specie payments the following December.[122]

The Independent Treasury had two important implications at the onset of the Civil War. First, it concentrated public funds in diffuse locations and rendered them only as secure as the rectitude and loyalty of their keepers. This facilitated the spoliation that occurred in New Orleans and throughout the southern states during the secession crisis. Officials with access to the Treasury vaults in the seceding states could, and did, take the customs revenue, minted coins and other government receipts and transfer them to the Confederate state governments without any intervention from a third party (such as bank officials). Employees in Washington grabbed all they could before the change in administrations.

Second, the government had to sell its own loans. Before 1846, banks 'sold' government loans, and provided credit while holding the issued notes and bonds.[123] Banks not only facilitated these transactions, but 'private bank note companies' printed the securities (the actual pieces of paper that constituted the bonds), a duty the Treasury had to assume.[124] Under the Independent Treasury, banks could no longer act in this intermediary role. Instead they had to purchase the bonds with specie, then turn around and resell them to the public. The loans taken to prosecute the Mexican–American war totalled only $49 million, during a period when the economy showed strength and promising future. Senator Thomas Hart Benton noted that the 'Sub-treasury system' sold more bonds for that war than expected. 'Government bills were [sold] above par! And every loan taken at a premium! ...this is the crown and seal upon the triumph of the gold currency.'[125]

James Cummings noted that during the Mexican–American War, the Independent Treasury 'performed adequately, in receiving, safeguarding, paying out, and transferring the government's money.'[126] However, the government needed more money at the onset of the Civil War, and the system in place could not handle the burden. Enriching his 'finance capitalist' acquaintances concerned Chase less than obtaining the funds he needed to prosecute the war.[127] The limitations imposed by the Independent Treasury created, according to Bray Hammond, a 'stunted government' that greatly circumscribed the operations of the Treasury. These institutional restrictions, erected purposefully, minimized the role of government in the economy and society. Subsequently, this system limited the options available to rectify the 'embarrassments' faced by the Treasury on the eve of the Civil War.[128]

Congress revised the Independent Treasury law on 5 August 1861 to allow the government to borrow from banks and keep funds lent in bank vaults until the Treasury disbursed it. However, the 'specie clause' instructing the government to pay for its goods in gold remained in place. In practical terms, this meant that the government could not use checks, state bank notes or other 'paper heresies' to purchase war goods or pay soldiers; disbursements by the Treasury still had to be made in specie or Treasury notes. The Treasury only held only $3.6 million when Chase came to office. Because of the dearth of coin, beginning in August 1861:

[Treasury notes were used] for salaries in Washington. They were received with reluctance, and the merchants and shopkeepers endeavored to discredit them. Railroad corporations refused them in payment of fares and freight; and leading banks in the city of New York refused to receive them except on special deposit. The Secretary [Chase] and other officers of the treasury signed a paper agreeing to accept them in payment of salaries...General Scott issued a circular on September 3, 1861, announcing to the army that treasury notes in five, ten, and twenty dollars would be used to pay troops...The available coin [was needed] in payment of the interest upon the public debt.[129]

The 'Paper Anarchy'

According to Stephen Mihm, the policy of 'benign neglect on monetary matters' before the Civil War had two results. The first was a 'sprawling system' of decentralized state-chartered banks. The second was the 'proliferation of bogus bank bills.'[130] The revulsion against banks that manifested after the Panic of 1837 greatly affected state banks. The demise of the Second Bank of the United States effectively ended the national government's oversight of banking procedures until 1863. Each state established its own set of rules for chartering banks. From this void emerged the system of 'free banking'.[131]

New York state instituted a Free Banking law in 1838 that soon became the basis of banking reform at the state level (and the model for the National Bank system introduced by Chase in 1863). Sixteen of the thirty-four states adopted free banking laws by 1860. Free banks could open without a state legislative charter as a limited liability company. Any individual or consortium could open a bank if he/they could accumulate the capital required by the state. Once incorporated, the free banks would deposit bonds or mortgages with a state auditor as security against any notes they issued. The composition of these securities varied from state to state; originally most relied on state bonds, but federal issues also fulfilled the requirement. Increasingly after the mid-1840s, railroad bonds became an acceptable form of security.[132]

Banks proliferated under this state-centred system. The number of banks in the United States jumped from 829 in 1838 to 1601 in 1861. This lack of oversight and ready access to liquidity and credit spurred economic development in many parts of the country, but created economic instability in other regions.[133] A study conducted of the free banking system in Minnesota, Indiana, Wisconsin and New York found that 104 of 709 free banks established before 1861 failed. Nationally, about half the banks formed under this deregulated system closed within ten years of opening.[134]

The pubic tolerated this spurious system of public finance because banks in all states during the antebellum era served a different function than they do today. 'The most important public function which banks perform is the creation of a currency for the people', noted an 1860 Treasury report.[135] Article I, Section X of the Constitution disallows states to 'coin money, emit Bills of Credit, make anything but gold and silver coin a tender in payment of debts'; however this limitation did not prevent state chartered banks or private entities from issuing script or notes. Since states could not disseminate money, and the federal government relied predominately on specie payments, banks throughout the country filled the currency void. This practice began in the colonial era, when Great Britain banned the incorporation of banks in British North America. In order to have some form of money, Americans adopted a loose system of paper currency, another sign of American pragmatism with regard to fiscal policy. After independence, state banks circulated their own notes as a form of currency to keep pace with the growing demands of commerce.[136]

In 1860, approximately $180 million in state bank notes circulated, most of this 'money' controlled by 'a relatively large number of incorporated banks operated in the interests of their owners'.[137] The Treasury estimated that over 7,000 various forms of legitimate bills circulated in 1860.[138] Moreover, 80 per cent of these individual bills had been successfully counterfeited. This meant that various 'forms of money may have performed as a reasonably effective medium of exchange within localities', where fake bills could be recognized, but 'they were unacceptable at par outside the local community'.[139] A 'paper anarchy' ensued.[140]

Theoretically, the states required free banks to pay specie on demand for any of their circulating notes; in practice states did not enforce this regulation. Gold and silver coin constituted only one quarter of the money in the United States, with deposits and bank notes comprising the remainder.[141] Louisiana, the state with the tightest 'free' banking laws, required banks to maintain a specie-to-deposit ratio of 33 per cent. Most state banks had only 10 per cent of their notes guaranteed by reserves, according to Paul Trescott.[142] 'It is not possible', noted Schuckers, 'that these state institutions' could act as 'auxiliaries to the financial measures of the government' during the course of the war.[143]

'Currency, not credit' became the distinctive problem in American commerce, especially in the western states.[144] 'Manufacturers had always done business in an atmosphere of monetary uncertainty ... forced to use money issued by banks, customers, and merchants. Expenses required immediate payment, whereas income trickled in through the credit cycle', Porter and Livesay related.[145] And when funds arrived, distinguishing the good money from bad became a business in itself. Publications that focused on 'counterfeit detection' proliferated. Private banks that functioned without a charter and whose principals bore the liability if the bank failed, often acted as 'note shavers', validating and converting state bank notes to specie for a premium. Businesses employed 'note detectors' to examine the notes they received and determine their validity:

The note detector scrutinized the worn and dirty scrap for two or three minutes ...
turned it up to the light and looked through it, because it was the custom of banks
to file the notes on slender pins which made holes through them. If there were many
such holes, the notes had been often in the bank and its genuineness was ratified.[146]

'Runs on banks' in the antebellum era, John Knox related, 'were not made by
depositors, but by note holders' eager to reclaim what they could from the issuing bank at the first sign of weakness.[147]

The Coinage Act of 1834 abetted the emergence of this crazy monetary system. This legislation reduced the gold content of the dollar, which changed the
ratio of silver to gold from 15:1 to 16:1, making silver cutlery and jewellery more
valuable than silver coins. Gold coins soon overwhelmed the undervalued silver
coins, which circulated less frequently. Substituting for silver coins, a variety of
small 'change' notes exacerbated the proliferation of paper currency. The intent
had been to fortify the bimetallism but instead silver coins, the only official
monetary instrument under the value of $2.50, were hoarded or exported. This
mistake was corrected in 1853, when the silver ratio was lowered so the coins
were no longer squirrelled away or shipped to England for bullion. But the use of
postage stamps, 'shinplasters' and fractional notes for change continued in many
parts of the country. 'We never had money enough in this country for the proper
conduct of business', Samuel Hooper (R. MA) complained in 1866. 'The effect
of the bank notes, under the old system of state banks, was to expel the money
from the country. Those notes were not money but only used as substitutes for
it within certain localities'.[148] Not only did the government face the challenge of
trying to utilize this peculiar monetary system to pay for munitions, supplies,
and soldiers, but an estimated one quarter of the circulating currency had left the
Union with the seceded states.[149]

This created the second great structural challenge from the antebellum
period that the Treasury had to overcome on the eve of the Civil War: how do
you pay for a war when your vaults are nearly empty, your credit impaired and
the 'money' of the nation is comprised of 7,000 different types of hole-ridden
scraps of paper? Approximately $253 million was deposited in banks in 1860,
$104 million in New York alone. Banks held roughly $83 million in specie. The
government had no claim or ready access to this wealth; the coins circulated or
were hoarded at their owner's discretion. The currency held value in its locality
only, where those familiar with it could detect counterfeits. Once it left the area,
the value depreciated. The state was prostrate, weakened not only by the political and economic turmoil, but also by the limitations of the government's fiscal
structure.[150]

Conclusion

Salmon P. Chase faced these challenges when he was sworn in as Treasury Secretary on 7 March 1861. The Union began the war in a state of economic disarray. Rather than a unified vision for addressing the war finances, Republicans differed sharply over economic policy. Fiscal federalism proved a great impediment to harnessing the wealth of the nation at the onset of the crisis. The antebellum financial structure restricted the options at hand for addressing the Civil War fiscal crisis. We must evaluate Secretary Chase's initial decisions regarding war finance in this context. On 23 April 1861, the New York Times compared the new Republican administration to 'a person just aroused from sleep, and in a state of dreamy half-consciousness'.[151] The challenges of secession and war, coupled with the government's structural liabilities, influenced many of the policy decisions made during the four years of conflict. The limitations inherent in the American fiscal system of 1860 narrowed the choices open to the new administration. The constructed divorce of the national government from banks and local economies hindered Secretary Chase's ability to address the overwhelming pecuniary needs that hit the Treasury as the war began. Faulty credit limited their borrowing options; a spurious system of paper currency, and a Treasury secretary, who did not wish to invoke the 'implied powers' of the government, limited the options for war financing. Critics then and now claim that immediate and more aggressive taxation would have been the answer to the Union financing dilemmas.

At the onset of the war, officials feared that trade would slackened without cotton to export. Ships would bring fewer goods to the Union ports, and this would reduce the amount of customs revenue. The Confederate Congress, on 9 February 1861 enacted a new law based on the Tariff of 1857, and legislated lower rates on imports than the Morrill tariff. Suddenly, goods unloaded at Confederate ports paid a substantially lower duty than those delivered to New York. Ships returning to Europe from the South could fill their holds with bales of cotton, an advantage northern merchants feared they had lost. Thus the Union government's traditional source of income, customs duties, now seemed imperilled. After the secession of states with key customs houses, the legislators recognized that the precarious state of the government's finances required incisive action. The assembling congressmen confronted a problem no Congress had faced since 1816: how best to levy internal taxes.[152]

3 THE MAGNITUDE OF THE CONTEST

The fiscal legislation passed during the four years of Civil War transformed the social, political and economic landscape of the post-bellum era. The United States adopted a uniform currency, established a national banking system, embraced an aggressive, protectionist revenue policy and created an internal revenue system. Before the Civil War, the national government never collected more than $74 million in revenue; after the Civil War, the Treasury never collected less than $257 million in receipts.[1] In 1861, the Treasury department employed roughly 4,000 workers nationwide; by 1866, the number had ballooned to over 10,390.[2]

When the Lincoln administration arrived in Washington, DC, the Union carried the largest debt the government had ever accumulated without engaging in war. Empty vaults, unpaid bills, and large outlays awaited them. Creditors expected their interest payments as scheduled, a demand that would have to be met to keep investor confidence from sinking any lower. The law bound the Treasury to a fiscal system that barred it from using anything but coin and Treasury notes as a means of paying its obligations, including the pay promised to the thousands of soldiers assembling and preparing for battle. The currency circulating in the country worked where it was issued, but depreciated quickly once it left its locality. Congress had adjourned, so no immediate remedies to the financial problem were foreseen. Indeed, after his inauguration, President Abraham Lincoln 'had hoped to cool passions and buy time ... to organize his administration, to prove his pacific intent, to allow the seeds of voluntary reconstruction to sprout'. However, the president, and his cabinet, soon found themselves presiding over the deadliest war in American history.[3]

The Secretary's Choices

The limitations inherent in fiscal federalism placed Secretary Chase in an awkward position. He could only sell bonds that Congress had authorized while in session. Because the war began after the close of the Thirty-sixth Congress, no additional revenue or loan measures could be enacted. President Lincoln did not want Congress to convene until July, because 'he thought it best for the administration to have a free hand in coping with the emergency'.[4] Chase could only acquire needed funds by selling undersubscribed loans approved during the Buchanan administration. Further, Chase determined that the Treasury would not to sell the issues at 'market price', which at that time meant well below par, as the Buchanan administration had done. This decision greatly vexed the domestic bankers whose capital Chase needed. '[Mr. Chase] determined to accept par bids for Treasury notes rather than dispose of [them] at any considerable discount', according to Jay Cooke.[5] Selling them at a discount would have reaped profits for the 'finance capitalists', and incurred greater expense for the nation. In the past, during times of war, the Treasury had sold government securities below par to a few wealthy individuals, who would later resell the issues for a handsome profit. Chase wanted to break that pattern. The secretary explained his reasoning in his initial report to the Congress:

> as the contest in which the government is now engaged is a contest for national existence and the sovereignty of the people, it is eminently proper that the appeal for the means of prosecuting it... should be made to the people themselves.

He wanted to extend the 'circle of contribution' as widely as possible, to make the 'burden press as lightly as practicable upon each individual contributor, and if possible, to transmute the burden into a benefit'.[6] He wanted the 'people' not just a handful of 'finance capitalists' to benefit from holding the bonds. Chase secured just over $15 million by the end of May. His 'puritanical' nature and obsession with economy did help rally the bond market. However, the position of the Treasury deteriorated so rapidly that by June, Treasury notes could not be sold at par. Chase instead used them as collateral for a $5 million, sixty-day loan. Not until 17 July 1861 did the Thirty-seventh Congress authorize the first 'war' loan that allowed the secretary to borrow anew.[7]

Chase faced limited options in his efforts to borrow money. Traditionally foreign markets had provided a reliable outlet for US government bonds. However, 'no money could be borrowed on the other side of the Atlantic', Hugh McCulloch recounted. '[During the 1860 bond sales] not a bond could be sold in either English or French markets. Mr. Chase perceived that the home market was the only one in which the United States securities could be disposed of – that to the people of the loyal states he must look for support of the Treasury.'[8] Remembering the defaults that occurred on state bonds in the early 1840s, foreign investors, particularly the English, remained cautious when investing in US securities. August Belmont, a friend of Secretary Chase, and US agent for the Rothschild family, visited England in July 1861 to try to secure support for the Union cause. He met privately with Prime Minister Viscount Palmerston in July 1861 who told Belmont that, 'We do not like slavery, but we want cotton and dislike very much your Morrill Tariff'. Belmont later reported to Secretary of State Seward that 'I am more than ever convinced that we have nothing to hope from the sympathy of the English government and people in our struggle'.[9] Indeed, by 1866, foreigners held only 13 per cent of the US debt, the lowest percentage of overseas investment in US history until that time. Once confident of Union victory, foreign investment resumed its historic pace: by 1869, foreigners owned over $1 billion, or approximately 45 per cent, of US debt.[10] Foreign investment also brought fresh specie into the country; the dearth of this European coin further exacerbated the difficulties in the bond market.

Chase did not trust state banks as a source of steady investment for government bonds. 'As a chief reliance in the varying fortunes of war, they were clearly inadequate', Shuckers related. 'They were located in widely separated places, they were managed by men of every shade of political opinion; their capital varied largely; they were bound by no public purpose and were subject to no common direction'.[11] Also, the state banks would use their own notes to purchase government bonds as they had done during the War of 1812. John Sherman noted that the lessons of the past had not been forgotten. 'With the terrible lessons of 1815 and 1837 staring us in the face, no one advised adopting as a standard value the issue of 1500 [state] banks'.[12]

> During the War of 1812, banks used state bank notes to purchase federal government bonds, with calamitous results. The notes depreciated to just half their value, causing considerable loss to the national government.[13]

The 'Superior Wisdom of Congress'

The emergency session opened on 4 July 1861, three months after the attack on Fort Sumter. Congress received Chase's report the next day. President Abraham Lincoln requested from Congress only the 'legal means for making this contest a short and decisive one'.[14] Because President Lincoln decided not to call members to Washington earlier, developing the initial finance plans fell to Chase. Because of the 'absence of valuations and the uncertainty of effective cooperation in all' and the lack of machinery in place to collect internal revenue, Chase recommended relying primarily on loans to finance the war, with taxes paying for the ordinary costs of running the administration, paying the interest on the loans, and building a 'sinking fund' to pay off the loans as soon as possible.

The secretary's plan did not represent a bold or innovative idea, but instead relied on the British tradition of borrowing for the 'extraordinary' costs of the war, while taxing for the 'ordinary' expenses of government, including servicing the interest on the debt. Dubbed 'Dutch finance', because it originated with during the reign of King William III, this system provided the means by which England funded its 'Long Century' of warfare from the Glorious Revolution through the final defeat of Napoleon.[15] This strategy followed a long and ultimately successful precedent for absorbing the overwhelming costs of war. Because most of the members of Congress agreed with the president that this would be a short and decisive contest, they felt that borrowing the initial funds would carry the nation through the contest. Implementing a tax system would be time consuming, and unnecessary if the contest was as short and decisive as the president predicted. Secretary Chase feared laying a heavy tax burden on an already divided nation; however, James G. Blaine later recorded that Congress did not accept all of Chase's recommendations, and agreed quickly that the crisis required a more reliable stream of revenue. However, 'the legislators were not inclined to go farther than the head of the Treasury suggested'.[16]

Secretary Chase estimated that the government would spend $318.5 million during the next fiscal year. He requested $240 million in loans and $80 million in tax revenue. This sum represented the single largest appropriation ever sought from Congress. To secure these loans, Chase recommended an interest rate of 7.3 per cent for three-year Treasury notes. Although historically high for US securities, this interest rate nevertheless fell below the demands made by lenders at the end of the Buchanan administration. Chase also requested authority to issue thirty-year bonds, carrying a 7 per cent interest rate. Senator William Pitt Fessenden (R, ME), now Chair of the Senate Finance committee, wrote to his son on 1 July 1861, 'We shall have to authorize a loan for $250 million and I am afraid it will be hard to get. We shall probably give Mr. Chase authority to get it in any way he can'[17] Part of 'getting it' meant enacting taxes that would pay steady interest. 'Public credit can only be supported by public faith, and public faith can only be maintained ... by prompt and punctual fulfillment of every public obligation', Chase stated in his report to Congress.

Chase left it to 'the superior wisdom of Congress' to determine how to raise the $80 million in tax revenue. In the past, the executive branch had often taken the lead in pushing desired revenue schemes. Treasury secretaries Alexander Hamilton, Albert Gallatin and Robert J. Walker wrote, or significantly influenced, the development of tax or tariff policy from their perch in the Treasury. Though Congress had constitutional authority to enact all tax legislation, the secretaries often exerted an authority not vested to the executive branch in the Constitution. Although Chase aspired to assume the same activist role in the nation's fiscal policy, throughout his tenure he practised a narrow interpretation of the Constitution, especially with regard to Congress's authority in revenue policy. This reveals another irony of Civil War governance; although the Lincoln administration expanded many of the powers of the federal government, in this other important area of governance, Chase deferred to Congress.[18] A believer in a narrow interpretation of the Constitution, Chase knew that revenue measures would ultimately come from Congress and did not wish to encroach on their authority. Also, as an opportunist who wished to protect his own political future, one can imagine Chase was happy to leave this volatile issue with Congress. Further, President Lincoln, overwhelmed by his role as the Commander and Chief of the military, left financial policies to Chase.[19] He moved cautiously forward on the tax initiatives.

To secure the revenue to cover the ordinary expenses, the secretary suggested levying taxes on stills and distilled liquors, tobacco, carriages, jewellery and inheritances. He also requested an increase on the duties charged to various types of alcohol. These recommendations represented traditional means of raising short-term revenue. Chase also recommended passage of a direct tax. This request betrayed the secretary's Democratic heritage and economic principles. Although acknowledging that it might entail extra expenses to collect, Chase spoke favourably of the direct tax. Chase believed the best tax system relied on, 'the manifest equity of the distribution of burdens in proportion to means, rather than in proportion to consumption'. He acknowledged that in some states, the local system of taxation would make for a 'certain and convenient method of collection'. Chase expressed his displeasure with the Morrill tariff, suggesting it hindered the 'prosperity of the nation', and urged its repeal or at least adjusting duties so 'the articles now exempt' would carry a 'light' tax. This would allow for lower duties on wool and other protected articles. Chase wanted coffee, tea and sugar taxed, and estimated that these duties would raise an additional $20 million, 'while the burden of this revenue will be mitigated by participation on the part of the foreign producers'.[20]

Finally, Chase also set forth a theme he would repeat constantly during the war. 'The Secretary respectfully asks ... whether the current disbursements of government may not be themselves diminished?' He continually urged economy in government, another Democratic principle that often put him at odds with his Whig cohorts.[21] Although this emphasis on restrained spending bothered his colleagues, Chase's vigilance against 'extravagance' impressed others. 'The secretary's reputation for efficiency and integrity', David H. Donald noted, played a decisive role in 'the gradual restoration of federal credit in 1861' and played an instrumental role in securing the loans the government contracted between Lincoln's inauguration and the opening of the Special Session.[22] The greatest consideration in financing the war remained the need to bring fresh funds into the Treasury.

'Why Stickle About Terms?'

Congress enacted three comprehensive revenue measures during the course of the war: House Resolutions (HR) 71 (1861), HR 312 (1862), and HR 405 (1864). Adopted during the July special session, the first measure, HR 71, represented an important bridge between antebellum fiscal policy and the demands of a modern government. Based on legislation written for the War of 1812, HR 71 initially relied on direct taxes collected in all the states, including those in rebellion. The congressmen assembling in Washington faced the challenge of reuniting a nation consumed by civil war. Bereft of funds, and its credit impaired, all knew that the crisis necessitated some form of internal taxation. For seventy years, the United States had relied on duties collected from imports as the primary source of revenue. Obtaining loans from foreign countries had cushioned the financial 'embarrassments' that occurred when tariffs did not meet all the expenses. Yet, these two traditional sources of revenue now seemed threatened.

The legislators who assembled in Washington for the special session, faced the challenge of reuniting a financially hobbled nation consumed by Civil War. As they had always done in the past, the House concentrated first on the tariff legislation. They passed a measure on 25 July 1861 that reaffirmed the structure and revenue outlines of the Morrill Tariff, but increased many of the rates. Congress removed coffee, tea and sugar from the free list. As the Treasury secretary recommended, they fixed specific rates to these articles to generate guaranteed revenue. Clement L. Vallandigham (D. OH) charged that these duties on coffee, tea and sugar unfairly taxed the 'necessaries of life' and 'subjects of universal consumption'. He demanded they remain on the free list instead of bearing a tax. Thaddeus Stevens (R. PA), Chairman of the Ways and Means Committee retorted that the necessity to 'sustain' the government for the 'prosecution of the war' made these duties inevitable. This move as well represented a traditional remedy to short-term needs. Raising duties on these staple 'luxuries' had been a favourite revenue device during the antebellum era to correct budget shortfalls.

With the tariff adjusted, Congress turned to the internal revenue measures. At the onset of the war, most of the political leaders in both the Union and the Confederate states believed this would be a short war. As John Sherman (R, OH) would later recollect in a speech, 'None of us appreciated the magnitude of the contest – the enormous armies demanded and the vast sums required...when the war came, we were without a currency and without a system of revenue'.[23] In designing these internal revenue measures, Congress never assumed that this would be a protracted war; instead, during the first session of the Thirty-seventh Congress, most predicted victory within thirty days.[24] The revenue measures passed in the session reflected this belief. They passed a tariff adjustment that would readily, and quickly, provide more revenue. The purpose of the Internal Revenue Bill was to assure lenders that the government had a plan to pay the interest on government bonds, and provide a mechanism for establishing a 'sinking fund' that would, eventually, extinguish.

Because of the brevity of the session, the House Ways and Means Committee felt compelled to borrow from the past and adopt a law that had already been written. The measure copied 'section by section' from the 1813 and 1815 Direct

Tax Bills penned by former Treasury secretary Albert Gallatin. When critics characterized the bill as 'undigested', Thaddeus Stevens, retorted that 'this undigested, ill-considered bill is an exact copy of [Gallatin's]'.[25] Hoping to use the old bill, and only readjust the apportionment based on current census figures, the Committee hastily reworked the earlier statute. They introduced HR 71 on 23 July 1861, two days after the Union army's humiliating defeat at the Battle of Bull Run. A group of congressmen moved for the postponement of HR 71 until the next session to give members more time to craft a new, more comprehensive tax bill. Justin S. Morrill (R. VT), Chair of the Subcommittee on Taxation, who became instrumental in developing the national internal revenue programme, rose to address this challenge. 'We want to pass something now promptly', he extorted, 'something that will enable the Secretary of the Treasury to negotiate a loan ... [otherwise] he will not be able to negotiate a single dollar'. Morrill tied the success of future loans to the passage of the tax bill.[26] In its first draft, HR 71 called for $30 million in direct taxes from all the states, with $20 million divided amongst the 'loyal' states and $10 million from the states 'in rebellion'. This reflected the broader Union policy of not recognizing or acknowledging the independence of the Confederate states. All the internal revenue measures passed during the war pertained to the states in rebellion as well. This would have implications for the nation later when the two sections reunited.

Although this bill represented the fifth time Congress proposed a direct tax, because the population and economy of the country had changed significantly, the debates on this bill were more contentious than the earlier statutes. Representatives from western states, and states with rural populations, reacted with hostility to direct taxes. Three main objections to HR 71 emerged during the course of the five days of intermittent debate. First, the original direct tax assessed only real property, and did not tax any wealth in the form of capital. This reflected the origins of the direct tax in the late eighteenth century when wealth equated with land and property (houses and slaves) ownership. The transition from an agrarian to a more mercantile and industrial economy, well underway by 1861, moved more and more Americans toward a new source of income. The western states comprised small populations with extensive land holdings, thus the tax would place a high quota on the citizens they represent. Congress apportioned the 1813 direct tax by population and the assessed value of 'all lands, lots of ground and their improvements, dwelling-houses, and slaves'.[27] Created in a time when scattered farms comprised the base of the economy, the formula for direct taxes no longer matched the demographics of the country. Sixteen southern and western states had joined the United States since 1815, and most of these states had small populations of farmers who owned large tracts of land. As originally presented, the direct tax would fall heavily on these individuals. Western representatives realized immediately that this bill would disproportionately tax their land rich but cash poor constituents. The increased urbanization of the East, and accompanying concentration of capital and non-agricultural wealth that occurred after the first Industrial Revolution in the 1840s and 50s, created a class of urban residents who did not count their holdings in acres. These differences in national demographics meant the tax would fall 'discriminately' on the western states.

Second, the 1861 bill changed Gallatin's system of using state officials to assess and collect the taxes to one that used federal government officials. A group of congressmen, led by New York Republican Roscoe Conkling, raised the fear that 'an army of [federal] officers whose business it is to collect these taxes' would swarm across the country. They suggested employing state tax collectors who could double as the federal revenue officers, a scheme that would avoid having to construct a new bureaucracy. Conkling wanted to rely on the precedent of 1813, when Congress requested that state tax officials act as their emissaries, collecting their quota then submitting it to the Treasury for a discount on their portion of the tax.[28] Finally, each direct tax measure before 1861 included slaves in the assessments. Abolitionist Congressmen objected to collecting the direct tax on slaves because it validated their status as property. They did not wish to sanction slavery by formally recognizing slaves as property that others could own 'like a horse'.[29] This signalled the more aggressive position that many northerners had taken against slavery since the Early Republic.

Schuyler Colfax (R. IN) led a group of western representatives in fighting for tax on capital as well as land. 'The most odious tax of all we can levy is going to be the tax upon the land', objected Colfax on 24 July. He continued, '[I cannot vote for a bill] that would allow a millionaire, who had put his entire property into stock, to be exempt from taxation, while a farmer who lives by his side must pay a tax'. Colfax insisted on dropping the direct tax and instead taxing stocks, bonds and mortgages. 'Put this burden upon the men who are best able to bear it'.[30] John A. Bingham (R. OH) answered Colfax's concerns. Bingham, a former county district attorney and member of the Judiciary committee, had served in Congress since 1855. He had established his reputation as an authority on the Constitution and the law. Bingham countered Colfax's proposal by observing that the Constitution and the Supreme Court decision in *Hylton v. the United States* did not allow for a direct tax on incomes or capital; their only options included levying a direct tax apportioned by population, or indirect taxes that had to be uniform throughout the United States. 'This is not the time', he lectured, 'for friends of the country and the Constitution to undertake to establish a new construction ... There is no power conferred upon the Constitution to impose direct taxes upon personal property'. John A. McClerland (D. IL) renewed Colfax's objection that the tax would weigh 'very heavy, if not ruinous' upon the 'great agricultural states'. Owen Lovejoy (R. IL) joined the fray, and demanded that the tax extend to 'luxury' articles as well as property. Frederick A. Pike (R. ME) called for scrapping the tax on land and instead 'raising the sum by an income tax'.[31]

Based on these strong objections the House voted to return the bill to the Ways and Means Committee to see if they could include some form of tax on capital.[32] Stevens reported back the next day that they could not find any method for sanctioning this. Senator Thomas M. Edwards (R. ME) advocated moving beyond the Constitution and determining a way to tax all property, not just land. 'Why stickle about terms?' he asked.[33] While acknowledging that the Constitution did not allow assessing incomes under the direct tax provisions, Bingham suggested using the indirect taxing authority, and treating income taxes as excises or duties.[34] Anxious to move the bill forward, the members accepted this compromise.

The Ways and Means Committee sent the measure back to Congress with the direct tax apportionment dropped to $20 million, and a 3 per cent tax on all incomes above $600. They accepted Bingham's contrivance of terms, and henceforth referred to this tax as the 'income duty' during subsequent congressional debates.[35] For this reason, the income tax became an indirect, rather than direct tax, according to the provisions in the Constitution. Economic historian Edwin Seligman noted that referring to the measure as an income 'duty' derived from British precedent, where a 'duty was a generic term applied to every source of revenue' and taxes and duties remained 'interchangeable'.[36] The measure passed the House on 29 July 1861. Justin S. Morrill, acknowledging that taxing incomes would 'be the most just and equitable' means of taxation, worried that 'we have no time in this session to mature an income tax'. In an acknowledgement that this measure reflected immediate needs, rather than a long-term change in American financing, Morrill added that, 'I have no doubt [an income tax] will be adopted ... But now, for this emergency, it is necessary that we have something.' The bill moved to the Senate.[37]

Senators did not 'stickle with terms' and voiced immediate support for incorporating an income tax into the revenue measure. 'Let us tax property in the last resort', suggested Senator James F. Simmons (R. RI), member of the Senate Finance Committee. 'We can meet all the exigencies ... with a moderate duty on importations and a moderate tax on incomes', he predicted.[38] Simmons introduced an amendment for the income tax on 29 July. As he announced the amendment, he encouraged the Senate to abandon 'old notions' and replace a land tax for national income tax.[39]

The first American income duty owed much of its heritage to the British income tax statute. Senator Simmons (R, RI) wrote the bill for Congress and noted that 'the time constraints' he faced necessitated using the British legislation as an early template. Simmons served in the Civil War Senate briefly. Elected as a Whig representing Rhode Island from 1841–7, he became very involved in formulating the Tariff of 1842. Later, he lost his re-election bid and resumed his career in yarn manufacturing. Re-elected to the Senate in 1856 as a Republican, Simmons joined the Finance Committee and emerged as an influential participant in their deliberations. Jerold Waltham has shown that Simmons wrote the income tax provisions that became incorporated into HR 71. Scandal, however, smote this legacy; forced to resign in 1862 rather than face censure for a bribery charge, Simmons's work on the income tax has receded from attention.

Before the start of the July emergency session of Congress, Simmons had requested a list of 'references on the subject of the British Income Tax' from the State Department and used it in writing the legislation. 'I could not write such a bill from new till January', he stated.[40] Many of the terms in the US income tax law, including the outline of what sources could be evaluated in determining taxable income (any 'profession, trade, employment, or vocation') came directly from the British statutes.[41] Portions of the income tax law followed those of the British statutes, word for word, although Waltham noted that the British tax 'was not copied verbatim; rather it served as a fountainhead for ideas'.[42] Like most of the revenue measures passed during the Civil War, the income tax would have a profound effect on the financial future of the country, yet the measure was passed as an expedient; it borrowed from the past, while reshaping the future.

The British implemented their first income tax in 1799, to shift the burden of financing the Napoleonic Wars from consumption to income. The British set high exemptions to the tax so the working poor would have some protection from the tax. Repealed in 1802 after the short-term Peace of Amiens was signed, then reintroduced in 1803, the British income duty continued until 1816. Although graduated and with high exemptions, the income tax raised the ire of the British 'because payments are visible and made in comparatively large sums at fixed intervals', according to Arthur Hope-Jones. Indirect taxes, on the other hand, 'although unfair, are often unnoticed and always paid in the form of small additions to the price of the article taxes'. The income tax did not become a permanent fixture in British fiscal policy until 1842.[43]

Because the Constitution requires Congress to apportion all direct taxes in the United States, lawmakers had to classify the US 'income duty' as an indirect tax; in England, as in other European countries since, the income tax has always been referred to as a 'direct tax'. This became a significant difference later in the nineteenth century, when the Supreme Court declared the income tax a direct tax, and therefore unconstitutional. Indirect taxes are restricted only in that the rates have to be 'uniform' across the country. In order to make the income tax graduated, and exempt individuals of lower incomes Congress continually referred to this measure as an indirect tax or an income duty.

The income tax provisions of HR 71 were not debated at length in either the House or the Senate. The modifications made in the upper chamber necessitated a conference committee, from which the final version of HR 71 emerged. When completed, HR 71 levied an income tax of 3 per cent on all incomes above $800 derived from 'any kind of property, or from any profession, trade, employment or vocation carried on in the United States'. This amount was well above a wage earner's salary, so most Americans did not pay any income tax during the Civil War. Income derived from property owned by Americans living abroad was taxed at 5 per cent. In an effort to keep the bond market afloat, income derived from US securities was only taxed 1.5 per cent. In setting uniform rates, Congress followed the Constitution's rules on indirect taxes. 'The indirect or income tax which is to be raised by this bill will be, in my judgment, at least twice as much as they shall raise by direct taxation', Justin S. Morrill predicted. Citizens did not have to pay the income 'duty' until 30 July 1862, again showing that this measure represented a symbolic revenue bill.[44] The first income duty levied in the United States would touch few citizens because of the exemptions.

Although the income tax passed without further delay, the direct tax portion of the bill continued to vex the legislators. The debates centred on how the government would collect the tax. With eleven states in 'rebellion', many fretted that state revenue officers would not have sufficient loyalty to the United States to render the moneys collected. The 1813 and 1815 direct tax legislation had allowed states to collect their quota for the national government, a system that proved more efficient than the earlier Federalist method of sending federal revenue officers to districts throughout the country. The first draft of this bill included the stipulation that federal revenue officers would collect the tax, and it did not permit states to pay their quota in advance for a discount. The recent experience with the southern customs officers had left some members with the belief that only national tax collectors should be used to secure the funds from these tax measures. This change from the 1813 statute had less to do with building patronage opportunities and extending the reach of the government, than making sure that the money collected from the tax measures actually reached Washington. Members of Congress wanted to mollify creditors worried about the security of their interest payments.

Conkling led the dissent on this portion of the bill. Conkling insisted the 'state machinery' would prove more effective in collecting the needed revenue. While Conkling's suggestion seemed to concern itself with a reliable and cost-effective means of collecting revenue, one can also look at this as part of the federalist struggle between state and national control over local governance. Conkling, an ambitious sophomore representative, had won election as the mayor of Utica, New York in 1858 and accepted the Republican nomination to the House months later. 'Boss Conkling', as his biographer David M. Jordan refers to him, integrated well into the New York political system. During the Gilded Age, 'he succeeded to the place that [Thurlow] Weed held' as master of the fetid New York spoils system. '[Conkling] dominated politics' through his control of the New York Custom House.[45] As the nation's busiest port, New York's customs officials supervised the flow of a large share of the revenue from imports. 'The New York Customs House afforded unequal opportunities for graft and extortion and lay at the center of the spoils system'. As one federal employee in the New York customs house stated, 'we clerks ... consider ourselves as in the service of the collector and not in the service of the United States'.[46]

Conkling emerged in the decades after the Civil War as a notorious lord of Gilded Age corruption and political patronage. He also became embroiled in one of most famous love triangles of the nineteenth century; his extramarital affair with Kate Chase Sprague, the daughter of Salmon P. Chase and wife of Rhode Island Senator William Sprague, created a sensation in the years after the war.[47] In 1880, he led the Stalwarts, a faction in the Republican Party that wanted to perpetuate the spoils system against the growing agitation for civil service reform. Conkling resigned from the Senate in 1881 over a dispute regarding federal appointments to the New York City customs house; clearly, control of the collection system in New York long remained a matter of great concern to him. By keeping control of the 'state machinery', and control of appointments, he strengthened his base, and provided himself with the vehicle to ascend to higher political positions. In the nineteenth century, because state legislatures, not the voting public, elected senators, keeping a grip on state based positions secured a politician's power. Opening similar positions to federal power would undermine his authority in New York State, and would provide him with the vehicle to move beyond the House of Representatives to the Senate and beyond. Here we find the merging of public and personal interests in the development of national fiscal policy, and the efforts to retain fiscal federalism to secure state-based political influence.[48]

Regarding the question of how to collect the tax in the Confederate states, the rejection of Conkling's protest relied on a more immediate concern. The direct taxes levied in 1813 and 1815 had not fulfilled expectations. Intended to generate $12 million, the tax produced only $10.5 million total. Not all states collected their share, and no mechanism for enforcement existed. Thaddeus Stevens reminded the members that Civil War would exacerbate this problem. Stevens believed that granting only the federal government the authority to hire revenue officers would secure the necessary revenue.[49]

The third and most impassioned objection to the bill came from abolitionists who did not want Congress classifying slaves as property. Article I, Section II of the Constitution cites representation and direct taxes as the twin policies directly affected by the 'three-fifths' clause. Counting slaves as taxable property acknowledged the southern wealth invested in slaves. However, this policy provided federal recognition of the status of slaves as property, a concession that anti-slavery, 'Radical' members of Congress would not allow. The recent Dred Scott decision (1857) that granted Fifth Amendment protection to slave owners to bring their property into the territories gave this question added importance. Under Chief Justice Roger B. Taney's interpretation of the Constitution, classifying slaves as property might have opened the free states to slaves. Owen Lovejoy, one of President Lincoln's trusted friends on Capitol Hill 'found the word 'slaves' in the bill 'with a good deal of surprise'. He noted that 'if we tax [slaves] as property, among dwelling-houses and horses, we are bound to protect them as property'. Stevens replied, 'If this provision is excluded from the bill, you exclude from taxation more than half the means of raising revenue in the rebel states'.[50] Determined to collect the southern states' share of the direct tax, Stevens would allow this concession for the broader goal of financing the effort to quell the rebellion and destroy the southern slave society.

As so often occurred with financial measures, compromise and efficacy prevailed over principle. Though acknowledged as a direct tax, the legislators accepted the income tax by redefining it as a 'duty'. The final version of the bill apportioned $20 million to all (including the seceded) states. The states would have the chance to collect their portion of the tax and submit the revenue in one payment to the federal government. If the states did not succeed in collecting their share, then the federal revenue officers would intervene and collect the outstanding amount. Striking the word 'slaves' from the bill, Congress instead allowed each state to determine what constituted taxable property. Justin S. Morrill acknowledged that of the $20 million estimated revenue; they expected to realize only $12 million from the Union states. The assessments for the tax would not begin until April 1862, another sign that many believed the war would end soon and that the bill served to assuage bondholders as much to collect revenue. President Lincoln signed the law on 5 August 1861.

HR 71 failed as a revenue measure. The states met their tax quota through their requisitions of troops and supplies, not with much-needed money. During the American Revolution, states failed to provide their requisitions because the central government had no means for compelling them to meet their obligations. In this case, the federal government used its limited resources to fight the war, and had neither the means nor the will to force the states to provide more than they did. The states in turn 'paid' their tax in goods, rather than the much-needed cash. Faced with the need to pass something into law, Congress accepted the expedient of a flawed tax bill. While understanding that they moved beyond the narrow constraints outlined in the Constitution, they chose not to 'stickle', but instead compromised with representatives from the 'new' western and southern states. They used both the direct tax and income tax because they had written statutes on hand they could use as templates, and would not have to create the legislation anew. The need to pass something in the short, emergency session forced them to accept these measures.

Finally, the dominance of one 'special interest' rose to the fore in these debates. While scholars tend to focus on the rising power of industrial and commercial concerns during the Civil War era, HR 71 and later tax laws show that the agrarian representatives exerted great power in designing these measures. No member got all he wanted, but the influence of 'farm interests' in the House held sway, demonstrating the predominance of agriculture both in representation and in the economy during that period.

Congress never collected any revenue under the first income tax. During the next session, they developed a more comprehensive and well-defined levy. However, through this initial attempt, the legislators came to understand that the needs and resources of the nation had changed since the War of 1812. The direct tax would neither be accepted nor practically enforced. The shortfall between expenses and receipts required them to ditch the antiquated and impractical direct tax and try something else. The central question as to whether the income tax constituted a direct or indirect tax did vex Congress briefly, but the exigencies of war, and the need to finish business during this short session, restricted the philosophical debate on this constitutional question. Once they accepted an income tax, this question did not trouble the lawmakers until the end of the century. They needed the money too much.

The Special Session, a remarkable though short assembly, adjourned the day after President Lincoln signed HR 71 into law. Aside from initiating internal taxation, Congress authorized Secretary Chase to borrow $250 million and imposed a tariff on coffee, tea and sugar, the favoured and most reliable revenue tariff of an earlier era. They took their first steps toward funding the Civil War.

'You Cannot Depend on Further Aid'

Congress had adjourned but Secretary Chase went to work to try to find money to borrow. With this new authorization from Congress to borrow funds, Chase had the opportunity now to replenish the Treasury coffers. In following the precedent of earlier wars, in August 1861 Secretary Chase began negotiations with an 'Association' of bankers from Philadelphia, New York and Boston. The secretary wanted the bankers to commit to providing $150 million of the $240 million in loans Congress had authorized. The bankers agreed to provide the Treasury with $50 million initially; to secure the loan, the banks would receive three-year treasury notes bearing 7.3 per cent interest. In turn, these would be marketed to the public, to keep the banks' reserves from dwindling too low. The bankers wanted the secretary to draw incrementally from the banks in the form of drafts.

However, Chase remained determined to follow the letter of the Independent Treasury law. He insisted that the banks provide specie to the Treasury, so the government could purchase war supplies with coin rather than cash. During the negotiations, the bankers also pressed Chase for a more aggressive programme of internal taxation. 'The success of the proposed loans will depend upon the enactment by Congress' of a programme of taxation 'adapted to the existing emergency', read a resolution of the New York Chamber of Commerce.[51]

Because the specie reserves that the banks held amounted to only $63 million at the start of the negotiations, the success of this plan depended on the rapid expenditure of the coin transferred from the banks to the Treasury, and success in marketing the treasury notes to the public. 'The plan would work in fair weather, but in the first storm, it was likely to collapse', commented Wesley C. Mitchell. Further jeopardizing this arrangement, the relationship between Secretary Chase and these bankers remained strained, each distrusting the other. Chase's demand that the bankers provide their funds in gold, rather than accepting bank notes or drafts irked them. On top of this, in order to pay the bills coming into the Treasury, Chase issued non-interest bearing demand notes in small denominations. These notes were used in part to pay the salaries of government employees and troops in the field. Because these government notes could be received for taxes and were redeemable for specie at any subtreasury, the bankers feared (justly) that these government-backed notes would drive their own bank notes out of circulation, depriving them of their primary form of steady income. They also feared the Treasury demand notes would depress the value of the bonds they received in exchange for their specie.[52]

This Association knew that the Union could not rely on foreign loans to finance the war, so Chase had few options. 'The credit of the government had become impaired to such a degree', remembered Moses Taylor, president of City Bank in New York, 'that a large loan could not be obtained in any ordinary fashion'.[53] They alone had sufficient resources to help the country through this peril; as capitalists in the past had done, the members of the Association also expected to earn a profit from their patriotism. Yet the Secretary of the Treasury continued to parry their demands.

Further, Chase expressed some odd opinions that portended a threat to the bankers' ability to profit from the war. He refused to sell the Treasury notes and bonds at the 'market price', instead insisting that the bankers take them at par. This stipulation cut directly into the bankers' potential earnings. Second, Chase kept saying curious things about 'the people' of the United States sharing the benefits of the Union debt, rather than relying on the established system of allowing a small circle of elite financiers to market and profit from the public debt. Finally, an upstart named Jay Cooke, who successfully pulled the state of Pennsylvania out of a fiscal crisis in 1858 by selling the state's bonds directly to the public, rather than through established financial channels, seemed to have the secretary's ear. All this troubled the cabal of bankers who felt they should run the financial show.[54]

These differences aside, the two parties reached an agreement. After relenting to Chase's terms for this first payment, the bankers agreed to pool their resources and provide $50 million in specie to the Treasury. John Stevens, a member of the Association, told Chase in a post-dinner speech, 'you have now received that vast sum of $50 million. We all earnestly hope this sum will be sufficient to end the war; should it not ... you cannot depend on further aid'.[55] The first $50 million installment of the loan arrived at the New York Subtreasury from late August through late September 1861. The Treasury quickly spent the money; as predicted, this kept the specie circulating. The rapid pace of war expenditures, and the generous interest rate they received for the Treasury notes they held, convinced the bankers they could afford to lend the Treasury an even more 'vast' sum of money. Initially, the plan worked as intended. 'The disbursements for the war were so rapid, and the consequent internal trade movement so intense, that the coin paid out upon each installment came back to the banks through the community in about one week', a New Yorker banker related. By mid-October, the association of banks had more specie in their vaults than they did that summer.[56]

On 1 October, they negotiated the second instalment of the $150 million loan. In exchange for another $50 million in specie, they received government bonds, paying a fair, if not generous interest rate above 7 per cent at par. All went well, so the third instalment began arriving on 15 November. On 7 December, the banks' specie reserves 'were actually stronger than in August when the first loan to the government was made', noted Robert Sharkey.[57] However, the banks' ability to provide specie to the government depended on public confidence. Banks sold many of the bonds obtained from the government to replenish their capital, but if no one purchased these bonds, or demanded more than the bankers had paid, this scheme would collapse, which it did in December 1861.

On 8 November 1861, Union naval Captain John Wilkes stopped the *Trent*, a British ship passing through international waters, and forcibly removed two Confederate emissaries who were traveling to Europe to secure money and diplomatic recognition for the Confederate nation. The *Trent* Affair, first greeted as symbol of Union strength, soon became a source of deep concern. The British believed (correctly) that the United States had violated international law by boarding their ship and removing diplomats. The Lincoln Administration's tepid response to their early protests pushed the British to consider declaring war against the Union government. British factories depended on southern cotton; from the beginning of the war, the British had refused to take sides, but many feared their economic dependence on King Cotton would induce them to support the Confederate cause. These events triggered a loss of confidence, in both the general population and the investment community. US bonds dropped 10 per cent on the London exchange as soon as news of the *Trent* Affair hit.[58] Tensions mounted when the British demanded the release of the envoys. Great Britain repositioned its troops in Canada and prepared its navy for a potential war with the Union. This stalemate lasted through January 1862. Although the Union avoided an open conflict with Great Britain, the threat of war had a deleterious impact on the Union's financial prospects.[59]

In the midst of the *Trent* Affair, Secretary Chase released his first *Annual Report* on the state of the nation's finances. This document raised deep scepticism amongst investors. They felt the Secretary did not address adequately the need for more vigorous war revenue measures. They wanted Secretary Chase to advocate a more productive programme of internal taxation. Bankers and investors saw two direct benefits to raising taxes: it would insure a steady source of income for interest payments, especially if the British decided to interfere with Union trade or, worse, declare war. Taxation would also help curb inflation, the bane of investors who hold long-term debt. Secretary Chase greeted the congressmen convening for the second session with more bad news. The Treasury could not keep pace with the expenses of the war. The tariff and internal revenue measures passed in the July session produced less income than anticipated. He reported that the deficit totaled $213 million and only $2.2 million remained in the Treasury. The government could not meet outstanding requisitions, including the Army payroll, despite having borrowing over $150 million that autumn. Chase did call for an increase in the direct tax and tariffs on selected items, but he did not advocate an extensive new internal revenue measure. He 'relied on the assurances from governors of the various states' that their internal machinery could collect the taxes, so no new 'federal agencies' need to intervene.

Chase also reaffirmed his belief that 'adequate provision by taxation for ordinary expenditures, for prompt payment of interest on the public debt ... and for the gradual extinction of the principal is indispensable to a sound system of finance'. In other words, he planned to continue financing the 'extraordinary' expenses of war through loans, while taxing for the ordinary expenses of government. To facilitate this, Chase repeated his call for a 'reduction in expenditure' as a means of alleviating the fiscal crisis. He also called for the distribution of more demand notes to help meet the immediate needs of the Treasury.[60]

In the most ambitious element of the report, Chase recommended the establishment of a national banking system. He saw many advantages that could result. 'Existing bank note circulation depends on the laws of thirty-four states and the character of some sixteen hundred private corporations'. He wished to replace these local notes 'gradually' with those that 'bear a common impression and [are] authenticated by a common authority'. He wanted to 'relieve the nation from competition with local circulation' by taxing bank notes. Chase also foresaw that the Treasury would need another $200 million in loans. He believed a national banking system would provide a steady outlet for the bonds needed to obtain this amount, because the new banks would take them as their reserve, then assist in marketing them nationwide. This would free the Treasury from its dependence on a small circle of bankers. Chase also wanted national banks to help facilitate the collection of taxes; national banks, rather than boxes in the shape of a coffin, would hold the collected taxes.[61]

This report angered the 'finance capitalists' from whom Chase had secured the initial funding for the war. They wanted the secretary to push for taxes. The bankers wanted the Independent Treasury Act suspended so they could act as depositories for government revenues. The secretary's call for a uniform currency and new system of national banks threatened their supremacy and long-term profits. For these reasons, Chase's report triggered a negative reaction amongst the investment community. Between 7 and 28 December, New York banks lost $13 million of their specie reserve to depositors who rushed to hoard their gold. On 28 December, banks in New York suspended their specie payments, and other banks soon followed.[62]

The previous July, Secretary Chase declared to Congress his intention to extend the 'circle of contribution' for the war as widely as possible in order to transmute the 'burden into a benefit'.[63] One can look at Chase's plans for the financing of the war as an attempt to create a system that is 'beneficial to the whole people' rather than just a small circle of financiers, as had been done in the past wars. However, at the beginning of 1862, these long-range plans of the Treasury secretary seemed to have been run aground by the immediate crisis. The 'poverty of the Treasury', which seemed so acute at the opening of the war, appeared more intractable now that all traditional mechanisms for carrying the Treasury through its financial embarrassments were closed.

Conclusion

We know that the United States emerged one hundred years after this catastrophe not only as a stronger country, but also as a dominant economic power. However, those who tended the nation's finances at the onset of the war had a different perspective. Soon after his return to Washington that December, Massachusetts Republican Henry Dawes wrote to her wife, 'Confidence in everyone is shaken to the very foundation. The credit of the country is ruined...and [the nation's] ruin inevitable'.[64] James McPherson notes a similar refrain in the president. Just a few days after Dawes wrote to his wife in despair, President Lincoln asked Montgomery Meigs, the Union army's quartermaster general, 'What shall

I do? The people are impatient; Chase has no money ... the bottom is out of the tub'.[65]

As the new year opened, and the hopes for a ninety-day conflict vanished, both Chase and many leaders in Congress abandoned their principles of political economy to do what they felt was needed to prosecute the war. Chase, the man who believed in 'economy' in government spending, oversaw the creation of the largest debt in American history. He trusted only 'sound' money, yet ran the Treasury when it introduced a fiat currency. In 1870, as Chief Justice of the Supreme Court, Chase wrote the majority decision that declared the 'Greenbacks' an unconstitutional violation of the Fifth Amendment.[66] As Treasury secretary, he supervised the inauguration of a system of permanent internal revenue measures, though he hoped at the beginning of the war to use only limited, direct taxation. Although he had committed to the principles of free trade throughout his career, a commitment that factored into his loss of the Republican nomination for the presidency that he so desperately wanted and felt he deserved, the United States developed an entrenched system of protection during his term as Treasury secretary that endured throughout the remainder of the nineteenth century.

The challenges of secession and war, coupled with the financial limitations inherent in fiscal federalism, influenced many of the policy decisions made during the four years of conflict. The structural restrictions inherent in the American fiscal system of 1860 narrowed the choices opened to the new administration. The constructed divorce of the national government from banks and local economies hindered Secretary Chase's ability to address the overwhelming pecuniary needs that hit the Treasury during the course of the war. Because most believed the war would not last long, the government delayed in introducing a broad, productive series of tax measures. The poor credit they inherited from the Buchanan administration impeded their ability to borrow funds for more reasonable rates and under better terms. These difficulties cost the reunited nation millions from inflated currency and added interest payments.

4 THE POVERTY OF THE TREASURY

When Congress reconvened on 2 December 1861, caution and concern had replaced the bravado that characterized the emergency session the previous summer. The war continued, but optimism waned. The Union army had suffered a series of losses throughout the fall; the troops seemed disorganized and the leadership bereft of talent. The Confederate army had triumphed in most land battles, some of which ended with humiliating defeats for the Yankees. Confederate soldiers camped in Virginia, not far from Washington, DC. General George McClellan, in whom the Union had placed its hopes for a quick and decisive victory, drilled and marched, but did not attack.[1] 'McClellan is a dear luxury', Secretary Chase complained in his diary that winter. 'Fifty days, fifty miles, fifty millions of dollars – easy arithmetic, but not satisfactory.'[2]

Chase's December 1861 *Annual Report to Congress* outlining the state of the Treasury reiterated his commitment to 'Dutch finance'; he wanted to depend on borrowed funds to finance the 'extraordinary' costs of war, while levying minimal taxes to pay the 'ordinary' expenses of government, including the interest payments on the war loans, and the establishment of a sinking fund to help pay down the principal on the debt. But from whom could the Union borrow these funds? Banks had suspended specie payments. Chase's refusal to market bonds below par had 'broken' the relationship with the capitalists upon whom he had relied upon that fall to lend the Union the 'extraordinary sum' of $150 million.[3] In January 1862, 'several prominent New York City bankers, headed by James Gallatin, met with Chase and Congressional leaders ... to argue vehemently for suspension of the Independent Treasury Act, use of state banks as public depositories, and new loans offered at prevailing market rates [meaning below par], and heavier taxation.'[4] Prepared to deal with those he disliked in order to keep funds coming into the Treasury coffers, Chase was surprised when congressional Republicans refused to acquiesce to the demands of these 'finance capitalists'. Many in Congress believed that marketing the bonds below par would signal a lack of faith in the government's credit; with the prospect of a prolonged conflict, this would greatly hamper the Union's ability to raise money. Also, they did not wish to repeat the mistakes of the past and accept the notes of state-chartered banks for the purchase of bonds. 'For the banks to finance the war was henceforth impossible' because of their misgivings about the government's policy, and their pessimism about the future.[5] Although the Union had averted war with Great Britain, the *Trent* Affair had sent a chill throughout the European exchanges. Union bonds could not be marketed across the Atlantic.[6] Chase recommended a new national banking system to remedy this situation, but most members of Congress were reluctant to endorse such a sweeping change to the Union's financial structure. Besides, this did not address the immediate, and desperate, needs of the government.

In analysing the 'revolutionary' changes that occurred with regard to the nation's economic future, 1862 represents the year of demarcation between antebellum practices and the beginning of a new fiscal structure for the national government. During this year, the Republicans pushed the limits of fiscal federalism in an attempt to meet the exigencies of war. The Union adopted fiat currency, launched the first national public bond campaign that became the blueprint for future war financing in the United States, inaugurated permanent internal taxation, and began the planning for a banking system that would create a national currency. All these measures were adopted reluctantly to address the burgeoning expenses of Civil War. The government needed money, so Congress initiated a series of financial measures that dismantled the seventy years of fiscal federalism erected during the course of the antebellum era.

The Greenbacks

Upon their return to Washington, lawmakers moved quickly to address the Union's financial 'embarrassments'. The financial calamity they faced prompted them to adopt a more ambitious stance regarding taxation. Secretary Chase had reaffirmed his commitment to rely on borrowed funds to pay the expenses of the war. Although increasing the overall cost of the conflict, it also mitigated the potential for a backlash by overtaxed citizens against the premise of the war. 'Adequate provision by taxation for ordinary expenditures, for prompt payment of interest on the public debt, existing and authorized, and for the gradual extinction of the principal is indispensable to a sound system of finance. The idea of perpetual debt is not of American nativity, and should not be naturalized.' He proposed raising an additional $50 million in internal taxes, primarily from duties on 'stills and distilled liquors, on tobacco, bank notes, carriages, on legacies, on paper evidences of debt'. He endorsed the income tax, and predicted it would yield $10 million. He did not wish to raise the general tariff rates, but instead concentrate on raising rates on key articles, primarily coffee, tea and sugar. He restated his belief that the direct tax should continue, and with states 'collecting and paying [the taxes], through existing State agencies'. He reiterated his hesitation to 'put into operation, at great cost, the machinery' necessary to collect internal taxes, if the states can take responsibility for gathering this revenue.[7] As noted in the previous chapter, the financial community reacted to the secretary's report, and his hesitancy regarding taxes, by suspending specie payments. Sensing that the situation called for immediate action, Congress took a more aggressive stance regarding the nation's finances.

On 15 January, the House passed a resolution requesting the Ways and Means Committee to formulate a $150 million internal revenue plan, trebling the amount of additional revenue Chase had requested. Clement L Vallandigham (D, OH) called for a delay in pushing through the resolution so the committee members would have time to develop a more comprehensive proposal. 'Taxation, heavy taxation, but upon sound principle, and in the right way, can alone save us'. What Vallandigham meant by the 'right way' remained unclear, because the members rejected his call for postponement. The public debt had reached $300 million, with $100 million in interest payments and military expenditures due by the end of January.[8] Since the war began, Congress had been in session for only two and a half months when they approved this resolution. Already they had increased tariff duties twice, approved over $250 million in loans and $80 million in taxes, with another $150 million to follow. Contrary to the belief that Republicans did not move quickly enough to levy taxes and raise revenue for the war, this represents an extraordinary commitment of resources in a brief period of time. Within months, Congress had abandoned the strictures of a system of fiscal federalism that had taken decades to fortify. The urgency of meeting the expenses of the war, and the upcoming payments on the interest, compelled members in Congress to go one step further and remake the American fiscal system.

Printing the Greenbacks remains one of the most criticized financial decisions made by Secretary Chase and Republican lawmakers during the war. This expedient, taken as a short-term resolution to pending crises, became a source of dramatic political conflict during the late nineteenth century. However, at the time, the urgency of paying the bills that had arrived at the Treasury superseded other concerns. Aside from fulfilling an immediate need, the legislation authorizing the issue of the Greenbacks gave citizens a standard medium to purchase bonds, and the government to pay its bills. The greatest irony of the Greenback story remains that the most hesitant advocate of the legislation became the one who bore the most opprobrium. Secretary Chase became a reluctant, and temporary, advocate for the issue of Greenbacks. In his December 1861 report to Congress, Chase proposed a 'circulation of notes bearing a common impression and authenticated by a common authority'. He wanted a system of national banks established that would facilitate the distribution of this common note that would become a national currency. He wanted to replace the 'paper anarchy' of the antebellum era with a more secure type of money that any citizen could use. He did not wish to create an innovative model of banks; nor did he wish to resurrect the Bank of the United States. Instead he based his vision of this system on the New York Free Banking law, and ultimately this antebellum measure would become the blueprint for the national banks. The difference between old and new would come from consistency and oversight. As Chase noted in his report, 'The value of the existing bank note circulation depends on the laws of thirty-four States and the character of some sixteen hundred private corporations'.[9] The individual states had a spurious system of regulation, whereas the National Bank system would have federal government oversight. Bonds of the national government, not state bonds or speculative railroad bonds, would provide the reserves for these banks. 'The people in their ordinary business would find the advantages of uniformity in currency; uniformity in security', and have a 'safeguard against depreciation', said Chase.[10] His recommendation gained no support. His colleagues in Congress, both Republican and Democratic, did not wish to tamper with the banking system. Bankers, particularly in New York City, bitterly opposed this challenge to their supremacy. The idea lay dormant for the remainder of the year.

The problems facing the Treasury could not lie dormant. By early 1862, the Lincoln administration needed to purchase more than stationery, but they had no funds from which to draw. They had run out of money. The Greenbacks were issued solely to meet the demands upon the Treasury, including the military payroll. Elbridge G. Spaulding (R, NY), who took the lead in pushing for passage of the act that validated the Greenbacks, explained his rationale: 'The army and navy now in service must be paid. They must be supplied with food, clothing, arms, ammunition, and all other material of war to render them effective in maintaining the government and putting down the rebellion'. Having exhausted other means of meeting their obligations, the Greenbacks provided 'the best that can be devised in the present exigency to relieve the necessities of the Treasury'.[11] On 7 January, Congress announced its intention to allow the Treasury to issue $100 million in non-interest bearing Treasury notes in denominations as small as $5. The bill also encompassed $50 million of the Treasury Demand Notes approved during the emergency session, proposing a total of $150 million in legal tender. This gave the Treasury a medium for paying the bills that it could not pay otherwise. The 'exhausted condition of the Treasury' at the start of the war led directly to the introduction of the Greenbacks.[12]

In addition to legitimizing the Greenbacks, the Legal Tender Bill drawn by Spaulding authorized the Treasury to issue a new series of bonds. Later known as the 'five-twenties', this bill allowed the Treasury to raise $500 million in bonds at 6 per cent interest that were callable in five years, and matured in twenty. These bonds could be sold at market value, meaning well below par. The bill allowed convertibility; individuals could exchange their Greenbacks for the five-twenty bonds. 'The five-twenties were meant to serve the double purpose of making the legal tender paper money more acceptable because of its convertibility into five-twenty bonds and of furnishing the government with funds'.[13] Lawmakers reasoned that issuing Greenbacks was preferable to selling bonds below par.

Debate on the bill began on 28 January 1862. Secretary Chase, who wanted to provide a uniform currency based on government assets, not just government will, resisted the expedient of issuing Greenbacks. Later, as Chief Justice of the Supreme Court, in the 'Legal Tender cases' Chase opined, 'We have no hesitation in declaring our conviction that the making of these notes a legal tender was not a necessary or proper means to the carrying on war or to the exercise of any express power in government'.[14] But in February 1862, Chase wrote a public letter of support for passage of the Greenbacks in which he stated, 'Immediate action is of great importance. The Treasury is nearly empty ... I fear the banks generally will refuse to receive the United States notes. You will see the necessity of urging the bill through without more delay'.[15] The House approved the measure on 6 February 1862.

The Senate fine-tuned the legislation, making Greenbacks receivable for all demands and claims against the government except the interest on government bonds, which still had to be paid in gold. They did not stipulate that the principal of the bonds had to be paid in coin, an oversight that would later cause great turmoil. Senator John Sherman spoke in favor of the legal tenders, reasoning, 'Where will the purchasers of your bonds get the gold and silver coin' to complete the sale? 'There is no such thing as gold and silver coin circulating in the country to any large amount'.[16] The Greenbacks were needed to provide a mechanism to purchase Union bonds.

The first issue of Greenbacks allowed Chase to restore a balance in the Treasury accounts. However, the placated secretary soon saw this calm go awry. Within months, the Treasury hit the wall again, and the highly principled man who would later declare the Greenbacks unconstitutional asked Congress to issue another $150 million in fiat currency. The expenses of the war had reached over $1 million per day, and receipts from customs and the five-twenty bond sales amounted to only $380,000 daily.[17] By the end of July 1862, only weeks after paying all the bills that had arrived at the Treasury, the government owed Union soldiers and defence contractors over $36 million in back pay.[18] At Chase's urging the government printed a second batch of Greenbacks, bringing the total circulation to $300 million before the end of the summer. Prices began to rise, although wages did not, and the sale of bonds, a barometer of faith in the nation's future, dwindled. 'It was on the passage of arms that the confidence of the people in their government actually depended', Robert Sharkey noted. 'The greenbacks were issued on the credit of the nation, and it was victory or defeat that determined the standing of that credit'.[19] In 1862, the confidence of the nation in a quick and victorious resolution to the Rebellion had been strained.

Aside from the concerns about public opinion, other complications emerged and forced the development of a unified fiscal system. The first related to the currencies of the nation. Despite the introduction of the greenbacks, notes of various types continued to trade as currency. Silver coins disappeared from circulation, creating great difficulties in managing small day-to-day transactions. Forced to produce some type of medium for these exchanges, the Treasury authorized the use of postage stamps as a currency on 17 July 1862. This expedient proved less helpful than anticipated, since the stamps had a 'propensity for sticking together and getting crumpled'.[20] People took to cutting small denomination bank notes into quarters or tenths, to replace quarters and dimes.

Shinplasters, private notes issued by 'hotels and transportation companies, but also barber shops and drug stores', circulated widely, although the state governments declared them illegal.[21] Banks chartered by states still printed their own notes, responding to the need for fractional currency. The Treasury began circulating copper coins and fractional bills by late 1863, but the currency situation continued to create 'disorder and much inconvenience to public business', throughout the course of the war. Thus, when first introduced, the Greenbacks neither stabilized the economy nor nationalized the currency.[22]

Some historians have theorized that the Union engaged in monetary espionage during the war. Samuel Upham, the owner of a newspaper stand and hawker of souvenirs and patent medicines, realized in 1862 that he could sell counterfeit Confederate currency to individuals who would later trade with Confederate agents and dealers. Upham printed nearly $15 million in Confederate bills, many of which returned to the Confederate states through the illicit cotton trade. Although there is no evidence showing that Upham received official sanction for his activities, the Union government apparently knew of his activities, and did not discourage him.[23]

The National Banking Act of 1863 allowed the banks that received a national charter to print notes. State banks continued to produce their own notes, since the demand for them continued. Western states did not have a supply of either greenbacks or national banks, so they continued to handle their money affairs as they had always, with a jumble of local currencies. The internal revenue laws taxed the state bank notes, but not until 1865, when Congress imposed the 'death tax' of 10 per cent on these renegade notes, did they begin to disappear.[24] Approximately $179.2 million in state bank notes circulated in 1864, but only $20 million by 1866.[25] As the supply dwindled, the remaining notes became 'dirty, greasy, and repulsive to use'.[26] However, state banks remained an important part of the local economies, particularly in the western states. State banks still outnumbered national banks as late as 1892.[27]

Economic historians Willard, Gunnanc and Rosen have argued persuasively that the fluctuating value of the Greenbacks during the course of the war provides a good indicator of the public's perception of the Union's ability to win the war and reunite the nation. 'Any event that increased the expected future cost of the war decreased the likelihood that Greenbacks would eventually be redeemed with gold at par ... the gold price of Greenbacks is a potential source of information on opinions regarding the progress of the war'. They found, for example, the Union victory at the Battle of Antietam involved so much loss of life, and squandered opportunity in General McClellan's decision not to press forward and destroy Confederate General Robert E. Lee's army, that it led people to 'revise upward their estimates' of the costs and duration of the war. The announcement soon thereafter that the Lincoln administration would press for emancipation of the slaves held in the South, but not in the Border States, reinforced the belief within the financial community that victory could only be achieved through 'Total War' and the destruction of the southern way of life.[28] The Greenbacks became the most controversial expedient to which the Republicans resorted to keep the Treasury afloat during the war.

Few analysts of this policy compare the Greenback issues with the currency policies of the Confederate States of America. To relieve their 'embarrassments', the Confederacy adopted a more aggressive with regard to issuing paper currency. The Confederacy printed $1070 million in currency during the war, and suffered from debilitating hyperinflation. In comparison, the Union printed less than half that amount.[29] The Confederate States also remained more hesitant to levy internal taxes than did the Union. This is a valid comparison, because both governments emerged from the same ancestry; the Union relieved themselves of the burdens of fiscal federalism sooner than the CSA, and this decoupling helped them achieve victory in what became a war of attrition. In retrospect, one can argue, the Union Congress showed great restraint in not issuing more fiat currency, especially compared to the Confederacy. Critics of this policy often overlooked the obstacles the administration faced in meeting the 'exigencies of war'. Yet at the time, the Treasury had no other means available to resolve its critical needs. Justin S. Morrill opposed the first issue of Greenbacks, and became a firm advocate of contraction after the war; however he voted for the second authorization of fiat currency. While never abandoning his 'repugnance' for this expedient, Morrill acquiesced in order to keep the Treasury solvent. 'It is not my will', he conceded, 'but the poverty of the Treasury that compels me to follow the only path left open'.[30] The 'poverty of the Treasury' compelled the Republican legislators to adopt many measures they would have avoided and, more than any other factor, directed Republican fiscal policy during the Civil War.

This infusion of freshly printed cash permitted Chase to pay some of his bills, which he could not do otherwise. By 1 July 1862, 'Not a single requisition from any department upon the Treasury remained unanswered. Every audited and settled claim and every quartermaster's check for supplies ... had been met', he reported with relief.[31] The relief Chase felt that July after paying his bills with Greenbacks quickly dissipated. 'Expenses are enormous, increasing instead of diminishing', wrote an anguished Secretary Chase in September 1862. 'It is a bad state of things; neither the President, his counselors, nor his commanding generals seem to care. They rush on from expense to expense and from defeat to defeat, heedless of the abyss of bankruptcy and ruin which yawns before us'.[32] Soon after Chase penned these concerns in his diary, the London *Economist* predicted in October 1862 that, 'the independence of the southern states was as certain as any future event could be'.[33]

By mid-1863, the Treasury had emitted a total of $450 million in Greenbacks in three separate pieces of legislation. The first two measures contained a convertibility clause, allowing holders of Greenbacks to convert them into Treasury bonds that paid 6 per cent interest. In the last act authorizing Greenbacks, passed in March 1863, this convertibility was removed. This change adversely affected the value of the Greenbacks, and accelerated the depreciation that continued until the end of the war. Because the Greenbacks could no longer be converted into gold-backed bonds, an aggressive policy of currency contraction ensued after the war ended, and sparked some of the great political agitation of the late nineteenth century.[34]

The 'Five-Twenties'

One provision of the first Legal Tenders Act authorized the issue of a new series of bonds. The 'five-twenties' became one of the most important, and productive, elements of the Union's Civil War financial scheme. In following the concept he floated in his first report to Congress, Chase wanted to distribute the 'benefits' of war finance as widely as possible. This entailed marketing the government bonds to the American public. During the previous fall, the Treasury had contracted sales agents to market the 'seven-thirties', with little result. Despite this initial disappointment, in March 1862 Chase opened the five-twenty loans nationally through sales agents and Treasury offices across the country. Henrietta Larson noted, 'Nobody in the United States knew how to sell hundreds of millions of bonds. Such a thing had never been done'.[35]

One agent, Jay Cooke, whose brother Henry was a friend of Salmon P. Chase, subsequently become a friend to Chase as well. Their relationship often strained the modern understanding of ethical behavior for public officials, but never crossed the line of nineteenth-century corruption or illegality. Cooke often lent money to Chase and his family, helping the Chases to live grandly while he served in the Cabinet on a public salary.

Jay Cooke became a partner in the firm of E. W. Clarke and Company, the investment group that helped finance the Mexican–American War. He had participated in the financing of that war, but in the traditional method of providing the [formidable] front capital to finance the public debt, then marketing the resulting bonds to institutional investors. Cooke formed his own firm in 1857. His first great success came from marketing the public bond drives of Pennsylvania in 1860. He developed a series of public relations vehicles for selling these state bonds – he used newspaper advertisements, well-placed editorials and a network of sales agents who went into little towns throughout the state to sell the bonds. Although the historiography suggests that Cooke 'invented the modern bond drive,' in fact he copied this idea from Napoleon III, who sold securities to the French public to finance the Crimean War. 'A scrapbook sent to Secretary Chase by Cooke contained clippings which referred to the selling of the French loans in 1854–55 when the government offices of the French departments were 'besieged by crowds of peasant subscribers".[36] Commonly regarded as the most innovative feature of Union financing, Cooke's sales effort copied a European precedent.

Marketing the bonds to the general public required 'two stupendous tasks: 1) educate the small investor in the buying of bonds and the value of the securities, and 2) create an organization for the distribution of the bonds'.[37] Cooke succeeded at both. By October 1862, Cooke had managed to outsell any of the other agents, so Secretary Chase named the primary agent to market the five-twenties. By January 1864, Cooke's network of sales agents had sold $360 million in bonds nationally. Cooke himself only received about $200,000 in commissions, far less than the bankers and capitalists who helped finance earlier wars.

The 'confused state of monetary circulation' impeded the bond drives.[38] Cooke and his agents sold $361 million of the five-twenties in communities across the country. As one of the first national financial campaigns of any kind, he came across the same difficulties with the various currencies in use. 'The most serious problem, when sales were large, was that of securing the proper means for making payments to the government.' Required to make payments 'in lawful money', Cooke often had trouble finding enough acceptable currency to transfer to the Subtreasury in New York or the Treasury in Washington. In the fall of 1863, the sales of bonds outpaced the Treasury's ability to print greenbacks, and Cooke's agents often had to hold these various local currencies until shipments of fresh greenbacks arrived. In smaller towns where suspect currencies circulated, Cooke's agent had to absorb the cost of exchanging these moneys into greenbacks or Treasury notes.[39]

Throughout the course of US history, Europeans had invested heavily in American bonds, both private (such as railroad and canal companies) and public (state and national). Foreign investors poured over $500 million into the United States in the decades before the Civil War. British investors in particular liked US debt because 'faith in the nation's resources were so great' and Americans were 'so frugal'.[40] Americans had a very good record of servicing their debt; providing steady interest payments, in gold and on time.

This expectation received its first great trial after the Depression of 1837. 'One after another' of the state budgets collapsed under the weight of their indebtedness. Combined, the states carried a debt of $230 million at the time and could not keep up with the interest payments. Florida and Mississippi completely repudiated their obligations. Arkansas, Indiana, Illinois, Maryland, Michigan, Pennsylvania and Louisiana all defaulted on interest payments. This defalcation created a great backlash, both within the state and abroad. Jefferson Davis, the governor of Mississippi when the state defaulted, would later regret his indifference to the 'crocodile tears' shed by British investors who lost thousands on the bonds issued by his state. During the American Civil War, English investors who remembered Davis's role in the default hesitated to lend money to the Confederate States of America. The enthusiasm foreign capitalists had for all types of 'American things' soured. When questioned on why American railroad securities sold poorly on the British market in 1859, an Englishman replied that, 'the record of the experience [states defaulting] now operated as a bugbear to Englishmen to this day'.[41]

Although British investors shied away from Union bonds during the Civil War, Robert J. Walker agreed to serve as an agent in Europe for marketing Union bonds. Walker was a friend of Salmon P. Chase. Although he attracted a great deal of publicity, Walker had little luck marketing US securities. Despite the general lull in foreign investors, millions in US securities did sell on the Continent. In Holland and Germany, US bonds that had been purchased stateside began to appear on the exchanges by late 1863. By 1864, Sexton estimates that $2 million a week was generated in these financial centers. Most of the bonds were purchased in the US then shipped to these markets for resale. 'The dramatic Union victories in July 1863 led to increased speculation in five-twenty bonds on the Continent', according to Sexton.[42] This surge of interest in US securities still fell short of the demand foreign investors had shown in US investments during the antebellum era.

The Treasury depended on the domestic sales of bonds. Chase and members of Congress knew they could not rely on foreign capital to invest in US securities, and thus needed the support and cooperation of American citizens. 'It is vain to look abroad' for funds, Chase noted in a 13 October 1861 letter to General William T. Sherman.[43] Wedded to borrowing at home, the government needed to provide some consistent means for customers to pay for their bond purchases.

'Laying No Burden on those with Small Means'

In accordance with the resolution that passed earlier that year, the Republican Congress set out to create a new internal revenue system. The resulting bill came about through compromise. The pragmatism that played a decisive role in establishing the fiscal federalism of the antebellum era also guided the Civil War internal revenue legislation. This becomes evident from the beginning of the debates on HR 71 and extends through the other two pieces of tax legislation passed during the war. Lawmakers relied on taxes they knew they could enact and thought they could collect. Too often this practical basis for taxation is ignored.

That March, Justin S. Morrill, acting as spokesman for the Ways and Means Committee, opened the debate on House Resolution 312 (HR 312). Raised in a small town in Vermont, Morrill worked as a shop clerk during his teens and later owned a number of small markets, as well as a business that supplied goods to shopkeepers. He sold his business in 1848, dabbled in farming, and then decided to run as a Whig for office in 1854, winning a seat to the House of Representatives. Because he never went to college, Morrill wanted to help others obtain that privilege. Education had remained the responsibility of state governments throughout the antebellum era; however Morrill believed that the federal government should help provide the opportunity for those who could not afford to attend college. He wanted farmers and labourers, who otherwise could not afford to matriculate at a college or university, to have exposure to the latest developments in these areas. His legacy with the public remains his stewardship of the Morrill Land Grant Act, which led to the establishment of seventy public colleges and universities for teaching 'agriculture and the mechanical arts'.[44]

Establishing the Land Grant universities emerged as Morrill's greatest legacy, however his House, then Senate colleagues respected him most as a master of public finances. He served on both the House Ways and Means Committee and later the Senate Finance Committee during his forty-four years in Congress. He wrote the Tariff of 1861, also known as the Morrill Tariff that moved the United States away from taxing imports on an *ad valorem* basis, relying instead on specific duties.[45] Morrill advocating using tariff schedules to protect raw materials, grown or produced from fields, stables and mines, instead of manufactured goods. For this reason, he supported high import duties on iron, lumber, and farm products, particularly wool that Vermont farmers raised. Although a 'protectionist', Morrill's form of protection had little to do with the industrial interests of the country; instead he aspired to keep the prices of agricultural products competitive. As Richard Hofstadter pointed out in 1938, the conflict in pre-Civil War tariff debates focused less on the sectional tensions between slave and free labour and instead pitted manufacturers, who wanted cheap raw materials to transform into goods, against farmers, who wanted to keep the price on their agricultural products competitive with imports.[46] In this debate, Morrill sided with the farmers, not the industrialists.

Subsequently, the revenue programmes that Morrill helped design relied on taxing industry and not raw materials. A general 3 per cent duty on manufacturers would provide the 'largest item of revenue', Morrill foresaw as he outlined the bill. 'A burden that would paralyze the agriculturalists of the country will be taken on the backs of the steam giants with alacrity and confidence', he predicted.[47] Inherent in this programme remained the goal to 'propose duties upon a large number of objects, rather than confine them to a narrow field'.[48] Instead of laying taxes on a few articles, the Ways and Means Committee determined to make the taxes 'diffuse'. The fundamental principle of this bill was to levy moderate duties on a broad selection of goods rather than heavy duties on a few. Morrill believed this would help the citizens absorb the taxes better, and it would lead to more compliance with the law, and eventually produce more revenue.

This diffuseness helped to break down the barrier between state and national taxation. The federal government would now tax citizens 'individually'. When one considers the scope of this tax measure, it is surprising that the debates on the bill did not focus more on the expansion of government power that would result from this legislation. Border state representatives raised this concern first by reviving the antebellum fears that expanded government power would inevitably lead to emancipation. 'Shall reserved rights be surrendered to a consolidated government?' asked William H. Wadsworth (U. KY). 'I am here to resist this new and overshadowing danger, this tendency of the federal government to swallow up the powers reserved to the states and the people respectively'.[49] Bingham countered that, 'because certain madmen have taken up arms against the Republic', that the Congress wishes to expand government power. 'The word centralization has no meaning in reference to American institutions ... so long as we recognize the supremacy of the written Constitution'.[50]

While the tax on manufacturers would produce the most revenue 'few taxable articles or forms of wealth were permitted to escape'.[51] Relying on long-recognized principles that 'sin' taxes on articles with inelastic demand generated steady revenue, the bill levied a twenty cents per gallon against distilled spirits; beer, ale, malt liquors, and fermented liquors would pay one dollar a barrel. 'A tax dependent on the habits or vices of men is the most reliable of all taxes', Morrill told the House.[52] Graduated rates applied to different grades of tobacco and tobacco products (cigars, cigarettes and chewing tobacco). Taxing luxuries also provided a substantial portion of the revenue generated by this measure. The legislators drew up 'Schedule A' upon which appeared the articles that had long been considered luxuries of the wealthy: carriages, yachts, billiard tables, gold watches, pianos and gold or silver plate. Under the provisions of this bill, people

had to purchase licences to become auctioneers, butchers, jugglers, lawyers, peddlers and soap makers. Traveling circuses had to pay taxes on their receipts. All
contracts, insurance policies, bank checks, wills and loans now required a stamp
for authorization. To ensure that 'men with large incomes pay more in proportion to what they have than those with limited means who live by the work of
their own hands', the bill included taxes on gross receipts of corporations, inheritance and succession taxes, and a new, more robust, income tax.[53]

'The committee has thought it best to propose duties upon a large number of
objects rather than confine them to a narrow field', Morrill explained.[54] Albert S.
White (R. IN) proclaimed, 'this tax is to be the touchstone of our patriotism. It
is the price that we are to pay for being true and loyal to our country.'[55] Thaddeus
Stevens, Chair of the Ways and Means Committee articulated the broad principles in this tax plan when he brought the measure to a vote in the House:

> The [Ways and Means] committee have found it necessary to visit many articles which
> they would have gladly spared. They have, however laid no burdens on those with
> small means...They have attempted to raise the largest sums from articles of luxury,
> and from the large profits of wealthy men...while the rich and thrifty will be obliged
> to contribute largely from the abundance of their means, we have the consolation to
> know that no burdens have been imposed on the industrious laborer and mechanic;
> that the food of the poor is untaxed; and that no one will be affected by the provisions
> of this bill whose living depends solely on his manual labor.[56]

In sparing the 'food of the poor', agricultural products, especially farm produce,
implements, 'breadstuff and flour', remained untouched by this bill. So too,
did the raw material used for production (iron and wool, in particular). Sparing these articles fit with Morrill's ideal of 'protecting' raw materials used for
industry, and sparing farmers from the burden of taxation. This also served the
communities that both Morrill and his good friend 'Thad' represented, a fact not
lost on other congressmen during the debates. The 'economic interests' of these
lawmakers did play a role, but not in the way the Beards suggested. In the initial
collection of the taxes, the 'industrial capitalists' bore the largest burden, while
sparing the northern 'agricultural interests'.[57]

In this bill, Congress attempted to keep the 'agricultural interests' of the country and rural residents from bearing a large portion of the tax. The collection of
the direct tax continued in a very lackluster manner. Congress passed a series of
resolutions to halt the collection of the direct tax, determining instead to rely
on indirect taxes. The revenue generated up to that time had disappointed, and
assembling the 'machinery' to collect the remainder would be cumbersome. This
shift left the land of farmers, as well as their produce, exempt from these taxes.
Agriculture still represented the largest segment of the economy and farmers,
by far, the largest portion of the population. They had many representatives in
the House. A practical element guided this development as well. Trying to tax

agricultural products would require an extensive 'machinery' of collection, with assessors patrolling the farmstead scattered all across the vast territory of the nation. Instead of taxing farmers specifically, the bill aimed to collect from the subsidiary economic activity of farmers, such as slaughterhouses, peddlers and the clothing worn by farmers, through the tax on manufacturers. Because of the extent of territory and the need to raise the money quickly, the bill was framed to collect revenue in a manner that would be efficient. Collecting taxes at established businesses that had ease of access would require less effort than trying to assess and collect from farmers spread across the country. Senator William Pitt Fessenden expressed his frustration with this system:

> We are obliged to pay tax on our salaries and our income of any other description, and we pay it on the gross income, and are not permitted to take out the expenses of living. But a farmer as he goes along supports his family out of the produce of his farm from day to day and regards as his income only the surplus, that which he sells and puts in the shape of money...under this bill the farmer must inevitably be the best off, and he will escape easier than others, though as a general rule, he is abler to pay and more independent than any other class of men in the community.[58]

Not all agricultural products remained untouched: corn (used for making distilled liquors), tobacco and cotton felt the taxman's sting.[59] Responsible representation of the needs and interests of constituents often became conflated with base lobbying to protect narrower concerns and personal interests. Although the Beards correctly identified the corruptibility of human weaknesses, they overemphasized the role of 'industrial' interests in these debates. The industrialists won some minor victories in framing the tax legislation but they did not achieve the escape from taxes that they had desired. The government collected more internal revenue from the tax on manufacturers than any other levy segment of the economy during the Civil War.

As the debates on this bill began, 'A swarm of lobbyists arrived to press their concerns on the congressmen,' lamented John Law (D, IN) in March, 1862. He chided the Ways and Means Committee for not working on the tax bill more diligently during the recess, thus clearing from Congress, 'the army who are now here besieging [us] from having ... every conceivable description of article exempted from duty'.[60] Delegations from the New York City Chamber of Commerce and the Boards of Trade from Boston and Philadelphia arrived to press their concerns 'As many as fifty or sixty interested parties were milling about the door of the room occupied by the [Ways and Means Committee]', asking for tax relief for their various clients.[61]

Intensive lobbying of this nature had occurred at the state level throughout the antebellum era, because states controlled the purse strings on most development projects. State governments, not the national government, provided funds for the mix of private and public development that characterized this period of history.[62] At the national level, lobbyists descended on Congress during tariff debates. John Pincus noted, 'the pressure group successes' in tariff measures affected local concerns, more than national, even as these local industries tried to tie their fortunes to the nation's well being.[63] This changed once HR 312 was introduced in Congress. The bill began a process of shifting tremendous sums of money from the private sector to the public economy, and from state to national government control. Now the central government, not just the states, would have discretionary power over private goods and services. The scale of this power shifted as well. Before the Civil War, public officials never had more than tens of millions at their disposal. Hence, Congress had at its disposal hundreds of millions. While allocated to set public expenses, the change represented a significant movement of goods and services from the private economy to the public. No one understood this better than the various industries and services whose prices and fees the national government would begin to tap for revenue. The national government would never return to the 'pinchpenny' budgets of the antebellum era.

During the debates on this bill, representatives focused on trying to keep their constituents from carrying the tax burden. Charles A. Wickliffe (U. KY), who represented tobacco farmers who would soon pay heavy taxes, urged Congress to hit bankers, brokers and other money men, 'who suck the vitals of society'.[64] Often petty local concerns became the center of the debate. On 20 March a prolonged discussion occurred between James R. Morris, Harrison G. Blake and John Hutchins, all Republicans from Ohio, over the merits of taxing different types of cheese. Throughout the tax debates, lofty moral, ideological and political issues mixed with base personal influence peddling. Senator Charles Sumner, recovered from the caning he received from Preston Brooks on the floor of the Senate in 1856, emerged as one of the more forceful and eloquent spokesmen for emancipation, then freedman's rights. During the tax debates, he advocated placing a high 'excise' tax on slaves, with the idea of forcing manumissions (exactly what James Madison had assured the Virginia Constitutional Convention would never happen because of the direct tax). Yet, he strongly opposed a moderate three cents per pound tax on cotton, which would have hit the same slaveholders he sought to punish in other ways, but also squeeze the textile manufacturers in his state. Later, he can be found pleading to remove the tax on paper, another product of the mills of Massachusetts.[65] Historians love to quote Schuyler Colfax's fiery rhetoric as he defended farmers and attacked capitalists in his call for the first income tax in HR 71, yet Colfax also fought with equal vigour during the second session to have the tax removed from newspapers and the advertisements that finance them. As a part owner in the *South Bend Free Press*, this tax cut directly into his profits.[66]

Rested after the long recess, Roscoe Conkling returned to Congress ready to defend his patronage castle once again. Conkling persisted in his desire to have state officers collect the federal taxes, pressing the point the day after the debate opened on this bill. New York alone would need 3,600 revenue officers, Conkling insisted. Thomas D. Eliot (R. MA), John S. Phelps (R. CA), Samuel Shellabarger (R. OH) and George H. Pendleton (R. OH) all concurred that state officers, rather than the national government should collect these taxes. 'It is not the taxgather [citizens] hate so much as the taxes', Thaddeus Stevens replied. In reference to the inclusion of the Confederate states in the tax measure, Stevens asked, 'How can we [collect the taxes] if we allow those who have caused this trouble to make the assessments?' In response to the fear of 'centralization' that proponents of state collections identified, Bingham asserted, 'The word centralization has no meaning in reference to American institutions ... there is no such thing as centralization under our system so long as we recognize the supremacy of our written Constitution'.[67]

Efforts to retain local control of assessments and collections failed, primarily because a Civil War raged, and legislators feared that they would never see revenue from the seceded states if they relied on local officials to collect tax from their fellow confederates.[68] This did not represent an attempt by the Republicans to 'nationalize' the economy, but rather to keep the revenue needed for the war flowing into the Treasury. 'It is indispensable that the government have within its own control the means of meeting its all its vast engagements', Morrill concurred.[69] They could trust only federal tax officials, appointed by the president, to secure the payments from southerners. The economic interests of their constituents, as well as the personal interests of the lawmakers, played a role in developing this bill. However, this represented less of a 'breakdown in the old moral standards' than a shift in the theatre of money politics, from the state houses to Congress. Efforts to spare their constituents from paying high taxes mingled with less legitimate concerns. Despite these competing forces, the bill passed the House on 8 April by an overwhelming 125 to 14 count and moved to the Senate.[70]

The Senate received the bill on 10 April 1862, but did not start debating it until 6 May. The Finance Committee tinkered with the legislation, causing the committee's chair, William Pitt Fessenden, to 'crack the whip' and move the measure onto the Senate floor.[71] Regarding the 'infernal tax bill', Fessenden remarked in a 25 April letter that, 'There is no time to make a new one, and all we can do is to patch this. It will be odious'.[72] The Senate began consideration of the bill on 6 May.

This tax bill affords the opportunity to examine the balance of power between the House of Representatives and the Senate. Clearly the constitutional authority to levy taxes lies with the House of Representatives, where 'bills for raising revenue' originate. However, the Senate may 'propose or concur' on revenue measures. In theory, House members represented the interests of the people who elected them to office every two years. Senators, chosen by their state legislatures and standing for election every six years, often spoke for the broader interests of their state, not merely the concerns of one district.[73] An individual Senator could exert more influence within his chamber than any individual congressmen (except in cases like Thaddeus Stevens, the 'fearless leader in the House.').[74] The deliberations on HR 312 demonstrate this dichotomous relationship.

First, the Senate tarried with the bill once it reached the floor. The *New York Times* guessed that 'speculators and monopolists' delayed the bill in an attempt to make their deals with different Senators.[75] The *New York Herald* opined the abolitionist Senators wanted to delay the bill to punish the administration for their laxity on the slavery question and ineffective management of the war.[76] No clear answer comes forth, but the delay created frustration for other senators, whose tempers flared throughout the debates on this bill.

The 'economic interests' of the various states present themselves clearly during the Senate deliberations. Senators from tobacco-growing states disapproved of the tax on leaf tobacco. John Sherman, representing corn farmers, spoke against the liquor excises made from his constituents' corn.[77] New Englanders opposed the manufacturing duties, and advocated replacing them with a broader income tax or a general sales tax. However, all understood that they needed to introduce some form of taxation; they just hoped to keep the taxman out of their states or districts. The Senators did try to shift the burden of taxation from their state onto others.

The Senate sent the bill back to the House on 9 June, with 315 amendments. Thaddeus Stevens tried to get the Senate's amendments dropped by having the House declare that they did not concur with the changes. This attempt failed. A conference committee met, with both House and Senate members, and worked through the amendments. The Senate withdrew 16, and saw 253 of their amendments pass from the committee.

The Income Duty

The Senate had the greatest impact on the income tax portion of the bill. Debates on the income tax focused less on the merits or legitimacy of an income tax, and more on the particulars of collecting the tax. No more 'stickling' about whether the income tax represented a constitutional form of taxation. Once the Congress had decided to levy it as an indirect tax, this concern did not arise again until after the war. Lawmakers saw people 'employed on a fixed income' as the main targets for this tax. Justin S. Morrill described the tax as the 'least defensible' and most 'inquisitorial' portion of the bill, but the need for more revenue trumped these worries. He understood that this represented a bountiful form of taxation. 'Ought not men with large incomes pay more in proportion to what they have then those with limited means?' he asked.[78] Whether that tax would count 'gross' or 'net' income emerged as the first point of concern. Thaddeus Stevens explained that they meant 'net' income, but if they included that word in the bill, it would have opened the door to a multitude of frauds.

Fessenden advocated making the income 'duty' graduated. A 3 per cent tax applied to incomes up to $10,000; anyone with an income over $10,000 paid a 5 per cent tax, starting 30 June 1863. The Senate also recommended lowering the exemption to $600. Provisions agreed to by both chambers included levying a 5 per cent tax on all income from property held in the United States of American citizens residing abroad.[79] In a nod to the federalist system, those paying the income duty could deduct state and local taxes. Corporations paid taxes on their gross receipts, and railroads withheld for the tax collector 3 per cent of the interest payments they made to those who held their bonds. Government employees in 'civil, military, or naval services' had the income tax withheld from their paycheck, another extraordinary change in the relationship of the government to individual citizens, a process called 'tapping revenue at the source'. Although this applied to public officials, those employed by private companies did not experience the same intervention. This led tax historian Harry E. Smith to conclude that, 'after the depreciation of the greenbacks' government employees 'found the tax more burdensome than most other people'.[80] To assess the tax, the payer provided a report of his income, and then swore an oath on the accuracy of the statement. Self-assessment became the basis for determining the amount of the tax. This mode of self-reporting allowed for more fraud, but it also made the tax less 'inquisitorial' and more acceptable to the public.

President Lincoln signed the tax bill into law on 1 July 1862. In its final version, HR 312 contained many of the broad taxes first outlined by Morrill including the 3 per cent *ad valorem* duty on manufactured products, twenty cents per gallon tax on liquors, stamp tax on all legal documents, receipts on railroads, steam boats and ferry boats were taxed one to 3 per cent, interest on railroad bonds carried a 3 per cent tax whereas US government bonds only one percent. Income from $600–10,000 was taxed 3 per cent; from $10,000–50,000, 5 per cent, and over $50,000, 7.5 per cent. George Boutwell, former governor of Massachusetts, became the first Revenue Commissioner on 17 July 1862. He ran a small operation initially; in the first year, employing three clerks to count the taxes. Although Boutwell considered HR 312 was 'incomplete in parts' and an 'imperfect plan', he concluded it was the best one could expect 'under the circumstances'.[81] However, the early returns disappointed. Morrill had estimated the tax bill would generate $101 the first year; Chase, after hiring some 'practical men' to review the measure, guessed $85 million. The measure generated only

$37.6 million through 1863. The shortfall, Dewey noted, 'was largely due to the unsettled conditions of business as well as to the necessity of establishing at short notice an entirely new branch of treasury administration for the collection of duties'.[82]

The National Banking System

Of all the financial measures passed by the Congress during the Civil War, the national banking system remained the most controversial amongst the Republicans themselves. In his December 1861 report to Congress, Chase proposed a 'circulation of notes bearing a common impression and authenticated by a common authority'. He wanted a system of national banks established that would facilitate the distribution of this common money. He did not wish to create a new model of banks; nor did he wish to resurrect the Bank of the United States. Instead he based his vision of the national banks on the New York Free Banking law; ultimately this antebellum measure would become the basis for the national banking system. The difference would come from consistency and overseeing; whereas the individual states had a spurious system of regulation, the National Bank system would have national government overseeing. Bonds of the national government, not state bonds or speculative railroad bonds, would provide the basis for the reserves for these banks. 'The people in their ordinary business would find the advantages of uniformity in currency; uniformity in security', and have a 'safeguard against depreciation', said Chase.[83]

Secretary Chase devoted most of his December 1862 report to Congress to advocacy for establishing a national banking system. He advocated 'the support of a United States note circulation, and the reduction of the bank note circulation'. To accomplish this goal, Chase believed he needed a national banking system.[84] His first attempt to create a national banking system had fallen on fallow ground, so he altered his plan. The new measure obligated state banks to join the national system before they could issue bank notes. In October 1862 Chase articulated his strong belief that 'if the debt is kept within any reasonable limit by active prosecution of the war and tolerable economy in expenditure, the adoption of this system will furnish all the money that is needed, at reasonable rates'.[85] His efforts were bolstered by President Lincoln. In his address to Congress, the president described the two printing of Greenbacks as 'unavoidable'. Because of the proliferation of paper money across the country – in the form of Greenbacks, state bank notes and other heresies, the president noted that a new system of national currency would 'protect labour against the evils of a vicious currency and facilitate commerce by cheap and safe exchanges'.[86]

When introduced to Congress, the bill advocated by Chase faced considerable hostility from Eldridge Spaulding, the force behind the authorization of the Greenbacks. Spaulding believed quite correctly that Chase was trying to undermine the status of state banks across the nation. As a former banker, he did not wish to see the antebellum banking establishment upended. 'The key to the resurrection of the bill was the ability of Jay and Henry Cooke to induce Senator John Sherman to support Chase's plan'.[87] After much reluctance, and by a very close margin, Congress passed the national bank bill on 12 February 1863. Lawmakers continued to refer to the measure as the 'national currency bill'. The legislation required banks to hold US government bonds as their reserve; this stipulation became a crucial element in the passage of the measure, because the new banks had to take government bonds. In this early phase, state banks would be allowed to distribute national notes under original charter. This allowed the state banks to remain intact, while benefiting from the issuing of the new national currency. Finally, this bill created a new market for the bonds, which improved the flow of funds into the Treasury. By making the national government bonds the basis for the new banks' reserve, Chase hoped to stabilize the price of bonds because of the increase demand. Despite the success of Jay Cooke's popular campaign, bond sales did not keep pace with Treasury expenses, and Chase convinced lawmakers that a system of national banks would increase demand for bonds, and help keep their value stable.

A uniform and reliable currency, distributed by a new system of national banks, would also help Cooke's campaign; before the introduction of the national currency, his agents had to accept whatever 'lawful money' bond subscribers gave them, including the various local currencies that lost value once the bond salesmen sent them outside of the region. As David M. Gische observed, 'The key to the resurrection of the bill was the ability of Jay and Henry Cooke to induce Senator John Sherman to support' the plan.[88] Another factor in the passage of the bill resulted from the internal revenue measure. Where would the federal government keep the money collected through HR 312? The Treasury could not store tens of millions of dollars in tavern coffin boxes across the country. Under the Independent Treasury law, the funds could not be kept in state banks either. As noted earlier, Chase did not trust state banks, whose charters had been granted under a myriad of state laws, some more restrictive than others. Funds in state banks had no protection from 'runs' by depositors and Chase did not want to entrust the revenue generated for the war to such an unreliable system. Finally, he worried about the loyalty of bank officers during a time of Civil War. Only a year earlier, rumours had spread through Washington that members of President Buchanan's cabinet had facilitated the movement of funds and arms to southern depositories to aid the rebellion. Federal officials in customs houses across the South had shown that they put the interests of their states ahead of the Union, another remnant of fiscal federalism. Chase wanted secure depositories.[89]

The banking community strongly opposed the national banking system; a year after its passage only 450 banks had taken national charters. With Greenbacks, national bank notes and state banks notes circulating at once, the inflation in the Union rose. To increase the number of national banks, and help check inflation, Congress passed a 10 per cent tax imposed on state bank notes in March 1865, which was effective. By 1870, 1612 national banks had been established and the 'better-secured' national bank notes replaced the 'diverse issues of state bank notes'.[90] Only with the 'death tax' of 1865 did state bank notes begin to disappear and, as discussed above, state banks still outnumbered national banks as late as 1892.

The national bank system had significant flaws that hurt rural economies during the late nineteenth century; however, the urgency of the country at the start of the war 'made such banking legislation financially desirable and politically feasible'. The 'exhausted condition of the Treasury' that began before the war, and continued through 1863, compelled reluctant lawmakers to adopt a new system of national banking.[91] Chase expressed his earnest desire for a 'circulation of notes bearing a common impression and authenticated by a common authority', in both his 1861 and 1862 Annual Reports to Congress. He wanted a system of national banks established that would facilitate the distribution of this common money. He did not wish to create a new model of banks; nor did he wish to resurrect the Bank of the United States. Instead he based his vision of the national banks on the New York Free Banking law; ultimately this antebellum measure would become the basis for the national banking system. The difference would come from consistency and oversight; whereas the individual states had a spurious system of regulation, the National Bank system would have national government oversight. Bonds of the national government, not state bonds or speculative railroad bonds, would provide the basis for the reserves for these banks. 'The people in their ordinary business would find the advantages of uniformity in currency; uniformity in security', and have a 'safeguard against depreciation', said Chase.[92]

Conclusion

With the passage of the national banking legislation, the Republicans completed process of building a new infrastructure that would allow them to finance the war. Although their measures did not dismantle fiscal federalism, they did push the limits of antebellum finance in new directions. As the war continued, they would have to learn how to meld the past with the future in order to carry the nation through this crisis. The policies they enacted did not represent a new, innovative, or uniquely Republican way of looking at the economy. Instead, at each turn, they had turned to precedents. In the process, they altered the course for the public economy and financial structure of the government.

5 SPARING THE NECESSARIES OF LIFE

During the American Civil War, Congress inaugurated the system of national taxation that Americans 'enjoy' to this day. Throughout the antebellum era, tariffs provided the federal government with most of its revenue. The United States had not levied internal duties since the War of 1812, so representatives in neither the House nor the Senate had experience in formulating national tax policy. Yet the overwhelming costs of feeding, supplying and moving armies across the country forced Congress to develop new revenue sources quickly. To expedite the process, the lawmakers relied upon English tax precedents.

As we saw earlier, Secretary Chase determined to finance the war by adopting the system of 'Dutch finance'. He planned to borrow for the 'extraordinary' expenses of war while taxing for the 'ordinary' operations of government, the means by which England funded her 'Long Century' of warfare from the Glorious Revolution through the final defeat of Napoleon.[1] Historians of Civil War finances have derided Treasury Secretary Chase's decision to finance the war in this manner but this strategy followed a long, successful precedent for absorbing the overwhelming costs of war. The income 'duty' adopted by the emergency session of the Thirty-seventh Congress followed the example of the British income tax levied during the Napoleonic Wars; additionally, the Civil War internal revenue measures were also based on the British example. This becomes important when examining the structure of the tax measures and trying to determine how the burden of these taxes fell on Americans. Because the Civil War legislators decided to follow the example of levying 'diffuse' taxes on manufacturers, Congress agreed to provide greater tariff protection for these industries, and this set the course of tariff legislation for the remainder of the nineteenth century.

The current literature on taxation in the United States in the early Republic and Civil War eras suggests that an 'exceptional' system emerged based on the accommodation to slavery or because of the unique Republican ideology.[2] While aspects of these arguments have validity, neither appreciates the deep historic traditions upon which nineteenth-century Americans based their tax policy. Americans based their system of public finance on the English revenue model. More specifically, in designing the Civil War revenue measures, US lawmakers lifted specific terms and 'maxims' of taxation from English precedents, especially the goal of 'sparing the necessaries of life' from duties.[3] Taxing luxuries, while sparing necessaries, emerged as a tenet in English revenue policy during the latter half of the seventeenth century after Parliament first introduced excise taxes. Not only did Americans appropriate the framework of taxing luxuries while sparing necessaries or necessities, the term itself appears consistently in American discourse on taxation.

Historians describe the internal revenue legislation as a series of 'regressive' measures, relying predominantly on a variety of excise taxes.[4] I suggest, instead, that the Civil War revenue measures did not constitute a highly regressive system of taxation. 'Sin taxes' on liquor and tobacco did not generate most of the revenue during the war, as many believe, rather it was the general duty on manufacturing. However, the desire at the end of the war to implement policy that would spare American productivity eventually led to the regressive tax policies that emerged in the late nineteenth century.

Borrowing from English practices helped hasten the flow of needed funds into the Treasury. Rather than develop an innovative new set of laws, the necessity of generating enormous sums quickly induced Civil War legislators to adopt a wartime revenue system they knew and understood. Because of their urgency, the Republicans drew their inspiration for the new revenue measures from the English precedent. Robert A. Becker observed that Americans during the colonial era, 'developed no radically new form of taxation when they came to the New World for they took their taxes as they took most of their political and social institutions, from the mother country, but with a difference.'[5] I propose that the legislators of the Civil War era followed this example, creating a revenue system based on English precedents, with some distinctive American differences.

Anglo-American Taxation

Americans embraced the concept of direct and indirect taxation that had become the basis of the English fiscal system until 1641. Direct taxes are those paid by citizens directly to the government through assessments of real and personal property, as well as poll taxes. This provided the most tangible form of revenue collection. Citizens knew exactly how much they contributed and paid these taxes to local officials in predetermined amounts. On the other hand, indirect taxes on consumption remained intangible because they were collected through an intermediary, such as a customs officer at a distant port or a merchant. Since the tax became incorporated into the price of the good, the consumer paid his share in small increments (through each purchase) and remained unaware of the actual amount contributed to the Treasury. Customs duties, collected on imports and exports, remained the primary source of indirect tax revenue through most of early English history. Until the onset of the English Civil War in the mid-seventeenth century, direct taxes upon land and indirect taxes on imports and exports provided the government with its ordinary revenue. However, when these sources would not suffice, Parliament requisitioned 'extraordinary' sources of funds. Invoked most frequently for the 'defence of the realm', these extraordinary taxes 'were imposed on the nation only when war, or the likely prospect of it, could justify such exceptional burdens', according to historian G.L. Hariss.[6]

Although warfare spurred increased taxation, English barons established their prerogative over national revenue in a way that other European vassals did not. Adopted in 1215, the Magna Carta set forth 'the eloquence against arbitrary taxation [until] the acceptance of the United States Constitution', according to Shepard Morgan.[7] The twelfth provision of the document required that 'no scutage shall be imposed unless by common counsel'. Parliament affirmed this limitation during the Glorious Revolution. In 1689, William of Orange agreed to the 'Declaration of Rights' that placed limitations on imperial power. For the purposes of this study, Article IV proved most important. This strengthened the restriction that the Crown could not levy taxes without the consent of Parliament, and placed time constraints on the appropriations made. Americans followed this example as well. The Constitution grants Congress alone the power to 'raise revenue' and appropriate funds. John Sherman (R. OH), congressman and future Treasury secretary, echoed the sentiments of English tradition just before the American Civil War when he stated, 'The theory of our government is that a specific sum shall be appropriated by a law originating in this House [of Representatives] for a specific purpose and within a given fiscal year'.[8]

Americans would later replicate these elements of the English fiscal system. Both governments relied on custom duties as a primary source of national revenue. Direct taxes, in the form of apportioned taxes on land and 'movable property', provided the second major source of steady revenue. In both countries, apportionment and relying on local officials for assessment and collection reduced the need for a large, centralized bureaucracy of tax collecting 'dregs and scum'.[9] Historian D. M. Palliser estimated at the commencement of Queen Elizabeth's reign (1558–1603), England employed one royal officer for every 3,000 Britons, whereas the French monarchy employed one officer for every 400 citizens.[10] Because local officials determined the best means for collecting these national taxes, '[English] direct taxes appear in the records under a variety of names', according to O'Brien and Hunt.[11] In 1798, Treasury Secretary Oliver Wolcott commented on the same 'diversity of principles' used by American states in collecting their direct taxes.[12] Wars required extraordinary sacrifice. In both England and the United States, an intimate symbiosis between war and taxation emerged. Wars necessitated taxes, and these funds kept armies on the march.

Incrementally, these war taxes became permanent revenue machines. However, Britons and Americans bore their burdens well because the tax regimes relied on self-assessment in collecting taxes and the restrictions in the British tradition and American Constitution against arbitrary taxation. In generating national revenue through indirect taxes, the government could raise the needed funds through customs duties, a tax consumers pay unconsciously. As a Member of Parliament noted in 1756, 'When a tax is blended with the price of the commodity, the tax is forgot or its remembrance makes little impression, whereas if a tax is assessed directly on the consumer, it will be very disgustful'.[13] The excise remained one 'disgustful' tax that both Parliamentarians and congressmen sought to avoid until the advent of Civil War.

'The Key to the Fiscal Cupboard'

The English graduated their direct taxes to relieve the poor, representing a unique feature of their fiscal system compared to other European countries. The '[agricultural] income of the taxpayer became the standard for all who paid direct taxes by the seventeenth century', according to William Kennedy.[14] Not strictly collected 'per head', rates on poll taxes, for example, also took into account a person's wealth and status. The labouring poor did pay poll taxes, but at lower rates than 'dukes, earls and widowed countesses, barons and baronets and widowed baronesses, knights, esquires, lawyers, traders, franklins, and farmers'.[15] William Kennedy remarked that, 'Over a course of centuries [in English fiscal history] there was no uniform tradition regarding the taxation of the poor man', William Kennedy explained, 'but the tradition of exempting the poor from taxation reigned during Elizabethan and Stuart England'.[16]

With the outbreak of the English Civil War in 1642, Parliament needed more resources 'for the speedie raising of money', which led to the enactment of the first national excise taxes. These duties 'clearly fell upon all sectors of society'.[17] First adopted as a temporary wartime measure, soon excise taxes soon became permanent. Continental European countries had adopted an array of excise taxes earlier, but Parliament avoided these duties. Considered 'un-English…because of the inquisitorial activities of the excise man',[18] Britons paid no excise taxes before this conflict. Adopted as a temporary wartime measure, soon they became the 'key to the fiscal cupboard'.[19] The initial excise tax placed a duty on tobacco, wines, spirits, beer, soap, paper and other goods. Mass opposition to the excises, including a 1647 riot that started over the tax charged for the purchase of an ox, induced a reduction on the charge upon the 'prime necessities of life'. However taxing the sale of domestic and select imported goods (in addition to the custom duties), particularly beer, ale, cider, perry, French wines and coffee, continued.[20] 'The revenue from this source was so considerable and so indispensable', J. E. D.

Binney observed, 'that however unpopular the duties, it was virtually impossible to discontinue them'.[21]

From the time of the English Civil War onward, the poor in England paid taxes, 'regularly in excise duties, and at intervals in direct taxes'.[22] This initiated the practice of taxing all citizens, even the 'meanest in the kingdom'.[23] While this expediency arose from the nature of the excise, it soon evolved into the principle accepted both in England and later in the United States: that all citizens must contribute to the maintenance of government, to the best of their ability. Just taxation did not mean exempting people from paying taxes, but instead ensuring that all citizens, rich and poor, be charged in proportion to what they could pay. This principle became a component of the liberalism that evolved during the late seventeenth century, a legacy that 'was ongoing' to the 'end of the eighteenth century in the American colonies'.[24] The ideal of completely exempting the poor from taxation did not resurface again in the United States until the early twentieth century.

Sparing the Necessaries of the Poor

Permanent excise taxes inculcated the English to the practice of taxing all citizens; soon this matured into the conviction that all should contribute towards the support of the government. The poor ought to pay taxes to the best of their ability as part of their duty to society. John Locke, the political theorist intimately connected with the Glorious Revolution, whose writings served as the basis for the Declaration of Independence, strongly supported this idea. 'Governments cannot be supported without great charge and it is fit everyone who enjoys his share of protection should pay out of his estate his proportion for the maintenance of it'. The contract between government and its citizens, he believed, included an obligation on the part of each constituent for the maintenance of the state. This in turn meant that governments could 'not [to] raise taxes on the property of the people without the consent of the people'.[25] A century later Adam Smith would echo this sentiment; his first 'maxim of taxation' declared, 'The subjects of every state ought to contribute towards the support of the government, as nearly as possible, in proportion to their respective abilities'.[26]

The ubiquity of the excise, and the subsequent dependence of the British government on this revenue, fostered an acceptance of the idea that all members of society, even the poorest, would pay taxes, as long as their 'necessaries' were exempt.[27] In this spirit, one British pamphleteer, writing in 1690, proposed that if excises did not touch the food of the poor, 'there could be nothing said against this tax'. According to William Kennedy:

> The three ideas that most influenced eighteenth century view on taxation were, first, that everyone should pay taxes, including the poor man. Second, that necessaries of

his subsistence should, if possible, be exempted out of compassion. Third, exempting
these necessaries served not only a charitable purpose, but also prevented high wages
and benefited trade. These ideas led to the condemnation of taxes on necessaries,
...and the acceptance that the tax on luxuries represented the most 'ideal tax'.[28]

What constituted a 'necessary' as opposed to a luxury? This delineation became
less precise as England's imperial ambitions developed. The early excise targeted
imported goods such as tobacco, wine and silks as well as domestic goods such
as beer, ale, perry and cider.[29] However, as James Walvin has noted, the development of the 'social and personal habits' of the British people advanced in lockstep
with the course of 'imperial and commercial history'. The 'tropical staples that
began life as the expensive luxury of the wealthy eventually became the cheap,
commonplace pleasure and necessity of the masses'.[30] Facilitated by the expansion of trade and the military power of the empire, the rare exotic produced by
slave labour became the plentiful consumer good. By the late eighteenth century,
Adam Smith defined necessaries and luxuries as:

> Necessaries [are]...not only the commodities which are indispensably necessary for
> the support of life, but whatever the custom of the country renders it indecent for
> creditable people, even of the lowest order, to be without ... All other things I call
> luxuries," he continued. "Beer and ale, for example in Great Britain, and wine even
> in the wine countries, I call luxuries. A man of any rank may, without any reproach,
> abstain totally from tasting such liquors. Nature does not render them necessary for
> the support of life, and custom nowhere renders it indecent to live without them.[31]

During the course of the eighteenth century, an acceptable 'departure from the
principle' of exempting necessaries from taxation allowed a minimal tax on some
of these goods, such as salt, because of their ubiquity. A small tax on items of
great demand goes unnoticed to the taxpayer, but returns great revenue to the
Treasury. The taxes on sugar and tea, for example, started as a means to target
luxuries, but then became a potent revenue source as a small tax on a necessity.
When William Pitt became Chancellor of the Exchequer in 1784 he shifted the
tax burden by increasing the duties on 'luxuries of the well-to-do, including hats,
gloves, mittens, perfumery, female servants, and horses'. He championed the
idea of making taxes 'diffuse', by placing a light duty on articles in wide use. 'The
most equitable principle of taxation will be to render the objects as diffuse as
possible', he stated in 1796.[32] As noted above, this ideal became the foundation
of the Republican internal revenue measures during the war.

Liquor, lawmakers agreed, proved another ideal source of revenue because
the tax 'is paid finally by the different consumers exactly in proportion to their
respective consumption.' Alcohol has an 'infelicitous effect upon the health and
morals of the laboring classes,' and therefore the tax penalizes the intemperate.[33]
This belief resurfaced in the American concept of the ideal tax. Taxing 'ardent

spirits', Alexander Hamilton noted in *Federalist 12*, 'might furnish considerable revenue', and 'would tend to diminish the consumption of it', which would 'be favorable to the morals and health of the society. There is', he continued, 'nothing so much a subject of national extravagance as these spirits.'[34] Indeed, when launching internal tax programmes in the United States, Federalists in the Washington administration, Republicans in the Madison administration, then Republicans in the Lincoln administration, all turned first to indirect taxes (import duties and excises) on liquor. These principles of taxation embraced by the English became the creed in America: first that all must contribute to the support of government; second, that indirect taxes should spare the 'necessaries of the poor'; and finally, that taxing luxuries provided the 'ideal tax'.

Necessaries of Life

Antebellum Americans embraced the central tenets of British revenue policy. They replicated the practice of apportionment and self-assessment in levying direct taxes on property, and allowing local government to use this fount as its primary source of revenue. The national government relied predominantly on indirect taxes, primarily customs duties. During times of distress and war, 'extraordinary' taxes were levied to pay those expenses. In selecting articles to tax indirectly, Americans also employed the ideal of limiting taxes on the 'necessaries' or 'necessities' of the poor, while taxing 'luxuries'. In a 1775 letter to Samuel Osgood, John Adams fretted about the expense of the impending Revolution. 'We have no funds out of which even the interest can be paid and our people are not used to taxes upon the luxuries much less the conveniences and necessaries of life'.[35] From the Constitutional Convention forward, Americans associated selected goods (such as wine, silk) as luxuries, thus suitable targets for taxation.[36] 'The theory that luxuries are best fitted for...taxation has been followed consistently', throughout the nineteenth century, asserted Frederic C. Howe.[37]

Finally, Americans also accepted that all would contribute to the cost of government. 'It was desired that all should contribute in proportion to his abilities', observed Richard T. Ely.[38] Exempting the poor from taxation emerged a tenet of distributive justice in recent history; limiting, but not exempting, the poor from taxation remained the rule in American fiscal policy until the Great Depression era. To blunt the impact of this practice, lawmakers attempted to exempt the 'necessaries' or 'necessities' of the poor. This stated goal re-emerges consistently in discussions of early American political economy, but with a 'difference'. The American twist came through embracing the ideal, but redefining the term. In the United States, limiting the burden on the poor transformed into an attempt to spare the 'necessaries' or 'necessities of life'.

This reference appears over and over in both official and popular literature from the founding through the American Civil War.[39] In his *Report on the Public Credit*, Alexander Hamilton advocated taxing 'luxuries; foreign luxuries ... pernicious luxuries' including 'wines, spirits, teas and coffee' so to spare the 'objects [that] are more regarded as necessaries of life'.[40] Representative Felix McConnell (D., AL) asked the Twenty-ninth Congress to reduce the import duty on two 'necessaries of life: salt and iron'.[41] Andrew Jackson, in a January 1833 speech regarding the Nullification Crisis, urged Congress to change the tariff law because, 'enormous taxes are laid in the necessaries of life...' while 'articles of luxury, universally acknowledged to be the fittest subjects for taxation, are admitted free'.[42] President Jackson's Treasury secretary Thomas Ewing recommended that 'items of luxury not now, may very properly be taxed' while some 'necessaries of life might' move from dutiable to duty free.[43]

The emphasis on the 'necessities of life' demonstrates the inherent belief of many Americans that the richness and vastness of the country allowed any person willing and able to work could care for himself and his family, thus avoiding poverty. The dearth of labour across the country allowed workers to ask for higher wages, reinforcing the idea that American workers fared better than their contemporaries in Europe. 'Americans insisted that the political (not the economic) system determined the extent of poverty and maldistribution of wealth,' according to James L. Huston.[44] Although historians have demonstrated that both poverty and many dimensions of class structure permeated American society from the founding through the Civil War, this belief in upward mobility echoed throughout the literature and official reports of the era.[45] This ideal, expressed since the early Republic, became the basis of the free labour ideology articulated by the Civil War era Republicans. Rather than a new or unique concept, this belief in the ability of Americans to rise above their status at birth became a central feature of national identity.

'In a country where laborers are few and the means of employing industry to advantage are numerous', noted the *North American Review* in 1819, 'no man remains in poverty who possesses even moderate industry and economy'. Though wages may seem low in some places, the employer provides 'not wages alone, but the necessaries of life', so those who possess 'even moderate industry and economy' can advance.[46] Two decades later, the *United States Democratic Review*, a publication with a different political readership, extolled a similar message. 'The nation virtually bestows upon each of its poor citizens as much land as he can cultivate', author W. Kirkland asserted. 'We secure independence to all who are able and willing to work ... an enforced simplicity of living will prove a benefit instead of an injury to the farmer and his rising family ... the real lack of the Western farmer concerns the inner, not the outer man'.[47] Thus, the popular belief that any American could attain wealth if he lived worked hard, remained sober and lived frugally. Those who purchased 'luxuries', particularly 'pernicious luxuries' could pay the extra price. Sparing the 'necessities of life' allowed the industrious to prosper and advance.

What constituted the 'necessities of life' in antebellum America? This definition kept changing, expanding or contracting to fit different political needs. 'Articles which are of large consumption and rank among the necessaries of life', stated an 1825 congressional report, included 'coffee, teas, and cocoa'.[48] In 1833, residents of Westmoreland Co., Pennsylvania identified, 'clothing, salt, implements of husbandry' as necessities.[49] In 1853, during discussions over trade policy with Canada, 'cheap lumber', became a necessity.[50] Various congressional reports, especially the *Commerce and Navigation* reports, consistently listed 'bread and breadstuff' as 'necessities of life'.[51] Sometimes, though, the fiscal demands of the government made these everyday articles appropriate objects to tax as long as the duty did not fall too hard on individuals. In determining which taxes to eliminate after the War of 1812, the House Finance Committee recommended retaining the duty on salt, even though it represented 'a necessary of life', because the duty did not increase the price considerably.[52]

A revenue system based on public consent, rather than imperial or executive fiat, must make concessions to the public will. Americans adopted both the broad principles of taxation from the English as well as the more specific goal of 'sparing the necessaries of life'. Direct taxes, those most tangible to citizens, were administered locally where citizens knew the collector. Colin Brooks suggested that localism in collecting direct taxes helped to promote political stability. 'Under assessment made non payment less of a problem' and 'any attempts to inject ... those ideas of efficiency and executive professionalism [into collecting the direct tax] would meet with hostility of the political nation'.[53] Avoiding the 'hostility of the political nation', especially during a time of crisis, remained imperative.

Between the period of the Glorious Revolution (1688–9) and Napoleon Bonaparte's final defeat (1815), Great Britain 'plunged into financial commitments on level previously unimaginable'.[54] War became the centric force in British society and completely altered her political economy. This level of warfare required dramatic increases in revenue, and new sources of funds. The British embarked on the 'financial revolution', that transformed England into an international financial and military powerhouse. [55]

Taxes alone could not provide enough revenue to build this new 'fiscal-military state', so the British government inaugurated an intensive programme of deficit financing. The 'funding system' relied on a 'powerfully extractive fiscal system' to secure the interest payments for both the short and long term debt.[56] The British raised approximately 75 per cent of the finances needed for their eighteenth century wars (1702–13; 1739–48; 1756–63; 1775–83) by borrowing funds. They incorporated the Bank of England to facilitate the management of their debt.[57] The capacity of the English government to levy taxes efficiently provided a crucial element in this transformation. Without the excise machine constructed during the late seventeenth century, this rapid fiscal transformation would not have occurred so expeditiously.

As the demands for public revenue grew in the eighteenth century, the British government turned to indirect taxes, both excises and custom duties, as the primary source of funds. This reliance on indirect taxes, O'Brien suggested, made the new, more vigorous tax regime, more bearable to the citizens. 'Flexible administration, complemented by an expedition tolerance of evasion, and a prudent selection of the commodities and social groups 'picked upon' to bear the mounting exactions of the state are what made rising taxation tolerable and politically manageable from 1660 to 1815', O'Brien explains. 'In theory, and to some considerable degree in practice, wages and necessities consumed by the poor were exempt from taxes, direct and indirect alike', though the burden of taxation for British society escalated.[58] The debt encumbered the British with a system of permanent taxation, but as Brewer noted, 'The English system looked fairer than many other tax system because it did not have inequality built into its legal structure'.[59]

Taxation During the American Civil War

When it became clear the American Civil War would require more blood and money than originally anticipated, lawmakers turned to precedent to create the 'new' revenue system for the United States. Senator James F. Simmons predicted 'I suppose the House of Representatives propose to follow ... the rule of the British Parliament and their [tax] system ... I do not think it strange that statesmen in this country should conclude that that is best'.[60] These influences came forth when Republicans crafted their Civil War revenue legislation.

By January 1862, as the war continued and costs escalated, lawmakers realized they needed a more ambitious revenue system to meet the costs of the war. The task fell to Congressman Justin S. Morrill who took the lead in writing HR 312, the nation's first comprehensive internal revenue measure. Morrill followed British practice in adopting a set of 'diffuse' taxes. He wanted to tax industry, not 'food' or 'raw materials'. The general 3 per cent duty on manufactured articles would provide the 'largest item of revenue' Morrill foresaw as he outlined the bill. 'A burden that would paralyze the agriculturalists of the country will be taken on the backs of the steam giants with alacrity and confidence', he predicted.[61] Morrill wanted the burden of taxation to fall 'in proportion to [their] ability to pay ... ought not men with large incomes pay more in proportion to what they have than those with limited means?' he asked. However, in following British precedent, Morrill also believed that 'diffuse' taxes should be laid, so no single sector of the country or the economy should bear an undue burden of taxation. Morrill also acknowledged that because the 'habits of the world are fixed' the tax burden should 'rest heavily on spirits, malt liquor, and tobacco'. However, 'an American can still get drunk in our land on cheaper terms than in [any other nation] I know of', he asserted. Morrill cited specific figures regarding British excise tax and alcohol consumption, showing he had studied the English revenue system closely.[62]

As the debate over internal revenue legislation progressed during the course of the war, lawmakers defended their work by claiming they spared 'necessaries' or 'necessities'. Thaddeus Stevens (R., PA), Chair of the House Ways and Means Committee, defended the first Civil War excise taxes in 1862 by lamenting that, '[we] have attempted to raise the largest sums from articles of luxury ... we have the consolation to know that the food of the poor is untaxed'.[63] Joseph J. Lewis, the first Commissioner of Internal Revenue, boasted in his first report that Congress had succeeded in providing, 'relief from taxation on the common necessaries of life' and instead had targeted 'hurtful luxuries'.[64] Lewis also made direct comparisons between the new United States internal revenue measures and the British taxes on distilled spirits, malt liquor, tobacco and stamps. He cited and favourably contrasted British and American collection costs for taxes. Writing in support of the new income tax Lewis reasoned 'If the English people could tolerate without murmuring [an income tax], to sustain a war of conquest American citizens will certainly endure a lighter one for union and freedom'.[65]

As the costs of the Civil War outpaced the income from the early tax measures, Secretary Chase voiced his opinion that 'hurtful luxuries' and other 'voluntary products' including liquor and tobacco, provided the most appropriate sources of tax revenue. Wine, he described as a 'luxury, useless to the consumer'. By taxing these objects, 'relief could be given to the common necessaries of life'.[66] In 1864, Treasury secretary William Pitt Fessenden lamented that the 'great expansion of prices' on all 'necessaries of life' had placed a burden on the lower classes throughout the war, but luxuries had remained the primary target of taxes.[67] In the first comprehensive report outlining recommendations for the postwar revenue system, David A. Wells, the Special Commissioner for Revenue, in 1866 advised exempting from excise taxes 'articles of prime necessity' for all consumers.[68]

Aside from referring to 'necessaries' throughout the tax debates, lawmakers made many specific references to British practices while formulating the internal revenue legislation. The income duty passed by Congress owed much of its heritage to the original British income tax statute. Senator Simmons wrote the first income tax measure for the United States, and noted that 'the time constraints' faced by Congress in passing this legislation necessitated using the British bills as an early template for the American measures. Their income tax bill, he noted 'filled fifty-nine pages' of the Parliamentary record. 'I could not write such a bill from now till January', he stated.[69] Before the start of the July emergency session, Simmons had requested a list of 'references on the subject of the British Income Tax' from the State Department, and used it in writing the legislation.[70] Many of the terms in the US income tax law, including the outline of what sources can be evaluated in determining taxable income (any profession, trade, employment or vocation) were lifted directly from the British statutes.[71]

Throughout the Civil War, when discussing excise taxes on liquor, the income tax, licensing fees on insurance companies and taxes on specified commodities, lawmakers repeatedly referred the British precedent. Senator Charles Sumner (R. MA) quoted from *McCulloch's Commercial Dictionary*, 'which I have before me' during the debate on the cotton tax.[72] Senator John Sherman (R. OH), a member of the Finance Committee and future Treasury secretary, opposed the preliminary version of a tax on livestock sales by invoking three of Adam Smith's four maxims of taxation. Sherman charged that the tax under review 'was not certain', 'difficult to collect' and that it would not 'bear lightly on the people'. Sherman demonstrated his continued knowledge of the British tax policy when, six years later, in a speech advocating the retention of the income tax, he quoted extensively from Parliamentary speeches on the subject.[73] One observer with knowledge of both revenue systems immediately connected the British and American policies. 'With regard to the financial measures [passed by the Congress]', Karl Marx wrote to Frederick Engels in August 1862, 'they are clumsy, as they are bound to be in a country where up to now, no taxes have existed; but they are not nearly so idiotic as the measures taken by Pitt and Co'.[74]

HR 405

By the end of 1863, the government had collected only $37.6 million in internal revenue. The mounting debt became the concern of all lawmakers. Worrying because the 'vast expenditure' necessitated by the war caused 'fear in his mind', Secretary Chase admitted in a February 1864 letter, that 'I am anxious to have them provide for at least one-half of our whole expenses' through internal revenue, a dramatic shift from his earlier pronouncements.[75] However, he and Congress still remained at odds over how best to accomplish this. Chase wanted 'the largest possible proportion of expenditure [to] be provided by direct contributions from the property and incomes of the people'.[76] However, it became clear to the lawmakers that excise taxes, which played a significant, although secondary role in HR 312, would provide the 'key to the fiscal cupboard'. They knew from the experience of the British that a high tax on distilled spirits could produce more revenue than under the current statutes. Joseph J. Lewis, Commissioner of Internal Revenue lamented that the British liquor taxes raised 20 per cent of their revenue, while those in the United States less than 10 per cent.[77] 'England taxes spirits enormously, but has her drunkards still', Morrill noted during the earlier debates on the revenue bills.[78]

For this reason in 1864, Congress targeted the taxes on alcohol with particular zeal. They retained the idea of keeping taxes diffuse, but determined to target selected articles, particularly those that corrupt the 'morals of the community'.[79] On 7 March 1864 Congress increased the tax on distilled spirits from twenty cents per gallon to sixty cents per gallon on any alcohol produced between March and July that year. The rates would continue to increase through January 1865, to the level of eighty cents per gallon. As the debt grew, they determined to enact a more comprehensive bill. The result, HR 405, enacted in June 1864, built upon the foundation of HR 312, but increased duties on most articles. The tax on distilled spirits rose again to $1.50 per gallon. Licenses to sell all types of liquor increased. Tobacco also took a hit. They doubled the tax on smoking tobacco and increased the rate on leaf (unmanufactured) tobacco. The cigar duty soared from $3.50 to $40.00 per 1,000.

The 1864 debate on the liquor tax focused on whether or not to tax liquor 'on hand' that distillers had produced and warehoused in anticipation of a tax increase. Fernando Wood (D. NY) insinuated that 'unseemly influences' had lobbied Congress in order to shield the liquor on hand from the tax.[80] The *New York Herald Tribune* more explicitly charged that one 'mercantile house' in New York had paid 'certain parties operating in Washington' $72,000 to keep the tax off whiskey on hand. 'Judge then what must have been paid in all'. In 1868, when the 'Whiskey scandal' was revealed, the *New York Times* lamented that the 1864 bill 'was the beginning of the fearful corruption and demoralization' that engulfed public officials after the war.[81] The need for more revenue drove these adjustments to the taxes on alcohol.

The most productive tax thus far, the general duty on manufactured products, also increased from 3 to 5 per cent. Again they raised the income tax, to 5 per cent on incomes between $600–5000; 7.5 per cent for incomes ranging from $5,000–10,000; and 10 per cent for those over $10,000 per year. The top rate doubled the income tax duty from the earlier bill. In addition to this increase, Congress enacted a special income tax in October 1864 that went directly to paying bounties for soldiers who re-enlisted or volunteered. This one-time tax charged a rate of 5 per cent on all incomes over $600. This became the first direct transfer of income from one class in society to another.[82] William Pitt Fessenden advocated a further increase in income taxes by removing all exemptions. 'In a young and growing country the vast majority of incomes are small while all participate alike in the blessings of good government'.[83]

Although the general manufacturing tax remained the most productive through the course of the war, the shift towards excise taxes on selected goods, most notably alcohol and tobacco, had begun. By 1865, the tax on domestically produced alcohol had climbed to $2 per gallon. Considered luxuries, or at the least, non-necessities, they represented a fair tax, one that the taxpayer could avoid by not choosing to drink or smoke. When John Sherman complained that his corn raising constituents paid the 'heaviest tax in this bill (HR 312)' through the levy on distilled liquors, Fessenden snapped right back, 'That is a tax only on those who drink liquor'.[84] This remained a fundamental idea in American taxation since the Constitutional Convention: that taxes laid on consumption, particularly on items deemed 'luxuries', fell only on those who chose to purchase the good. When the base for taxation had to expand, Congress concentrated the 'diffuse' taxes on manufacturers that spread the burden of taxation through the broad range of goods produced. This attempted to bear upon the profits of the steam giants, and spread the incidence through most sectors of the economy. Rather than regressive taxes, laid upon the 'politically mute consumer who shouldered the tax burden',[85] the Republicans laid taxes that on manufacturers and wealth first, in the form of the manufacturing duty, income, legacy and corporate taxes. Second, they targeted excises taxes on, historically, the most productive sources of revenue that also proved to be destructive to the health and morals of society.

Regressive Taxes?

Once established, the Republican tax legislation focused on a 'diffuse' tax programme that attempted to place 'no burden on those with small means'.[86] The general duty on manufacturers provided the most revenue during the war, but lawmakers never agreed on who actually paid this tax. Justin S. Morrill insisted throughout the conflict that this duty did not fall on 'consumers', but instead draws from 'the profits made by manufacturers'.[87] However, Fernando Wood (D. NY) disagreed. 'Some gentlemen appear under the impression that the manufacturers are to bear the burden [of this tax.] That is not so. It is the consumer, and not the manufacturer'.[88]

Incidence, or where the burden of taxation falls, has always provided a compelling field of inquiry. Professor McCloskey has argued that, 'The question of incidence cannot be answered by inspecting the tax law or its revenue'.[89] Civil War historians often describe the incidence of the war taxes as 'regressive' because they assume that 'the excise tax was the major source of income' during the war, most specifically the excise taxes on liquor and tobacco, goods whose demand remains constant, or inelastic, even when the price increases.[90] As Manikiw suggests, the burden of taxation falls on:

the side of the market that is less elastic. The elasticity measures the willingness of buyers or sellers to leave the market when conditions become unfavorable. A small elasticity of demand means that buyers do not have good alternatives to consuming this particular good. A small elasticity of supply means that sellers do not have good alternatives to producing this particular good. When the good is taxed, the side of the market with fewer good alternatives cannot easily leave the market and must, therefore, bear more of the burden of the tax.[91]

Although levied on selected articles, certain taxes can be 'shifted'. Manufacturers, for example, can transfer the cost of the tax they pay to the price of the articles they produce. When demand is inelastic, as it has been historically with alcohol and tobacco, the consumer will absorb the increased cost in order to purchase the good. The legislators crafting the Civil War revenue laws struggled with the same question. 'There are and always whom it is levied and from whom it is collect, or whether it is somebody to whom he sells his goods and manufactures', lamented Senator Preston King (R. NY) in 1862. 'We shall never know'.[92] 'Until a few years ago, we were the most lightly taxed nation on the earth', remarked Congressman Henry J. Raymond (R. NY) in 1865. 'Now we are amongst the most heavily burdened of them all'.[93] Despite this burden, Congress marvelled that the public bore the taxes without any severe complaint. 'The present tax laws, on the whole, have been not merely endured, but welcomed by the people in a manner, it is believed, elsewhere unparalleled', noted the 1863 Annual Report from the Internal Revenue Commissioner.[94] But not all saw the taxes as a 'welcomed' addition to the civic life. Samuel S. Cox (D. OH) wondered in 1862 why Congress 'commenced this tax business at the wrong end'. First they levied a tax on 'tea, coffee, sugar, and other necessities of life', later they turned to the luxuries, like 'circuses', which had to pay a tax on their ticket sales beginning in 1862. The definition of what constitutes a necessity played a significant role determining which items to 'hit' with taxes. 'We must recollect that we have taxed the poorer classes of our people almost out of the power of social enjoyment [through the liquor/beer taxes,] stated Benjamin G. Brown (U. MO) in 1865.[95]

Even the income tax, clearly the most 'just' tax enacted during the war, fell hard on the 'middle class'. Amongst the first taxes levied during the Civil War, the income tax exempted all who made less than $800, then $600. The *Internal Revenue Recorder* reported in 1867 that the income tax in 1866 (its most productive year) brought in $61 million, of which $26 million paid by those with less than $5,000 in income. Over 300,000 people paid the $26 million, whereas only 50,000 individuals paid the remainder of the tax. 'It is unjust, unproductive, inequitable. It falls with crushing effect on salaried men.'[96] Adopting the method of collecting the income tax 'at the source' had made salaried individuals more susceptible to the tax than the 'honest' citizens who had to report their income. This policy hurt government employees in particular. Private companies did not always cooperate in reporting their charges' salaries.[97] The tax on interest from stocks and bonds issued by banks, railroad companies, insurance companies and other private corporations proved the most productive means of counting the 'hidden' income of the wealthy.[98]

Worries about tax incidence did not fall strictly on party lines; as Linden suggested, a geographic divide, depending on the tax and how it affected the constituency of the representative or senator, most influenced the lawmaker's concerns about where the tax fell. Nor did the same ideal of tax equity that we have now extend back to the Civil War era. 'In our age', Webber and Wildavsky observed, 'conceptions of equity comprise the central core of fiscal theory. Equity of incidence manifested as one measure of the goodness of a tax'. However, in an earlier time, 'fiscal equity meant, without exception, all men should pay taxes'.[99]

Describing the Civil War internal revenue measures as 'regressive' does not place the legislation in proper historical context. Congress did not tax agricultural produce, a remarkable conciliation when one remembers that America remained a decisively agrarian country until the late nineteenth century. They tried to spare the poor from bearing a large portion of the tax burden by avoiding taxes on the 'necessaries of life'. Instead, they designed the legislation to fall on manufacturers, then made these taxes as diffuse as possible to spread the burden of taxation between the profits of these businesses and a broad segment of the American population. Also, Republicans introduced the first national income tax and tax on inheritances, decisively progressive taxes. The tax on manufacturers generated more income than any other duty; and, as the table below indicates, most of the revenue from the Civil War taxes came from taxes that can be described as progressive in its origin (before shifting): progressive taxes paid: the manufacturing duty, the income tax, the tax on articles and occupations, the stamp tax, and the tax on banks and bankers, as noted in the table below.[100]

Table 5.1: Primary Sources of Internal Revenue 1863–72

Articles Taxed	Total Revenue
Manufactured products[101]	$403,175,721
Income Tax	$341,706,036
Distilled Spirits Excise	$336,138,546
Articles and Occupations[102]	$238,540,178
Tobacco Excise	$200,213,837
Stamp Taxes	$131,673,669
Fermented Liquor Excise	$52,954,800
Banks and Bankers	$28,644,495

Source: *Report of the Commissioner of Internal Revenue, 1873*

A closer examination of who paid taxes is shown in the chart below. The graph compares the percentage of national wealth held in each state in 1870 based on figures from the census taken that year. Further, it charts the cumulative tax paid by citizens in each state between 1863 and 1870. The lines move in tandem, showing that more taxes were collected in the states with greater wealth. While still an imperfect measure of the regressive nature of the Civil War taxes, the graph does indicate that on the broad scale of state wealth the Civil War internal revenue measures were more proportional than progressive or regressive. The states where the per cent of taxes collected were higher than their share of national wealth were predominantly the wealthier, Union states (New York, Massachusetts, and Ohio). Having citizens pay in proportion to their wealth remained the stated goal of Republicans leaders throughout the course of the war.

Chart 5.1: Per Cent of State Wealth Compared to Per Cent of Taxes Collected 1864–73

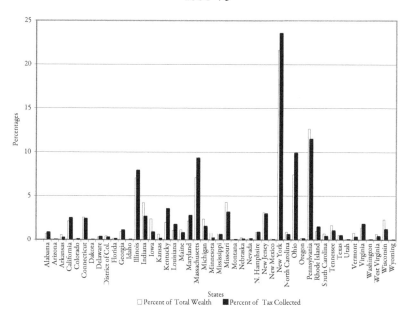

The Civil War represented the first 'modern' war in American history, but the fiscal policy used to fund that war retained elements of the archaic. The tax on manufacturers and the income tax augured future tax policies that would attempt to shift the incidence towards more progressive taxation. However, immediately after the war, Congress retained the ideal of taxing 'luxuries' or 'superfluities' as a fair form of taxation. This concept, borrowed from the past, wedded the United States to a more regressive tax programme in the late nineteenth century. The tariff policy that emerged during the war did as well.

The War Tariffs

Throughout the antebellum era, tariffs became the staple source of 'ordinary' government revenue. Andrew Jackson noted that income from 'luxuries, the fittest subjects for taxation' in the form of imported goods, spared the 'necessaries of the life'.[103] Only on rare occasions, because of war or the financial debt incurred by war, did the national government turn to internal taxation. When financial 'embarrassments' occurred in the government, adjusting tariff duties rather than resorting to other forms of taxation became the standard remedy.

Yet historians have been less inclined to treat tariffs as taxes than as a field for manipulation of certain 'economic interests'.[104] With due reason, of course. The first tariff measure passed by the Congress called for using those duties not only for revenue but also for the 'encouragement and protection of manufacturers'. Edward Stanwood, who sympathized with the protectionists' arguments, in 1903 described the tariff as the most 'persistent issue in American politics'.[105] F. W. Taussig, in his study of tariff policy in the United States, focused on the arguments for the 'protection of young industries', concentrating on the iron and textile industries.[106] Because most historians' references to tariff policy begin (and often end) with Taussig's work, and politicians representing Pennsylvania's iron smelters and Massachusetts's textile manufacturers played such a dominating role in the tariff debates, analysis of any given nineteenth-century tariff often centers on these two industries. Controversy over the degree to which tariffs would be employed for 'revenue only' or 'protection' became part of the growing sectional tensions of the antebellum period. Free trade advocates more likely hailed from slave states, whereas protectionist sentiments resided in the free states.[107] Historians John Commons and James L. Huston have argued that politicians also saw tariffs as a means to keep wages high for free labourers, rather than just a device to reward capitalist supporters.[108] Clearly, politicians have found ways of expanding the use of tariffs beyond revenue devices.

I concede readily that tariffs had many political purposes, and have been manipulated consistently to reach certain ends. As Jonathan J. Pincus has revealed, 'pressure groups' played a significant role in forging tariffs, at least the protectionist tariff of 1824.[109] All tariffs contain protection, whether incidental or overt, and will continue to as long as the First Amendment continues to guarantee the freedom to 'petition the government for a redress of grievances'.

Consider the tariff legislation enacted during the Civil War first and foremost as a series of revenue vehicles. I suggest that 'protectionism', imposing duties on imports in order to protect home industries from overseas competition, arose as a response to the fiscal demands of the Civil War, rather than the Republican leaders' primary motive. Analyses of the Republican Party's tariff legislation too often begin with the assumption that protectionism provided the basis for the Civil War tariff legislation. For example, historians routinely refer to the Morrill tariff, signed into law by President Buchanan two days before Abraham Lincoln's inauguration, as a 'protectionist measure' that 'nearly doubled the rates of import duties' and 'provided the if statement of a new protectionism peculiar to the Republicans,' thus inaugurating the protectionism agenda before the war began. As I have argued elsewhere, the Morrill tariff represented primarily a response to the fiscal malfeasance of the Buchanan administration, rather than a new statement of protectionism.[110]

Republican legislators who crafted the tariff bills kept four objectives in mind. First, the tariffs were used to balance the internal revenue measures enacted during the war. Second, the development of protectionism sprang from the movement of goods first from the free list to the dutiable list, then from adjusting these imposts from *ad valorem* to specific duties. Because tariff duties had to be paid in specie, continuing to increase the revenue from customs duties ensured that the government would have the ability to continue paying the interest on the federal debt in gold. These actions occurred to generate more revenue. Finally, at the conclusion of the war, tariffs were retained to help pay down and service the federal debt. Enacted to increase revenue to keep pace with the expenses of the war, each of these three steps helped clear the path for the development of the protectionism that burdened the American fiscal system for the remainder of the nineteenth century. The advent of protectionism came in June 1864 when Congress passed internal revenue and tariff legislation that taxed American citizens more than ever before. Manufacturers 'only had to declare what rate of duty them deemed essential, and that rate was accorded'.[111] Although I recognize the protectionism played a role during the course of the war, I suggest that coping with the overwhelming costs of the Civil War contributed more to the development of this policy.

Internal tax measures played in driving tariff policy. Indeed, few recognize that tariffs constitute 'taxes', but instead write about them as a separate device used for other purposes. When writing about the 'taxes' levied during the war, the reference is singularly focused on the internal revenue measures.[112] However, the internal taxes and the tariff measures emerged as two parts of the same revenue programme. Understanding the internal tax legislation launched during the war provides for a more complete comprehension of Civil War tariff financing.

In 1862, Congress decided to create an internal revenue system that taxed the 'steam giants' while attempting to 'lay no burden on those with small means'. The 3 then 5 per cent duty on manufacturers paid the greatest share of internal taxes. Manufacturers also paid licensing fees to keep their factories open, and paid higher rates on the raw materials they processed.[113] Congress attempted to provide 'relief' to industry for the tax burden they carried during the war. They wanted to tax fairly, and spread the burden of taxation 'diffusely'. However, they did not want to 'kill the goose that laid the golden egg'.[114] They used the tariff rates to create parity between the price of imports and the price of taxed domestic goods. The average rates of duty imposed by the tariff legislation reached 38.4 per cent by 1865. While high, this remained below the rates imposed by the 'Tariff of Abominations' passed in 1828. The per capita tax burden exacted by the Civil War tariffs averaged $2.33 between 1861 and 1865, whereas the custom duties per capita averaged $2.51 between 1802 and 1889.[115]

Tariff Rates 1800–99

Chart 5.2: Overall Tariff Rates

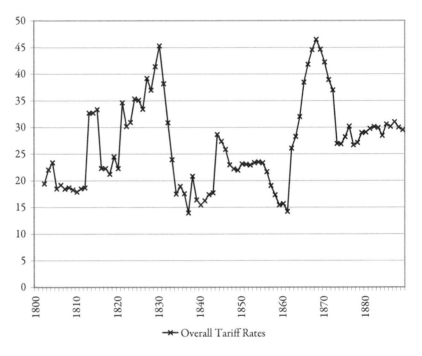

—✴— Overall Tariff Rates

By 1864, industry clamoured for relief. The general duty on manufacturers provided the most revenue during the war, and they insisted that shifting the taxes to consumers did not occur and that these taxes came out primarily out of their profits.[116]   Based on the prosperity manufacturers reported at the end of the war, few historians, including me, believe these tales of sorrow. However, their pleas to Congress did have an effect. Although the rates in the 1862 tariff bill raised average tariff rates to 28 per cent, the tariff legislation passed on 30 June 1864 shows the first significant increase in average rates. This statute was passed in conjunction with HR 405, the largest internal revenue measure of the war.

The internal revenue legislation drove the tariff rates in an attempt to blunt the impact of the internal taxes. Rightly this can be seen as form of protectionism, but protectionism primarily to offset the internal taxation.

As they adjusted these tariffs, the Republicans relied first on devices to increase revenue. These included 'shrinking' the free list. The value of imports for home consumption admitted into the United States free of duty declined from $68.3 million in 1860 to $15.1 million by 1868, or from 20 to 4 per cent of the value of all imported goods.[117] Moving articles from the 'free' to the 'dutiable' list helped generate more revenue, while not inherently increasing 'protection'. By concentrating on 'revenue producing' goods, which historically had included coffee, tea, sugar (including molasses, etc.), imported 'spirits' of all types (brandies, ales, wines), spices and tobacco, Congress maintained goals of providing 'relief from taxation on the common necessaries of life' while targeting 'hurtful luxuries'.[118] Treasury Secretary Chase in particular, sought to expand the duties on coffee, tea and sugar. Congress complied by December 1861 when they added a five cents per pound duty on coffee.[119]

Another means of boosting tariff revenue came from changing *ad valorem* duties to specific duties.[120] Free trade advocates preferred *ad valorem* duties because they fluctuated with the price of the import. If the price of the import decreases, so does the tax. However, these changes in prices, and the ability of merchants to skirt the tax by misrepresenting the value of the import, led to difficulty in securing a desired amount of customs income. Conversely, protectionists preferred specific duties. A decrease in the price of the imported good would still trigger the same tax, and help provide more insulation for the domestic product. Because the same tax would be levied on an import no matter what the value of the good, specific duties produced more reliable revenues. When trying to guarantee a desired amount of revenue, Congress often turned to specific duties.[121]

During the Civil War, Congress repeatedly altered the duties on goods from *ad valorem* to specific duties. This process began with the Morrill tariff, when 107 items were moved from the free to the dutiable list.[122] They would also levy 'compound duties' where 'in addition to the duties heretofore imposed by law' Congress would impose a general *ad valorem* duty (10 per cent in this case) to the existing duties.[123] On 29 April 1864, for example, Congress passed a joint resolution raising by 50 per cent 'of the rates of duties and imposts' on the 'present duties and imposts now charged on the importation of all goods, wares, merchandise and articles imported.'[124] Originally for only sixty days, this provision was increased to one year the following June in the scramble to find more money to pay the continuing costs for the war.

They also adjusted the tariff rates not only on manufactured goods but also on agricultural products. Hemp, wheat, flax and other agricultural goods were some of the first items to move from low *ad valorem* tariffs to higher specific duties. Justin S. Morrill (R. VT), repeatedly assured Congress that the rates introduced in the 1861 measure, 'though specific rates, are only equivalents for the Tariff of 1846', and that the 'highest duties in the bill are proposed for the purpose of revenue', not protection.[125] Throughout the course of the war, Morrill remained more sympathetic to his state's woolgrowers, rather than wool (textile) manufacturers, making him more inclined toward incidental protection of domestic raw materials than manufactured textiles. In this, Morrill clearly sided with agriculture.[126] This concern for the agricultural 'interest' also permeated the internal revenue legislation. Senator William Pitt Fessenden complained in 1862 that 'a farmer must inevitably be the best off ... he will escape [taxation] easier than others, though he is abler to pay and more independent than any other class of men in the community'.[127]

Chart 5.3: Per Capita Rates

As the chart above indicates, the per capita rate of tariff duties collected during the Civil War remained within the range of the antebellum era. Only after the cessation of the fighting did the amount each citizen paid, on average, rise considerably and stay high for the remainder of the century. This reflects the burden created by the Civil War debt. Generating revenue to pay the debt remained one of the key factors in the consideration of tariff rates.

The General Sales Tax

I have argued throughout this book that the war Congresses enacted revenue legislation out of necessity, rather than choice. To assess fully where volition ends and obligation begins, one must look not only at what measures each Congress passed into law, but those they did not. The proposal to introduce a general sales tax provides such a test. In writing both HR 312 and HR 405, legislators considered incorporating a sales tax to shift the burden of both the income tax and the tax on manufactured goods more directly to consumers. The sales tax would have placed a national *ad valorem* duty on sales, with rates of 1 per cent (recommended in 1862) to 1.5 per cent (1864). Advocated most strenuously by representatives from manufacturing states, and those with the highest contribution to the income tax, the sales tax would have lightened the duty on the manufacturers and the wealthy who paid the income tax and instead placed it consumers as they purchased finished goods and other articles.

Without doubt, manufacturers would have escaped from fronting the brunt of the Civil War internal taxes if the proposed amendments passed. While benefiting larger, vertically integrated enterprises, that handle distribution and sales without middlemen or jobbers, the tax would hurt smaller distributors, and those located in rural areas, particularly in the West, who generally purchased goods from intermediaries. These middlemen remained the 'most important men in the economy', according to Livesay and Porter. They not only sold goods, but provided capital and credit to both their suppliers and customers and helped spur regional development, and 'served as the primary economic integrators' for the developing western and rural communities.[128] In rural areas, they provided the 'simplest and most pleasant banking operations' for local farmers.[129] The merchant's centrality to the economy waned slightly in the pre-war years, as railroads facilitated the distribution of goods from producers to market without intermediaries. The introduction of the Greenbacks, which moved businesses off the 'credit treadmill' and onto a cash-only basis, played a significant role in the decline of mercantile influence, and the rise of corporate power, during the late nineteenth century.[130]

Instituting a national sales tax would have expedited this process. This tax, as Congressman James E. English noted, represented 'a great national measure intended to affect all the interests of the country'.[131] It would swiftly help create a more national economy by tying the government into transactions, large and small, throughout the nation. Government officials would scrutinize all sales, thus extending its reach into the economic process, a 'goal' of the Republicans, according to Arthur M. Lee.[132] The incidence of a national sales tax, Otto van Mering noted, 'is widely distributed', but then 'rights itself over time'. Prices increase, especially on goods with high, inelastic demand.[133]

The Boards of Trade in both Boston and Philadelphia called upon Congress to pass this legislation.[134] On 27 March 1862, William P. Sheffield (R. RI) offered an amendment to HR 312, seeking a 1 per cent tax on the sales of 'goods, wares, merchandise, property, and estates'. Although his initial amendment excluded 'sales to jobbers or middlemen' he later stated that he wanted 'all sales' to fall under this tax. Sheffield said that he offered the amendment to place both the receipts of the 'man who received $1 million in profits' with those of the 'the poor woman who sells a pig' (and has to pay a tax at the slaughterhouse) on the tax roll.[135] However, he soon dropped this populist pretext. 'I [want] my constituents to be relieved from an undue proportion of [war taxes]', he proclaimed. 'As [HR 312] now stands, it makes the workshops of New England pay one fourth of the tax. That sir, is unjust'. Rather than a concern about the poor woman and her pig, he offered the sales tax as a relief for the manufacturing duty.[136]

A brief but telling debate ensued. New England representatives, James E. English, Samuel Hooper and Alexander H. Rice, spoke in favour of the tax. 'Instead of singling out manufacturing interests of the country', Rice complained, 'it would be equally just and equally wise', to spread the tax more fairly, especially on 'articles furnished by nature'. Hooper suggested that the tax on manufacturers would act as 'a duty on consumers', so the sales tax would not represent a significant change from the current bill. Valentine B. Horton (R. OH) objected because the sales tax represented a measure that required 'a new principle' and 'new machinery'. William Kellogg (R. IL) added, 'There ought to be some justice and some far distribution', of the tax burden, 'so that it shall reach the capital of the country as well as individuals'. He protested that replacing the sales tax with one that the 'consumer' would bear through the 'actual necessaries of life'. Sheffield then withdrew his amendment, stating, 'My object has been accomplished'.[137] Although HR 312 did not incorporate a general sales tax, Congress did adopt taxes on selected sales including, auctions, real estate and securities (stocks and bonds) sales.

The idea of a national sales tax did not surface again until 1865. When the Finance Report of 1864 projected a $35 million shortfall between receipts and expenditures, Commissioner of Internal Revenue, Joseph L. Lewis, advocated implementing a general sales tax. Lewis stated in his report that,

> I can find [no other tax] which promises such a large yield of revenue, with so little disturbance to trade, and so slight a pressure on the tax payer...I am clearly of the opinion that the tax on sales...is greatly preferable to a supplementary duty on incomes [or] a direct tax.[138]

The Ways and Means Committee instead suggested raising the tax on manufacturers again, to reach an average duty of 5 per cent. George Boutwell (R. MA) countered by reviving the idea for a general sales tax. William P. Sheffield (U. RI) first introduced the sales tax as a means for taxing rich and poor alike. Boutwell, on the other hand, made no effort to hide his intentions with the tax. On the evening of 17 February 1865, he proposed adding a 1.5 per cent sales tax in place of an increase in the manufacturers duty. The debate on the amendment began the next day. 'When you analyze this system of taxation, whether on incomes, manufacturers, or sales, the producers and consumers of the country pay the tax'. Since the consumers represent 'a larger class', Boutwell continued, 'the tax should fall on them'.[139] Whereas manufacturing interests advocated the sales tax in 1862, representatives wishing to relieve their constituents from the income tax became part of the debate in 1865.

As with the debate in 1862, this became a contest between eastern and western interests, as well as urban against rural representatives. 67 per cent of the western representatives opposed this tax. California representatives William Higby and Thomas B. Shannon, both Republicans, favoured it, in hopes of relieving the tax on domestically produced wine. 'A tax on sales', James A. Garfield (R. OH) protested, 'is a tax on all necessaries of life'. Garfield also showed concern for enlarging the government's reach into the economy through this tax. '[The sales tax] would put property in a place where government can lay hands upon it in bulk'.[140] Although recognized in the 1862 deliberations that this measure would increase the role of the federal government in the economy, representatives showed far more concern about this issue in 1865. William A. Allison (R. IA) also worried about augmenting federal power through this tax. 'It would be a radical change in our system of raising revenue and would require the presence of the tax gatherer and collector in every district and hamlet in the country', to secure the revenue from a sales tax.[141]

Rather than a sectional split, the interests in this legislation fell more towards rural against urban representatives. Fernando Wood (D. NY) former mayor of New York city, whom Joel H. Silbey described as one of the Democrats who feared 'the impact the war was having on the country', and 'the centralization of power' incumbent in the war legislation, nevertheless did not see this augmentation of national taxing power as a part of this feared revolution.[142] Wood supported this measure. 'If you tax sales it does not necessarily follow that the tax imposed runs into the consumption of the articles and the consumer finally pays it', he offered.[143] Rufus P. Spalding (R. OH) said he supported the sales tax because 'the shoddy contractors' and 'men who buy houses ... would feel the tax'.[144] John A. Griswold (R. NY), hoping to relieve his state from the disproportionate national share of the income tax, supported the sales tax, while complaining that 'no mode of taxation is more unjust and unequal' than the income tax.[145]

Robert D. 'Pig Iron' Kelley, the outspoken defender of Pennsylvania iron also favoured replacing the taxes on iron and iron products with a sales tax. All the Massachusetts representatives, except Samuel Hooper (R. MA), who had a change of heart on this issue, voted for the tax, hoping to relieve the textile concerns in their state. Hooper noted that it hurt those in rural area who 'have to pay the tax many times over on flour and groceries.'[146] William Allison (R. IA) noted that another special interest would benefit from the sales tax. 'I am not surprised that gentlemen representing constituencies in New England and other great cities in eastern states are in favor of this tax upon sales...the tax will consolidate trade in those large cities and break down the smaller traders throughout the country.'[147] The amendment failed on 18 February 1865.

Justin S. Morrill emerged as the primary opponent to incorporating a national sales tax into the revenue bills, both in 1862 and 1865. As a former merchant and storeowner in a small Vermont town, Morrill, more than any other participant in the sales tax debate, understood the mechanisms needed to collect the tax, and the effect it would have on small businesses. He did not wish to see the augmentation of federal power inherent in this tax. 'Inspectors and collectors', Morrill warned, 'would have to run down every transaction in the country'.[148] Small-scale retailers, who would have to pay the tax to acquire items, then charge it again upon the sale, would face price competition, and eventually elimination, from larger distributors with national reach. Manufacturers and importers would undercut these merchants, and replace their businesses. Merchants did not keep detailed books that would allow the efficient collection of this tax. Finally, many 'sales' still occurred without money, as a form of barter.[149] How would a revenue officer determine the appropriate tax in these situations, Morrill wondered.

Applying some of the lessons of brief debate for an unsuccessful tax, we find that congressmen represented the interests of their constituents. Republicans from manufacturing districts favoured the legislation. Both Republicans and Democrats from rural areas opposed the legislation. Although Democrats voted overwhelmingly against this measure, urban Democrats favoured it. New Yorkers in particular, supported the measure as a substitute for the income and other progressive taxes that hit their constituents disproportionately. Thus constituent interests, some of whom were also strong economic interests in the district, played a key role in this vote. The sales tax would have facilitated the Republicans supposed goal of 'bolster[ing] a new national system',[150] both by concentrating the power within the economy, and extending the governments reach into the daily transactions. While acknowledged and understood that this would eventuate with the introduction of the sales tax, the proposal did not pass. The broader contention that 'industrial capitalism was now in control of the state' cannot be supported by this episode.[151] The sales tax clearly would have shifted the burden of taxation from the 'steam giants' and 'capitalists' and spread it on the citizenry. This did not happen. Also the generalization that the Union tax system constructed the 'most coercive civilian agency in the national government' needs moderation. Implementing the sales tax would have necessitated a larger, more coercive force of collectors, a fact recognized then rejected during the debates.[152] Morrill had the final word on this issue:

> The vast amount of sales of the country are purely and simply on the necessaries of life; you are therefore proposing to tax the poor man with a large family...the very men that we have exempted from license [fees], the very men that we have exempted from the income tax, will not escape this tax.[153]

The effort to shield the 'poor man with a large family' defeated the elitist interests on this measure.

The Demise of Secretary Chase

Salmon P. Chase served as Treasury Secretary until June 1864. His weariness from the trials of the job, and his determination to become president, caught up with him. In October 1863 he made a political trip to Ohio and Indiana, ostensibly to blunt the gubernatorial campaign and rising influence of the most vocal and acerbic Copperhead, Clement L. Vallandigham; in fact he used the occasion to launch his bid for the Republican nomination for the presidency in 1864. Enthusiastic crowds greeted him in both states; they affectionately referred to him as 'Old Greenbacks', a great irony, considering his initial reluctance to invoke fiat currency, and his later denunciation of it. Upon his return to Washington, Chase wrote to a friend that, 'never in my life have I felt such emotions as were excited by my recent visit to Ohio and Indiana.'[154] Encouraged by his coterie of longtime Democratic–Republican supporters, Chase hoped to capitalize on the public's war weariness. He began laying the groundwork for another run for the White House. To Chase's credit, he finally took the potentially unpopular step of calling for heavy taxation at the same time he began his presidential bid.

The release of the 'Pomeroy Circular' cut short his aspirations. This pamphlet, entitled *The Next Presidential Election*, written by Chase supporters, delivered a vitriolic attack on the president's administration of the war. President Lincoln dismissed Chase's intrigues: his Cabinet loyalists did not. An investigation was launched on charges of corruption and fraud in the Treasury department. Secretary Seward and his faction of the party attacked Chase's character, focusing on his relationship with Jay Cooke, and suggesting that Cooke profited too much from the Civil War bond drives. In February, 1864, when the Ohio and Indiana legislatures voted in favour of President Lincoln as the Republican nominee, Chase's bid for the presidency collapsed.

Chase lost the confidence of his last supporters in Congress, who forced him to remove Cooke as the exclusive agent for the sale of bonds. Concurrently, speculation on gold reached a feverish height in the first four months of 1864, driving up the price of specie and devaluing the Greenback. Chase began writing increasingly urgent letters to congressional leaders, newspaper editors and political operatives throughout the country, begging them to promote 'taxation to one-half the amount of our current expenditures'.[155] Chase lobbied both the House and Senate to adopt a tax measure that would raise at least $400 million in internal revenue, primarily from direct taxes. Instead, Congress passed HR 405, with the anticipated revenue from the bill totalling $220 million. Over Chase's objections, Congress passed the Tariff of 1864. Finally in June 1864, Chase had a patronage dispute with Secretary Seward; in a fit, he submitted his resignation, a step he had taken twice before during his tenure in the Cabinet. To his surprise, President Lincoln accepted it and made two announcements soon thereafter that Senator William Pitt Fessenden would assume leadership of the Treasury and that Salmon P. Chase would become the next Chief Justice of the Supreme Court 'when I have the opportunity'.[156]

The economy of government Chase had sought when he took charge of the Treasury died in the trenches of war.

Conclusion

The Republican lawmakers who crafted the internal revenue legislation during the Civil War relied on well-established precedents, rather than a new ideology. The resulting legislation 'raised the largest possible revenue in the least possible time without much regard to acknowledged politico-economic laws'.[157] Specifically, they levied taxes to guarantee payments on the interest rates for war loans rather than 'pay for the war'. Steady tax revenues assured lenders they would receive regular interest payments, which allowed officials to negotiate lower interest rates. In session for only thirteen months between 4 July 1861 and 3 March 1863, the Thirty-seventh Congress did not have much time to fashion a new revenue system from scratch, based on a unique ideology; instead they turned to the precedent of British tax policy. Meeting the demands of war required haste rather than deliberation. Writing comprehensive tax measures proved an enormous chore since four decades had passed since the last effort at internal taxation.

Many of the patterns the English established, Americans followed. Introducing permanent excise taxes during the Civil War provides one example. Invoking the income tax to balance and supplement direct taxes also manifested in the

United States. Americans also replicated the start-and-stop nature of the British income tax. The English income tax levied during the Napoleonic Wars lasted from 1798–1815; when, in 1842, Parliament 'arrived at the limits of taxation on articles of consumption', they reintroduced the income tax and it became permanent.[158] In the United States, Congress enacted the first income tax in 1861, then it 'died a natural death' in 1872, when the measure expired. The next American income tax passed in 1894, ending the next year when the Supreme Court declared it unconstitutional. Enacted again in 1913, after the passage of the Sixteenth Amendment to the Constitution, the tax became permanent. Twenty-seven years elapsed before the British resurrected their income tax to relieve another budget crisis exacerbated by war, while Americans took forty-one years to reintroduce theirs. In the interim, taxing luxuries while sparing necessaries, or necessities, emerged as a means of obtaining a 'just and equitable' distribution of taxes.[159] Most of the revenue collected through the Civil War tax measures did not, in fact, come from excises, but from a duties on manufactured products, the income tax and specific licences and fees levied specifically to limit the amount of tax paid by the poor. The effort remained to have citizens pay in proportion to their wealth and ability. In the aggregate, on a state level, this goal was accomplished. When members of Congress from the states where most of the taxes were collected tried a more brazen attempt to shift the burden of taxes across the general population through a national sales tax, the effort failed.

But the ironies and contradictions of Civil War finance persist. In the attempt to create a fair and proportional internal revenue system, Congress laid the groundwork for the onerous tariffs that would become such a divisive political concern in the late nineteenth century. The man who wanted to have economy in government left office having overseen the accumulation of the largest debt in US history. Salmon P. Chase, the man who wanted only 'sound' money brought a fiat currency to the national stage, basked in the glory of presenting it, then, much later, reverted to his old ways, and denounced the Greenback as Chief Justice of the Supreme Court. Finally, the secretary who supported free trade most of his career, and wanted to rely primarily on direct taxes during the Civil War, found in his wake a tax system that had rejected both. These changes did not occur because of Chase's weakness or inability but instead because the exigencies of war had pushed this highly principled man, and his fellow Republicans, into taking steps they would never had taken except to save the nation.

6 THE MOST BURDENED OF THEM ALL

On 9 April 1865, Robert E. Lee surrendered to Ulysses S. Grant at the Appomattox Court House. Although this event has come to represent the end of the Civil War, the Confederate president Jefferson Davis, who had fled Richmond the week before, urged his troops in the field to keep fighting. Many wished to see the Confederate forces disband and form guerrilla forces that would continue to resist Union occupation. However commanders in the field, who had fought and suffered most directly, followed their instincts. General Joe Johnston informed President Davis in late April that continuing to fight would be 'impractical' and would spread 'ruin all over the South'. He surrendered to General William T. Sherman on 26 April 1865. On 9 May Nathan Bedford Forrest, whose daring and cunning raids against Union forces throughout the western theatre had stymied commanders throughout the war, parried President Davis's call to resist. 'It is our duty to divest ourselves' of 'all feelings of animosity, hatred and revenge', he counselled his followers. 'Obey the laws, preserve your honor, and the government to which you have surrendered can afford to be and will be magnanimous'.[1]

But could the government of the reunited nation afford magnanimity? For four long years, lawmakers feared that the fiscal demands of the war would overburden, and eventually collapse, the effort to reunite the nation. Now that victory had been achieved, and the president's 'paramount object' seemed within reach, the question turned to how to recreate a nation that had been torn apart by Civil War.[2] Earlier that year, on 31 January 1865, Congress approved the Thirteenth Amendment, guaranteeing that slavery would no longer persist in the reunited nation. However, as Eric Foner observed, passage of the amendment 'closed one issue only to open a host of others'.[3]

As the war dragged on, longer and bloodier than anyone had anticipated, the public understood that they would have to shoulder the war costs. The *New York Tribune* predicted in December 1861 that loyal citizens will 'cheerfully submit' to a system of taxation to prosecute the war.[4] 'The tax gatherer will be received by every loyal man', the *Chicago Tribune* predicted in March 1862.[5] Thaddeus Stevens (R. PA), as Chair of the Ways and Means Committee, received letters from citizens suggesting a variety of tax measures to pay the costs of the war. 'My life and the little property I have is at the disposal of the government for the suppression of the rebellion', wrote Unak Bruner of Nebraska on 8 February 1862.[6] Revenue Commissioner Joseph J. Lewis noted in his first report to Congress in 1863 that, 'The present tax laws, on the whole, have been not merely endured, but welcomed by the people in a manner ... elsewhere unparalleled'.[7] Even with these expressions of popular support for a vital revenue programme, the Republicans had hesitated in disrupting the structure of fiscal federalism to enact a national programme of taxation. Contrary to the idea that they eagerly embraced opportunities to 'nationalize' the economy, the Republicans looked upon this as less of an opportunity than a challenge and a burden. Meeting the war costs, through loans and revenue, helped push the Treasury to initiate the programmes that posed the greatest threat to the localized economic structure of the antebellum era. To gather enough money to fund the Civil War, the Treasury needed some consistent medium of exchange, that could be collected anywhere in the country and recognizable in Washington. The mixed currencies of the country had greatly impaired the ability of the Treasury to harness the wealth of the nation in order to fight the war. Introducing the Greenback and creating a standard national currency in the form of notes issued through the new national banks gave the Treasury the ability to pay its bills, and Americans a consistent method for paying their taxes. The new monetary system emerged as part of the effort to save the nation rather than nationalize it.

The war left the Union citizenry wary and impatient, and lawmakers feared that the public would not comply with the new, invasive tax regulations. The United States government had not levied taxes since the War of 1812; throughout the war, political leaders feared inciting public outrage by imposing a heavy tax burden. After the first disastrous defeat at Bull Run, in August 1861, Chase opined in a letter to John C. Fremont that, 'there is great danger that, after a month or two the people in view of the magnitude of the burdens it [the war] is likely to entail, will refuse their support'.[8] As late as April, 1864 Gideon Welles recorded in his diary that, 'Congress is laboring on the tax bill. The members fear to do their duty because taxation is so unpopular. An old infirmity'.[9]

We know now that the public willingly accepted this new burden, but the lawmakers had no way of knowing how far they could reach into the pockets of the loyal citizens. Taxes roused public discontent in the past, and the amounts levied during the Civil War far exceeded any amount requested by any earlier Congress. The excise provisions of HR 312 taxed luxury goods citizens owned already (not just upon purchase), raising the potential for assessors to enter people's homes to find their treasure. Senator William Pitt Fessenden warned in 1862 that the 'general opinion of the people in all sections of the country', would find these provisions of the tax bill 'odious' and 'offensive'. Citizens will not like 'this going into people's houses to know whether they had pianos, or going in their yards to find whether they had a carriage'.[10]

Popular unrest did occur during the Civil War. Riots broke out in Wisconsin, Detroit, Chicago and Rutland, Vermont between the summers of 1862–3, precisely when the first revenue measure took effect. Officials never knew when they might go too far in taxing citizens and set up the next riot.[11] Anger against the Conscription Laws, passed in 1862 and 1863, which imposed the draft for the first time in United States, provoked these outbursts of popular anger. The announcement of the Emancipation Proclamation invoked mixed reactions across the country. John Sherman noted that 'the effect of this proclamation upon the (Autumn 1862) elections in Ohio was very injurious'.[12] The most violent demonstration of public frustration occurred in New York in July 1863, when a four day Draft Riot broke out, leaving 105 people dead. These periodic outbursts of violence 'can be viewed as a direct consequence of specific wartime tensions' but Republicans also feared that exorbitant taxes could further exacerbate the public fury. Chase noted in his 1863 *Annual Report*, written the fall after the New York draft riots, 'I can see clearly that we go no further without heavy taxation' and 'heavy taxes will excite discontent'.[13]

Inflation continued to plague the Union as well. By 1865, a myriad of paper currencies floated about the country. By 1865, $431 million in Greenbacks circulated; $142.9 in state bank notes; $146.1 in national bank notes; $671.6 million in seven-thirty Treasury notes, and $193 million in compound interest notes.[14] Prices rose significantly during the war – although estimates vary, consumer prices rose as a response to the flood of new paper issued from the government and the rise in taxes and tariffs. Milton Friedman suggested that the inflation rate during the Civil War is comparable to the World Wars of the twentieth century, but that provided no comfort to the Civil War lawmakers.[15] A war of attrition that dragged on for years could have devastated the Union economy and sapped the will of the citizens. Until the final surrender, this remained a true concern.

'The Most Lightly Taxed Nation on the Earth'

The Civil War represented the first 'modern war' in American history, but the fiscal policies established to fund that conflict retained elements of the archaic. The direct tax, enacted as the first internal revenue measure of the war, had origins in America's agrarian past. Wary of sending federal officers into states to assess and collect individuals' property, the tax became obsolete, even upon its passage. The two internal revenue bills, HR 312 and HR 405, created a 'diffuse' tax programme that had mirrored policies employed by the British government. The Republicans had attempted to place 'no burden on those with small means', and spare the 'necessaries of life'; by the end of the war, this changed. The need to meet the expanding costs of the war forced Republicans to develop a tax programme that 'resembled an Irishman on his visit to the Donnybrook fairs: "Whenever you see a head, hit it." Whenever you find an article, a product, a trade, a profession or a source of income, tax it!'[16] Congressman Henry J. Raymond (R. NY) lamented in 1865 that, 'Until a few years ago, we were the most lightly taxed nation on the earth. Now we are amongst the most heavily burdened of them all'.[17] The need to generate more revenue had changed the initial goal of sparing the 'necessaries of life' to one that encompassed most goods and services. The diffuseness of this system created many challenges for the lawmakers who faced the task of determining which taxes to repeal, and which they should retain. The tax on manufacturers and the income tax augured future tax policies that would attempt to shift the incidence towards a more progressive policy. However, immediately after the war, Congress retained the ideal of taxing 'luxuries' or 'superfluities' as a fair form of taxation. This concept, borrowed from the past, wedded the United States to a more regressive tax programme in the late nineteenth century.

President Lincoln died on 15 April 1865. Before his death, Lincoln clearly intimated that he hoped to restore the South to full participation in American civic society as soon as possible. This vision now fell to Andrew Johnson, his Democratic, intemperate Vice President. Yet before the Congress assembled, Johnson's policies showed signs of divergence from the Republicans' goals. By the opening of Congress, seven-and-a-half months after Johnson became president, southern states began working towards the enactment of 'Black codes', repressive laws that would evolve into a systemic repression of black Americans throughout the nation for the next 100 years.

Schuyler Colfax (R. IN), the new Speaker of the House, opened the session stating that Congress's duties appeared as 'obvious as the sun's pathway in the heavens'.[18] However, splits within the Republican Party emerged over just how far the government could move towards granting individual rights and economic independence for the freedmen. Soon President Johnson and Congress began a fervent battle over the Reconstruction policies of the South. Congress passed sweeping Civil Rights legislation, only to see it vetoed by the President. The Freedmen's Bureau soon became emasculated. Johnson, who initially proclaimed his desire to reshape the political and economic power structure of the former Confederacy, issued over 7,000 pardons during the Thirty-ninth Congress to former Confederate elites, who soon regained their political stranglehold over southern politics. As Foner noted, the Republicans held a majority in Congress that could overwhelm any of Johnson's vetoes. If they had shared a unified vision on the future course of Reconstruction, they would have reshaped the South and enabled the newfound, and fully funded, might of the national government to secure the social, political and economic future of the freedmen. However, the divisiveness within the party, ineptness of the president, malaise and war fatigue of northerners and intransigence of the southern white population, led to the resumption of state-based power in the South, and a beginning of a second tragic period of history for black Americans.[19]

Debt or Taxes

The social policies considered during the early Reconstruction Congresses were profoundly challenging and had a dramatic long-term impact on the future course of the nation. Behind the struggles between the president and Congress to reconstruct a nation battered by war, the secondary question emerged on how to settle the debt accumulated during the war. As noted in the previous chapter, Salmon P. Chase resigned his position as Treasury secretary in June 1864. William Pitt Fessenden, who had served in the Senate for over a decade, took over the Treasury at the urging of the president. Fessenden did not want the job, and stayed in it for only a year. President Lincoln had urged him to serve as secretary to soothe the concerns of 'orthodox money men' whom Salmon P. Chase had alienated. 'Fessenden's reputation as a hard-headed, hard money conservative led many [leading] commercial bankers to suppose that he would seek to return the United States to a specie basis and finance the war in a more responsible manner,' Robert Cook opined. Although many in the administration had hoped that Fessenden would dismantle many of Chase's policies, the secretary soon found that he could not undo what had been done. In his one annual report to Congress, Fessenden reasserted Chase's proposal to tax state bank notes with the goal of driving them out of circulation, a proposal that passed the following year.[20]

Fessenden tried to market a new issue of seven-thirty bonds, but the effort did not succeed. He was acutely aware of the criticism Secretary Chase had endured because of his close relationship with Jay Cooke, and did not want to re-enlist Cooke as the Treasury's primary bond agent. Without the marketing and sales machine Cooke had assembled, Fessenden had no luck raising funds for the Treasury. The problem became so severe that the Treasury resorted to paying Union soldiers with the bonds. After a series of intense and not too friendly negotiations, Fessenden and Cooke reached an agreement whose terms Cooke considered 'outrageous'. In January 1865 Cooke again became a general subscription agent for the Treasury department; by the end of April, Cooke and his network of 4,000–5,000 agents had placed over $830 million of the loan. Although Cooke's sales force played a significant role, the prospects of Union victory aided the effort considerably as well.[21] Within a year of taking office, Fessenden resumed his place in the Senate. Rather than dismantling Chase's

financial policies, he had bolstered many of the key elements. Fessenden's advocacy of the tax on state bank notes had strengthened the national banking system
and brought fresh funds into the Treasury through another successful loan campaign. Fessenden had 'cast his lot' with most of Chase's financial schemes, not
because he agreed with them, but because he found it impractical to try to dismantle them. Hugh McCulloch became the Treasury's new secretary.

In his capacity as the president of the State Bank of Indiana, McCulloch trav-
elled to Washington in 1863 to protest the Secretary Chase's new National Bank
system. Soon thereafter, Chase asked him to assume responsibility for implementing this new organization, a responsibility McCulloch accepted reluctantly.
His knowledge of the workings of state banks and his contacts with the leaders
of the banks helped smooth the inauguration of Chase's new policy. McCulloch
became Comptroller of the Currency overseeing the admittance and circulation of the Greenback and the new national currency. In another great irony of
Civil War finance, McCulloch assumed responsibility for two programmes he
initially distained; after arriving in Washington, and consulting with Chase, he
came to believe that this would be the most practical means for bolstering the
finances of the country during the war (another example of how the exigencies
of war finance held more sway than preconceived fiscal principles). Like Chase,
McCulloch remained an avowed free trader. Thus, two of the first three Treasury
secretaries in a Republican administration advocated free trade, not protectionism.[22]

McCulloch became Treasury secretary on 9 March 1865 and occupied the
office until the beginning of the Grant administration. During his tenure, he
forcefully advocated two policies: first, a return to 'sound money' by contracting
the Greenbacks in circulation as quickly as possible and returning to the gold
standard; second, a reduction in the federal debt. Both policies aimed to thwart
the expansion of wartime inflation. When McCulloch took office in 1865, $100
in greenbacks purchased $51 in gold, the highest inflation rate in the country
since the War of 1812.[23] Although McCulloch launched an energetic contrac-
tion policy in 1866, the intense political reaction against this programme led to
a quick retreat two years later. This action opened the fissures within the Republican Party, and again demonstrated how deeply divided the party remained
with regard to economic matters. The question of expanding or contracting the
Greenback supply, and whether Greenbacks could be used to pay the principal
of the federal debt, opened a divisive political issue that rocked northern politics
for the next thirty years.[24]

Although most lawmakers agreed that the government could cut taxes, differences emerged quickly on how aggressively the government should reduce the
debt. In our post-Keynesian world, we often overlook what the congressional
leaders saw as one of the most formidable challenges they faced. By Febru-

ary 1866, the nation had accumulated a debt of $2.7 billion. Not only did it comprise the largest debt in the nation's history, but the magnitude of the debt dwarfed any of the previous encumbrances taken on by the government. Only five years before this time, members of Congress, many of whom still served, fretted over a $70 million debt. No one knew with certainty how much of a financial toll the interest payments and payment of the principal would take on the nation. Servicing the wartime debt, Robert Yearly observed, 'unquestionably posed a staggering task to men raised on the lackluster fiscal diet of pinchpenny government unaccustomed to taxing massively, spending lavishly, or borrowing feverishly'.[25] In evaluating the future course of fiscal policy and the level of taxation, Congress also considered a central question: should the United States stay with high, war-level taxes, using the surplus to shrink the debt, or should Congress reduce taxes, allowing the money to 'fructify in the pockets of the people?'[26]

Secretary McCulloch never equivocated. Inflation 'corrupts the public morals', declared the secretary. 'Men are getting rich while morality languishes and the productive industry of the country is being diminished'. He did not want drastic cuts in internal revenue, instead urging that the tax policy 'should be stable'. He noted the frequent changes in the tax and tariff laws showed 'the readiness of the people of the United States to adapt their business to the policy of the government, whatever it may be'. He wanted to use the accumulated revenue to pay down the debt. McCulloch also believed the high tariffs impeded trade and urged Congress to lower the tariff duties.[27] Regarding the debt, McCulloch declared his intentions in his first *Annual Report* as Treasury secretary:

> The debt is large; but if kept at home, as it is desirable it should be, with a judicious system of taxation, it need not be oppressive. It is, however, a debt. ... Neither its advantages nor its burdens are or can be shared or borne equally by the people. Its influences are anti-republican. It adds to the power of the executive by increasing federal patronage. It must be distasteful to the people because it fills the country with informers and tax-gatherers. It is dangerous to the public virtue, because it involves the collection and disbursement of vast sums of money, and renders rigid national economy almost impracticable. It is, in a word, a national burden, and the work of removing it, no matter how desirable it may be for individual investment, should not be long postponed. ... Various plans have been suggested for the payment of the debt; but the secretary sees no way of accomplishing it but by an increase of the national income beyond the national expenditures. In a matter of so great importance as this, experiments are out of place. The plain, beaten path of experience is the only safe one to tread.[28]

The American tradition of government carrying a low debt also played a role in this discussion. 'Those favoring a permanent debt or slow repayment [of the debt] remained in the minority', Robert Patterson noted. Tax revision did not become an 'important political objective' until the Panic of 1873 rocked the financial stability of the nation.[29] Justin S. Morrill suggested on 7 May 1866 that Congress reduce taxes by $75 million.[30] But 'arguments for the reduction of the debt' persisted. Since Albert Gallatin's tenure in the Treasury, 'the American people have manifested a strong dislike to the perpetuation of a funded debt', Henry C. Adams noted. As long as 'conditions remained prosperous' and 'industry had become adjusted to high taxes' there seemed little reason to reduce taxes, and great historical precedent to reduce the debt.[31]

In *Cash Nexus*, Niall Ferguson linked the rise of democratic institutions in Europe to the need to finance and service the national debt. James MacDonald goes further, suggesting that the 'earlier forms of democracy' arose in conjunction with the need for public borrowing. 'As long as a state borrows from its citizens, there is no divergence of interest between borrowers and lenders, for the two are one and the same', he explains.[32] Robert E. Wright recently demonstrated that the American national debt created by the controversial assumption of the state debts after the American Revolution contributed significantly to the stabilization of the early national government. 'One way for a government to show that it is capable of sticking by its commitments is to sell negotiable bonds, then service them as promised...Credit worthiness becomes a proxy for credibility', Wright asserted.[33] As noted in the chart below, interest payments as a percentage of the federal expenditures soared after the cessation of hostilities. Although Ferguson suggests that American interest payments remained relatively 'low' compared to the American government experience, the significant increase in federal obligations after the war created concern on Capitol Hill. The government's obligations as a percentage of their expenditures had not been as high since the early nineteenth century; and size of the debt meant that the obligations would continue (as they did) for well over a decade. Another complication with the post-Civil War debt involved the novel way in which Jay Cooke had marketed the debt. As noted previously, before the Civil War, federal loans were marketed through a small network of wealthy investors who would take the loan, then distribute it through other institutional investors. Because the Civil War debt had been marketed through a public bond drive, literally millions of Americans owned these bonds. James Macdonald estimates that over two million subscriptions in denominations of $50 to $100 were held by individuals across the country; 90 per cent of the total subscriptions were for amounts of $500 or less. Prior to the Civil War, investors in government bonds represented the wealthiest individuals in the country. Now, millions of Americans of all classes had lent money to the government and, as Chase had hoped, received a small benefit from this terrible tragedy of war. Even Karl Marx 'speculated partly in American funds' during the Civil War.[34] Retiring the many different securities held by so many people would be logistically difficult and a politically volatile issue. As Macdonald noted,

'Who is to say that in an electorate of 8 million (of which only 5.7 million actually voted), a nucleus of two to three million public creditors would not have constituted the decisive element in the outcome of the election'. For many of these citizens, the debt also came to represent the loyalty and patriotism of many who supported the war effort.[35] Although not an innovative or new idea unique to Jay Cooke or the Republican Party, the manner in which the Civil War debt had been marketed to the American people forever changed the way in which the government financed wars. The immediate concern for lawmakers in 1865 was how best to manage this new type of debt.

Chart 6.1: Interest Payments as a Per Cent of Federal Expenses 1800–99

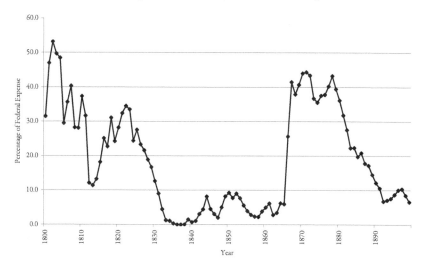

The war compelled the movement from this 'pinchpenny', antebellum system of finances to the 'modern' fiscal state of debt and taxation. As indicated above, servicing the debt remained a high percentage of federal expenditure through the 1880s, at which time, the rapid sinking of the debt helped relieve pressure on government expenses. How best to reduce the debt, relieve the country from the 'shackles which the internal taxes have thrown around it',[36] and help nurture the future prosperity of the country tested the Republican leaders. While most advocated reducing taxes as quickly as possible, some moved to keep taxes high in order to provide revenue to extinguish the debt. 'I believe that if there is anything the people desire more than [any other]', proclaimed John B. Alley (R. MA) on 11 February 1865, 'is that our taxes should be increased to such a degree that the credit of the country should be preserved and protected'.[37] To solve the conundrum of debt or taxes, the administration decided to enlist the help of an 'expert'.

David A. Wells

Although a frequent occurrence now, turning to a group of laymen to help resolve thorny financial or political issues represented 'a novelty in American experience' at the time of the Civil War. This development is associated with the Progressive Era, when using 'experts' to facilitate 'scientific management' of business and other large-scale processes became a regular feature of bureaucracies.[38] But the size of the debt, and complexity and diffuseness of the internal revenue system, convinced the administration and congressional leaders that they needed to seek advice. On 3 March 1865 Congress authorized Secretary McCulloch to appoint a commission to 'inquire and report, at the earliest practical moment, upon the subject of raising such taxation as may be necessary in order to supply the wants of government'.[39] Congress asked the commission to propose the best means for increasing taxes, rather than devising a way to make them more effective. Since the war ended before the commission began work, their purpose changed to a review and report of the revenue system. McCulloch asked David A. Wells to serve as the chair.

Born in 1828 from 'good New England stock', Wells's family came to America during the early Puritan migrations. Thomas Welles, his forebear, served as the governor of the Connecticut colony from 1655–8.[40] His father James married Rebecca Ames, the daughter of a prominent and wealthy paper manufacturer. Despite this pedigree, and fortuitous union, James Wells suffered financial ruin when his dry goods store went bankrupt during the Depression of 1837. He abandoned his family. Rebecca moved David and his two siblings into her father's home in Springfield, Massachusetts, where David lived until his adulthood. Rebecca Ames Wells 'burned with shame at her husband's failure'. Tapping her father's resources, she made sure her sons received the best education possible, and pushed them to succeed.[41]

Wells attended Williams College and graduated in 1847, then accepted a position as a reporter in Springfield for two years. There he honed his skills as a writer and earned his first small fortune. While working in the paper's pressroom, Wells invented a machine that folded newspapers. He obtained a patent for the device, which he quickly sold for a handsome profit. He decided to resume his schooling and enrolled at Harvard to further his 'scientific education'. He graduated in 1851, then accepted a teaching position at Groton Academy. Anxious to secure a better income for himself, Wells began his writing career. He launched a successful series of annual almanacs that catalogued scientific discoveries and current literature on agricultural progress. The series became a hit and Wells subsequently published a new volume each year until 1866. He earned enough to quit his teaching position and soon devoted himself entirely to his career as a scientific writer, concentrating on texts for schools and colleges. He married the heiress of a mercantile fortune in 1860; this allowed him to enjoy an affluent lifestyle while concentrating on his writing career. He became the editor of an agricultural journal, and soon a partner in the Putnam publishing house. Through his authorship of many magazine articles on trends in agriculture, Wells developed a national reputation as an authority on the most important component of the American economy.[42]

Wells invested heavily in Union bonds during the Civil War. As the conflict dragged on, and the debt of the government rose, unease seeped into the bond market. Two loan measures passed in 1864 that allowed the Treasury secretary to borrow $600 million and receive 'any lawful money or treasury notes, certificates of indebtedness or certificates of deposit', in payment for these bonds. This arrangement exacerbated this disquiet, because of the many different forms of 'lawful money' still floating in the economy, including state bank notes. During the War of 1812, the government used similar legislation to sell bonds, and then lost tremendously when much of the 'lawful money' collected turned out to have little value. Employing such a drastic payment device, John Sherman noted, would only pass under the 'extremity of the measures deemed necessary at this period of the war'. Secretary Chase worried publicly that the debt could rise as high as $3 billion, what seemed at the time as an insurmountable amount.[43] Both Greenbacks and bonds declined in value. Concerned for the fortunes of the nation, as well as his own investment, Wells decided to write a patriotic brochure to rally support for the government securities. *Our Burden and Our Strength* resulted.[44]

This pamphlet argued that the future prosperity of the nation in terms of resources and productivity coupled with the continued population growth would enable the government to readily meet the interest payments on the debt and retire the principal without forfeiture or any repudiation. Although a great 'burden' strained the nation, Wells predicted that the country's many 'strengths' would enable Americans to carry the debt without inhibiting future growth and economic success. 'With a virgin soil, enormous emigration, a system of land tenure which conduces to the highest prosperity of the greatest number, and a condition of society in which individual enterprise is encouraged and fostered', the United States would bear and retire the debt without impeding future prosperity, Wells wrote.[45] Per capita wealth would continue to grow, as it had throughout the antebellum era, through the increase in population, opening of new agricultural lands, continued industrial expansion, revival of the cotton trade and release of slaves from bondage into more productive labour. His command of the current agricultural and industrial conditions gave his argument great weight.

Wells used 'scientific' reasoning in studying the nation's productivity to demonstrate that the United States would carry its debt far better than the British had managed theirs. Wells provided statistical analysis that showed if rapid population growth continued the per capita interest payments would fall from $5.35 in 1865 to $2.00 by 1900, roughly half what the British paid on their debt.[46] The British debt and funding system became the template from which Wells based his comments, just as Congress had followed British precedent in developing the tax system. Wells's 'perky little book' reassured his friends. George Putnam, his former partner in publishing, saw great potential, and set his presses to work. Subsequently, over 200,000 copies circulated both domestically and abroad. Wells received accolades for restoring faith in the bond market.[47] President Lincoln requested a private interview with Wells to ask his advice about post-war finances. During the meeting, Wells observed that the tax structure needed revision based on the 'resources of the nation'. He then suggested that the president establish a commission to study the matter and make formal recommendations. 'That's a pretty good idea', Lincoln replied.[48] Three months later, Congress asked the commission to propose the best means for increasing taxes rather than devising a way to make them more effective. Since the war ended before the commission began work, their purpose changed to a review and report of the revenue system. Wells received the appointment as chair of the US Revenue Commission.[49]

Secretary McCulloch wanted the different members of the Revenue Commission to represent the primary economic forces and sections of the country. Wells, a native New Englander, former paper manufacturer, and resident of New York at the time the commission formed, spoke for the commercial interests of the Northeast. Stephen Colwell, an iron manufacturer from Pennsylvania, joined the commission and became its most outspoken proponent of protective tariffs. McCulloch, in his autobiography, stated that 'congressional representatives' had recommended Colwell to him. However, with his usual humility, Henry C. Carey claimed credit for securing his friend Colwell's appointment. 'Advanced in years and feeble in thought', Colwell contributed little of the work of the Commission. Samuel S. Hayes, Chicago's comptroller, represented the agricultural interests. McCulloch wished to have a 'western man' who would add more diverse political views to the committee. Hayes joined the commission as a Democrat and a 'copperhead', although 'amiable' and helpful in 'arriving at facts'.[50] Pleased with the composition of the commission, *Harper's Weekly* declared 'we may be sure that there will be neither jobbery, nor ignorance, nor political prejudice', with their deliberations.[51]

Wells and his commission subsequently produced one comprehensive report on the internal revenue system, plus thirteen 'Special Reports' focusing on taxation of specific articles. Remarkably, the commissioners produced these lengthy reports between March 1865 and January 1866. The process expedited by reports they received, upon request, from industries across the country providing details on their status, and soliciting recommendations on how the government should proceed. Credited with writing most of these reports, Wells unabashedly accepted the praise the Commission received. 'The diffuseness of the present revenue system is doubtless one of its greatest imperfections', the preliminary report noted.[52] Instead of a tax scheme that would 'hit every head', they urged Congress to abolish or pass a 'speedy reduction of all taxes which tend to check development, and the retention of all those which, like the income tax, falls chiefly upon realized wealth'.[53] Excise taxes on specific articles of 'indulgence' would generate large revenue without harming the 'industriousness' of the people. 'Securing large revenue from distilled spirits ... is absolutely necessary to insure the successful carrying out of any plan for simplifying the internal revenue system', they reported.[54] By placing a light duty on 'articles of necessary and large consumption', such as tea and coffee, Congress could collect great revenue without disrupting public consumption. They recommended retaining the tax on cotton. Preserving the income tax, although an obnoxious tax, would not hurt future economic growth because it 'falls mainly on accumulation' and would prove the least 'detrimental to the country than any other form of taxation'.[55]

If adopted, this new tax 'edifice' would grant 'entire exemption of the manufacturing industry' from all taxation; this would help to 'equalize' the tariff and internal revenue. Wells worried about the 'continued assaults' and 'deprived elements of stability' that the high war tariffs created. By cancelling the tax on manufacturers, Congress would not have to raise tariff rates. Although he advocated a reduction in the high wartime tariff rates, Wells urged caution in fixing new rates too soon, but indicated that Congress could lower them in the future. He did not wish to disturb the current trade structure, but did wish to see the trade barriers lowered to ensure future prosperity. Since the manufacturing duties accounted for most of the internal revenue during the war, removing those taxes and placing the burden instead on well-selected excise taxes, plus the stamp duties and licence taxes, could provide enough revenue to avoid the 'duplication' in the existing revenue system, and eventually lead to lower tariff rates.[56]

The report aimed to remove the 'diffuse' taxes and replace them with more 'concrete' ones that 'can be easily, cheaply, and surely collected, and distributed themselves with a satisfying equality'. Wells elaborated on this theme:

> We must draw our revenue from few sources, and avoid the error of many and useless perforations. [We must attain] freedom from multitudinous taxes, espionage, and vexations ... freedom from needless official inquisitions and intrusions; freedom

for industry, circulation, competition everywhere. Deprive the people of freedom in
industry and there will be disappointing revenues, discontent, embarrassment, and
demoralization everywhere – cheerfulness and prosperity nowhere.[57]

The commissioners recommended limiting taxes to a few select, but productive,
items, cutting the manufacturing tax, and being cautious in making any changes
in the tariff schedule. Indeed, the report suggested that in looking for a model to
follow for a balance of taxation and debt reduction, 'the British statesmen for at
least the last quarter of a century' have best shown 'what ought to be the future
revenue policy of the United States'.[58] All three men signed the commission's
report, although 'a difference of opinion exist[ed]' among the Commissioners.[59] Colwell and Hayes soon issued dissenting addendums. Colwell agreed
with Wells's recommendation to remove the taxes on manufacturers, however
he issued a strong appeal for protective tariffs. The revenue policy of the nation
needed to 'uphold and cherish that industry' which provides 'nearly all that meets
the wants of civilized life', Colwell argued. He advocated limiting the influx of
foreign trade, in order to boost industry and free 'domestic laborers' from the
'destructive' competition in Europe. This suggestion 'completely contradicted'
Wells's recommendations in the first report, to make few, if any changes, in the
tariff schedule.[60] Samuel Hayes wanted to base the new revenue system on taxes
on 'wealth', specifically the income and the inheritance taxes.

Wells, through the commission, launched a criticism of the revenue agents,
suggesting they were not 'competent men'. By adopting a system based on limited
taxes, the Internal Revenue Bureau could reduce the number of its employees.
These thoughts also signalled a future development in post-bellum politics.
Wells emerged as a 'nineteenth-century American liberal'.[61] He became a leader
of the 'Mugwumps', a group of Republican politicians who left the party in protest during the 1880s to support Grover Cleveland, and subsequent Democratic
candidates. These dissenters, predominantly prosperous men from the northeast, believed it their duty to direct American 'virtue, civilization, and progress'.[62]
Appalled by the corruption that had infiltrated both political parties, they advocated Civil Service reform and the re-establishment of a 'sound' currency by
returning to the gold standard. Signaling this future political evolution, Wells
stated in an 1866 letter, 'I am utterly disgusted with the rapacity and selfishness
which I have seen displayed by Pennsylvania people with regard to setting tariff
rates'.[63] By the 1890s, the Mugwumps became outspoken anti-imperialists. Wells
emerged as their chief critic of the high protectionist tariffs that gripped the
American fiscal system by the late nineteenth century. He abhorred the growing
influence of special interests in directing American fiscal policy, a distaste that
began during his early years as the Special Commissioner. By the time of his

death, in 1898, the Democratic Party had incorporated Wells's tariff position into their party platform.

While Congress accepted the general ideas espoused by Wells and the commission report, they differed on a few key provisions. Wells had recommended lowering the tax on whiskey from $2.00 per gallon to $1.00. Congress explicitly rejected this idea. 'Experience in England has shown that as the duty was raised on spirits ... it never seriously affected the consumption. In other words, men will drink, no matter what it costs', stated Thaddeus Stevens in the session before the release of the report.[64] More explicitly, Justin S. Morrill suggested after reading the report that Congress retain the liquor tax at $2.00 per gallon as a way of testing 'its real value for revenue purposes, and incidentally... as a mode of repression in consumption of intoxicating beverages'.[65]

Wells argued in *Our Burden and Our Strength* that the United States would grow out of its debt, without any direct fiscal intervention. On the question of debt or taxes, Wells urged lowering taxes as rapidly as possible. 'The rapid reduction of taxation, rather than a rapid reduction of the principal of the public debt', should become the 'true policy of the government', Wells stated.[66] Future growth and prosperity would enable the United States to carry a debt without stifling production. Securing lower taxes, Wells believed, would provide the first step in that direction. Members of Congress did not completely accept this optimistic outcome. Henry J. Raymond (R. NY), founder of the *New York Times*, insisted that taxes cover not only the interest, but start attacking the principal on the debt as well. 'When erecting the tax system we followed the example of the nation which has had more experience of internal taxation than any other, Great Britain'. Congress must follow Britain's lead in reducing the debt as well.[67] Yet cutting taxes had popular support. Voters experienced tax breaks directly, where debt reduction was less tangible. While lawmakers accepted the idea that some taxes needed to stay in place to cut the deficit, they wanted to provide as much tax relief as possible for their constituents. As with enacting taxes, the lawmakers now vied to reduce the burden as much as possible for their voters.

Between 1866 and 1870, internal revenue receipts fell from $309.2 to $184 million annually. After 1875, of the taxes that remained, most came from three main sources: liquor, tobacco and stamp duties. All accepted the premise that Wells suggested: making the system less 'diffuse' and settling instead on a few objects that would produce the greatest revenue without injuring the productiveness of the American worker or economy. William Lawrence (R. OH) summarized the goals of the Thirty-ninth Congress in winnowing the revenue system: 'The theory upon which [the revenue system] proceeds is that it is not our policy to tax sources of productive industry, except so far as they produce luxuries'.[68] Liquor and tobacco fit these requirements. Years later, John Sherman explained how the tax system came to rely so heavily on so few objects:

'As the necessity for excessive taxation diminished after the war was over, taxes on various articles were gradually repealed...by 1894, they consisted of practically four items: spirits, tobacco, fermented liquors, and oleomargarine'. The oleomargarine tax was not intended as a material revenue tax. The purpose was especially to prevent the fraudulent imitation of butter by using an extract of beef. None of these is an article of necessity, but all are used purely to gratify an appetite, in many cases indulged to excess. All civilized nations have come to regard these articles of the best subjects of taxation. To the extent that whiskey is used as a beverage it is hurtful in its influence upon the individual and upon society at large. The tax on tobacco and cigars is a moderate one, but the consumption of them is far less dangerous than of spirits in their influence upon society. No complaint is made of it. Its consumption is so general that the tax is fairly distributed and falls mainly upon the richer classes, as the tax is increased in proportion to the value of the tobacco.[69]

Liquor and tobacco, objects 'injurious' to the person, as well as society, became the primary targets of the future revenue acts. Both Congress and Wells based the immediate tax system on revenue collected from indirect taxes on liquor, tobacco, cotton and income, with the understanding that a reduction in tariffs would follow. The progress of the cotton tax demonstrates how the revenue system came to rely on so few taxes.

The course of events regarding the tax on cotton demonstrates the shifting attitudes of lawmakers in their attempts to distribute the burden of taxation during the war, then reconcile the revenue and debt plans after the fighting ceased. First considered during the debates on the manufacturing tax, lawmakers wanted to tax cotton because they believed the tax would fall on southern producers. Since the Union government did not recognize the independence of the southern states, the tax on cotton was seen as the one politically feasible way to have southerners contribute toward the costs of the war. Although originally proposed as a three cents per pound tax, in the final version of HR 312 the amount was lowered to half a cent per pound, primarily at the behest of New Englanders, who worried that the tax would fall heaviest upon textile manufacturers with mills in the New England states. Determining who would pay a tax on cotton became a central question in the debates. New England 'Radical' Republicans, such as Charles Sumner, Benjamin Butler and James Simmons, all associated with policies to punish the South for instigating the conflict, nevertheless consistently thundered against the tax on cotton in order to spare the textile mills in New England from assuming any portion of this tax.[70] Justin S. Morrill fought for a lower cotton tax in 1862, expressing his hope that the tax code would not be used for 'grinding the South'.[71] Samuel S. Marshall (D. IL) claimed the tax on cotton would 'shift the burdens of government from the rich to the poor'.[72] Abner Harding (R. IL), who served in the war with the 83rd Illinois Infantry, wanted the tax removed completely to spare 'the toiling millions', who would pay the tax through their clothes purchases. Senator Cowan also noted that taxing cotton would also tax consumer goods made with cotton. 'It is true that the poor people of the North are as willing to pay their tax on their shirt as on their tea and coffee; they are willing to pay their taxes, and perhaps more so than the rich people; but I say it is unjust to impose on them now all the heavy burdens of the nation; it is unjust to make them the great source of revenue'.[73]

When discussion opened on HR 405, John Lynch (R. ME) argued that if the cotton producer paid the tax, then the 1864 tax measure should allow for high exemption to spare the 'small producers, black and white' from the burden. Instead of levying any internal tax on cotton, Lynch suggested that Congress override the constitutional directive against levying duties against exports, and 'letting England pay' this tax.[74] Reminded that the Constitution banned a tax on exports, Lynch retreated. A brief discussion ensued about whether Congress could ignore the Constitution, since an export duty on cotton would provide tremendous revenue with little pain to any taxpayers. This discussion proved more theoretical than substantive, and the restriction on export duties was respected. As with the Greenback, Morrill re-evaluated his position on the cotton tax by the end of the war. Having spent far more than anticipated, Morrill looked for whatever opportunities possible to help meet the Treasury's needs. During the debates on HR 405, Morrill favoured a higher cotton tax, with limited exemptions, to ensure 'every piccaninny in the South' would not try to skirt the tax through these exemptions.[75] The House moved to raise the tax on cotton to six cents per pound, but the Senate again blocked this provision, and the rate remained the same in the 1864 tax measure.

After the war, the idea of raising the tax on cotton became more acceptable to the representatives of the textile interests if done in conjunction with the repeal of the manufacturing duty. In his Special Report on the cotton tax, Wells recommended a five cents per pound tax, collected by the trader or manufacturer, not the grower, because of the difficulty in collecting the tax in the former Confederate states. In the post-war tax adjustment, the tax was raised to three cents per pound paid by the producer. Adopted as a means of narrowing the 'diffuseness' of the tax codes, the increased tax on cotton was adopted to replace the general duty paid by manufacturers. Eventually Congress adopted a tax of two-and-a-half cents per pound. The following year, with cotton production lagging, they abated the cotton tax altogether for all cotton harvested after 1867, hoping that soon the South would be 'decorated and enlivened by factories'.[76] As Hugh McCulloch would later explain, 'liberal legislation' would help the South regain its standing economically and help promote 'harmony' in the country. Congress did not wish to wring the expenses of the war out of the southern 'rebels'.[77] Altogether, the federal government collected roughly $68 million in revenue from the cotton tax, or approximately 14 per cent of the tax collected on all manufactured goods.[78] The movement on the cotton tax demonstrates how Congress struggled to balance the needs of the country with the desire to generate as much revenue as possible from all sectors of the economy to pay the costs of the war. Less a window into the 'worldview' of the Republicans, the tax demonstrates how the struggle to pay the costs of the war often conflicted with the practical, and special interest, concerns of crafting legislation.[79]

The Tariffs

Congress embraced most of the Revenue Commissioner's suggestions, but with a 'difference'. Between 1865–72, most of the internal revenue measures that impacted the 'productivity' of the economy had been repealed, and the amount of funds generated from internal revenue fell dramatically, from $310.9 million in 1866 (the highest amount collected in a year) to $113.7 million in 1873, with the duty on manufacturers removed completely. Wells suggested implicitly at first, and more aggressively as time went on, that his proposed tax system would allow for a reduction in the tariffs enacted during the war. Because the burden had been lifted from the 'steam giants', they would no longer need the protection Congress granted them during the war. On this, Congress balked.

The House passed the first post-war tariff on 10 July 1866. As proposed, this legislation lowered the duties on some raw materials, but retained or raised the tariff level on most manufactured goods. The bill was received negatively throughout the country. When it arrived in the Senate, it was tabled until the next session. During the fall, William Pitt Fessenden, once again chair of the Senate Finance Committee, asked Wells to rewrite the bill. Wells sought to reduce the duties on raw materials and the chemicals, dyes and other material used to make clothing and other consumer goods. Wells's revision of the House bill passed the Senate, but failed to gain a two thirds vote in the House, which was needed to overcome the original measure. 'The result was not only that no general tariff bill was passed at this session, but the course of tariff reform for the future received a regrettable check'.[80] The House and the Senate split on the direction of tariff policy. No new tariff legislation, either increasing or decreasing duties, could pass the Thirty-ninth Congress. Congressmen could not reconcile the differences between those who wished to protect manufactured goods and those who wanted to guard against cheap raw materials coming into the country. Congress remained incapable of finding consensus on general tariff strategy until the Forty-first Congress. By then, the Treasury began accumulating surpluses well beyond the ordinary expenses and interest payments. Aggressive debt reduction became policy; this strategy of reducing the debt merged well with the embrace of protectionism. Between 1866 and 1873, the government reduced the debt by $604 million.[81]

The Tariff of 1870 produced the first comprehensive change in tariff rates. This bill focused on reducing 'revenue articles' such as tea, coffee, sugar, molasses and spices and expanding the free list. Congress lowered the duty on pig iron from $9.00 a ton to $7.00. But the duties on some manufactured articles increased, particularly steel. Awash in the 'comfortable feeling of prosperity', and providing ample funds for the reduction of the onerous debt, modifying the tariff became less urgent to the elected officials.

One member did get what he desired. Justin S. Morrill achieved his goal of providing a shield for the wool industry in Vermont. The Woolen Act of 1867 nearly doubled the import duty on the main commodity of his state. Morrill assembled a coalition of Ohio representatives (another wool state) and anti-protectionist Western representatives who saw this as a means of thwarting the manufacturers' efforts to increase the tariffs on manufactured goods. Subsequently, representatives succeeded in raising revenues on specific raw materials: copper in 1869; manufactured goods steel rails and marble in 1870.[82]

Two other factors contributed to the continued push for high tariff rates. First, as noted in the chart on p. 141, interest payments on the US debt grew dramatically after the war. In 1861, the United States paid $4 million in interest payments; by 1867, that figure increased to $143 million. Customs revenue in 1867 generated $176 million. All interest payments had to be paid in gold, and customs duties remained the most reliable source of coin for these payments. To generate reliable customs revenue, lawmakers levied higher tariff rates. The second relates to the decline of the premium on gold. The high price of gold made goods expensive, especially imports. As Secretary McCulloch's policy of contracting the currency took effect, the price of imports could undercut those of domestic produce. Because the expenses for materials and labour did not fall as quickly as the price of gold, imports could be sold more during this period of contraction than could domestically produced goods. Although lengthy, this quote from a manufacturing journal published in 1867, and reprinted in Robert Sharkey's study, provides a good explanation of the phenomenon:

> An English knife, the price of which in New York in July 1864 would have been $1.50 per dozen in gold, would have cost in US money, about $3.75 per dozen and, at the present rate of duty, would have paid about ninety cents in currency. Now the same knife will cost about $2.00 per dozen and the duty will be about forty eight cents in currency; the importer being thus enabled to sell his goods at nearly half the price he did then, and being relieved of nearly half the duty he paid then … the cost of living is the same as it was then; and while the foreign agent can reduce his price according to the decline in gold without loss, the American manufacturer is compelled, if he would meet this competition to do it at a loss.[83]

Manufacturers continued to press for protection because they saw the price of imported goods decline. Sharkey observed that protectionists of that era also favored the 'soft money' policies of low interest rates and increased consumption to keep American manufacturing profitable during the post war period.

Wells's ideal of making the tax system less 'diffuse', limiting taxes to a few 'indulgences', then lowering tariff rates worked in part. Congress accepted his suggestion of keeping taxes focused on liquor and tobacco, supplemented by taxes (such as stamp duties) that took little effort to collect and provided abundant revenue. He recommended keeping the income tax (they no longer bothered referring to it as a 'duty') that tapped accumulated wealth, rather than productivity. Wells proposed this system as a means to meet the interest payments while not curtailing American 'industriousness', and with the understanding that Congress would slowly reduce the tariff rates. On this second half of the tax readjustment, lawmakers could not reach agreement. Although Congress bequeathed to Americans a 'free breakfast' by reducing import duties on coffee and tea, and moving other goods to the free list in 1870, the bulk of the Civil War tariff rates remained in place. Customs revenue rose dramatically, from $84 million in 1865 to $194 million in 1870. No longer needed to offset the duties on manufacturers, the primary source of revenue during the war, these high tariffs shifted the burden of taxation completely to indirect taxes, the best hidden means of gaining public revenue. Ironically, the post-war reliance on the regressive alcohol and tobacco taxes sprang from the ideal of establishing justice and fostering American productiveness. Many believed these items hurt the health and well-being of the individual, as well as undermining the moral basis of society. In an effort to spare the 'necessaries of life', taxes fell on its small pleasures. Lawmakers readily whittled the internal revenue measures to give their voters a tax break in a manner that they could see and feel readily. Removing the taxes on everyday goods they purchased, food they ate, and clothes they wore gave the public a concrete break, and allowed lawmakers to claim credit for their actions. Professor O'Brien, in discussing the British reliance on these same taxes, noted, '[Lawmakers] considered each tax in isolation, and simply assumed that the "poor" needed to consume certain things and that if they chose to buy other highly taxed commodities they did so voluntarily and accepted the consequences'.[84]

The tariff continued as a result of congressional gridlock and the rationalization that high duties would generate enough revenue to sink the debt. 'High duties permitted debt reduction [and] the existence of the debt was itself an excuse for maintaining the high tariff', noted Patterson.[85] Hugh McCulloch, who considered protective tariffs as 'insidious' and 'unequal taxes', nevertheless, when writing his memoirs, effused that the tariff policy after the war helped reduce the debt. 'By the high duties, and taxes on whiskey and tobacco, more than one-half of the debt has been paid'.[86] Tied to debt reduction, as well as post-war prosperity, congressmen did not initially feel the pressure to enact tariff reform that would manifest later. As the chart above indicates, servicing the debt became a much smaller portion of federal expenditures in the 1880s. 'The protective system, which had been at the first a temporary expedient for aiding in the struggle for the Union, gradually became accepted as a permanent institution'.[87] While Congress felt pressure to reduce the internal revenue laws, they received many memorials and letters requesting that the tariff policy remain the same.

A second irony emerged. The continued policy of taxation after the war created surpluses well beyond the needs of prudent debt management. While Congress retreated from giving 'individual' assistance to the freedmen, they used the newfound cash to inaugurate the first national social welfare programme in the form of veteran's benefits. By 1888, the Republican platform declared, 'Congress should be so enlarged and extended as to provide against the possibility that any man who honorably wore the Federal uniform shall become the inmate of an almshouse, or dependent upon private charity'. The revenue generated from this tax legislation gave Congress the impetus to touch citizens 'individually' and launch what Theda Skocpol called the 'first phase of modern social provision in the United States'.[88] By 1890, the federal government spent 35 per cent of its budget on direct benefits for pensioners and their widows.[89] The Civil War revenue measures laid the base for this future policy.

What became of the two 'just' taxes enacted during the war?

The Direct Tax

No revenue measure failed as miserably as the first. The Direct Tax (HR 71) enacted during the emergency session in July 1861 did not fulfill its purpose. 'The government received nothing from the direct tax during the war which it would not have received otherwise', Charles Dunbar observed. The legislation followed the precedent established in the 1813 direct tax by allowing states to 'assume, assess, collect, and pay' the portion allocated to their citizens and receive a 15 per cent discount on the entire quota. Any amount allocated to the state that they did not pay would be collected by federal revenue officers. All the states that remained in the Union, except Delaware, took advantage of this incentive. Thus, the feared invasion of the 'army' of federal revenue collectors did not occur in most of the Union states.[90]

What the states paid to the government emerged as one problem with the direct tax. Instead of sending money, the states fulfilled their commitments through their military obligations, including the support for the regiments originating from the states. These 'payments' toward the direct taxes resembled the requisition system under the Articles of Confederation. States counted the supplies and provisions for the troops they sent to the war as part of their payment. Dispatching these materials over the course of the war meant that their quotas trickled into the Treasury, just as they had under the War of 1812 direct tax. By 1865 the states that remained in the Union and the territories had paid only 32 percent of the total amount allocated.[91]

Congress remained chary of the direct tax. Passed into law to assure bond investors that their principal remained secure, and their interest payments would arrive as promised, the direct tax represented an expedient that lawmakers soon abandoned. Unlike indirect taxes that remain hidden in the cost of the article purchased, the taxpayer knows what he pays under a direct tax and must produce his payment in one large sum, instead of incrementally through his purchases. Congressmen feared 'that their constituents would notice a direct tax more than an indirect tax', Smith noted.[92] Joseph A. Wright (U. IN) articulated the concerns of rousing the public with the direct tax when he stated in 1862, 'This is not the time to press upon the country this question of direct taxation, which, of all others, should be avoided if it can'.[93] Congress accepted the direct tax originally because, unlike other revenue laws, the statute existed. Lawmakers only had to reapportion the tax based on the current population. In contrast, it took members of Congress six months to write and agree upon the provisions of HR 312.

Written in 1813, the direct tax law applied to a much smaller country with a more even distribution of land in the states. Because of the addition of extensive land holdings in western and southern states, the burden of the direct tax would fall more unevenly on these sparsely populated areas. When dispersed evenly, through apportionment, legislators considered the direct tax the most fair, because it taxed the value of real and personal property. However, the change in the country's demographics rendered the tax more unfair than in an earlier era. The eastern states, with their greater concentrations of wealth, would dodge the brunt of the tax, leaving owners of large tracts of land to carry the weight of the tax. For these reasons, the Civil War direct tax floundered.

Congress repeatedly voted to delay collection of the direct tax, even as the states responded slowly to meet their obligations. In enacting HR 312 in 1862, Congress suspended the collection of the direct tax until 1865. In June 1864, they again deferred the tax, and in 1868, suspended the collection indefinitely since 'neither the legislative nor executive departments of the government have done anything regarding the collection of said tax'.[94] The laxness in enforcing this tax demonstrates, in part, the reluctance of the government to invoke its powers during the course of the war. They did not wish to rouse adverse public opinion, so delayed collecting the tax most tangible to the citizens.

The direct tax levy applied to all states, even those 'in rebellion'. As the Confederate states fell under federal control, the provisions of the direct tax applied. The landowner had sixty days to pay the tax after receiving notice from the assessor. Non-compliance resulted first in a heavy fine, then forfeiture. James G.

Randall described this portion of the direct tax statute as 'odious' and a form of 'virtual confiscation'. He claimed the direct tax law seemed more severe in terms of land seizures than the two Confiscation Acts enacted during the war.[95] Both acts had the provision that land could return to the owner's estate once he died. Attorney General Edward Bates did not strictly enforce these laws, and consequently seizures occurred on only a small portion of the former plantations. President Andrew Johnson restored most of this land to the original owners as he pardoned former Confederate leaders during the summer and fall of 1865.[96]

Like the Confiscation Acts, the direct tax did not inflict as much harm on the southern states as the legislation permitted. Only half the receipts from the lands confiscated for non-compliance returned to the Treasury. According to the 1862 legislation on collecting the direct tax in the southern states, one quarter of any receipts from seized lands remained in the state to support 'suppression of the rebellion'; another quarter went to a fund for the 'promotion of colonization [of freedmen] from the state'. Once northerners abandoned the idea of colonization, these funds were supposedly dedicated to education and support of the freed slaves. The Treasury only collected $2.3 million from the direct tax in the southern states. Forfeitures totaled approximately $2.4 million.[97] Robert E. Lee's estate in Arlington became the most famous of these forfeitures.

As soon as the war ended, the Treasury, now under the direction of Hugh McCullough, 'indefinitely postponed' the collection of the direct tax, and 'all internal taxes accrued before the establishment of revenue districts'. This exempted southerners from the back taxes accumulated during the war. Sales from forfeited land stopped. In an effort to 'promote harmony between the government' and citizens in the former Confederate states, the Treasury developed a lenient tax collection policy in the South.[98] This provides a clear indication of the reconciliatory attitude that the government extended to the former Confederate states, a remarkable turn, considering the blood and treasure that the war consumed. Indeed, McCulloch's tenure at the Treasury marks a period of leniency in collecting taxes in the former Confederate states. Despite the rhetoric of the Radicals in Congress, the power of the victorious North did not descend on the former Confederate states in a vindictive manner to collect back-taxes.

Legal complications with the direct tax continued until 1900. Some states, Georgia for example, never paid their quota, or paid only a small portion of their share. As the Treasury accumulated large surpluses, all recognized the impracticality of trying to collect this tax in the delinquent states. Absolving these truants from their obligation angered some citizens in the states where the tax had been paid in full (reminiscent of the reaction to Alexander Hamilton's policy of assumption after the American Revolution). Thus, Congress decided to refund the full amount collected to all the states, and forgive the outstanding balances from the delinquent states. Though this met with approval in Congress, in 1889 President Grover Cleveland vetoed this legislation. The Constitution does not have a provision allowing the federal government to give states money, he reasoned. The 1836 surplus distribution represented a loan, not a gift. These constitutional scruples did not trouble Cleveland's successor. President Benjamin Harrison signed the legislation into law soon after he became president. By 1896, Congress redistributed $15.2 million back to the states as a refund for the direct tax contribution. This legislation also permitted the Treasury to reimburse anyone who could prove he had owned land seized and sold for non-payment of taxes. The government settled the last of these claims in 1900.[99]

Now a curious relic of United States tax history, the direct tax demonstrates how the American economy matured; the provision could work in a uniformly rural, agricultural country but not in a large democracy with mixed economy and rural–urban population. The direct tax also provides an extended lesson in American fiscal pragmatism. Added to the Constitution to provide a 'bridge over a gulph' between slaveholding and non-slaveholding states, the direct tax provided one of the compromises necessary for ratification of the Constitution. Invoked only four times, the federal government used this power of the purse only in times of war, and in a manner that allowed states to maintain their sovereignty. Rather than enforcing the tax with a heavy hand, the national authorities allowed states to collect the tax, and in turn accepted lower than apportioned receipts. Rather than an 'odious' tax that afflicted the southern states after the war, the direct tax demonstrated the government's desire to reunite the nation and heal the war wounds.

The Income Tax

With regard to the income tax, David A. Wells wrote that, 'Although in many respects an obnoxious tax, falling as it does mainly on accumulation, it will probably be sustained with less detriment to the country than any other form of taxation – the excise on liquor and tobacco excepted'.[100] Wells and the Revenue Commission recommended keeping the income tax as part of the future revenue system. In 1864, Congress enacted an income tax that placed a 5 per cent duty on incomes over $600 but less than $5,000; 7.5 per cent on incomes between $5,000—$10,000; and 10 per cent on incomes over $10,000. Companies withheld five per cent from their stock dividend and bond interest payments for the Treasury. Government payroll clerks would withhold 5 per cent from the salaries of all officials making more than $600 a year. The tax would continue through 1870.[101]

As promoters of the income tax predicted, the measure provided a bountiful source of revenue. The income tax generated $20.2 million in 1864, $60.9 million in 1865, and $73.4 million in 1866. The special income tax passed in

October 1864, to pay bounties to recruit new soldiers and retain those serv-
ing, proved especially effective. The statute required an extra 3 per cent tax on
incomes up to $10,000 and 5 per cent on those over $10,000. This one-time
tax raised $29.8 million, and provided enough to enlist 200,000 men.[102] As its
opponents feared, the revenue generated from the income tax came primarily
from a small geographic area. In 1864, citizens in New York, Massachusetts, and
Pennsylvania alone contributed 61.3 per cent of all income tax revenue; 75 per
cent of the total income tax revenue came from all the northeastern states.[103]

When introduced, the 1864 income tax bill stirred debate because it graduated rates. Morrill in particular feared that levying a higher tax on the wealthy
would encourage fraud and evasion. 'The income tax, intrinsically the most just
of all taxes', he stated, 'will always be difficult in ascertaining the actual income of
reluctant taxpayers, and these will be sufficient in number to form a respectable
company of growlers'. Morrill recommended instead taxing all income above
$3,000 at 10 per cent. Fessenden, in his sole report as Treasury secretary, rec-
ommended removing all exemptions and making the income tax universal. 'All
participate alike in the blessings of good government', so all should contribute
towards its 'necessity', he suggested.[104]

When Congress considered how best to trim the tax burden, Morrill, now
Chair of the House Ways and Means Committee, recommended 'The abolition
or speedy reduction of all taxes which tend to check development, and the retention of all those which like the income tax fall chiefly on realized wealth',[105] a view
that echoed Wells's recommendations. The income tax had proven productive,
the costs of collection minimal, and, while falling on one group on individuals,
maintained broad appeal with the general population. The concern regarding
the constitutionality of the tax disappeared. Although still referring to it as the
'income duty', legislators no longer worried whether it constituted a direct or
indirect tax. Supreme Court Justice Roger B. Taney denounced it as unconstitutional because it 'diminished' the salary he received during his time in office,
but this complaint fell on unsympathetic ears.[106]

Instead of debating whether or not to retain the tax, Congress considered
ways to improve it. They moved to flatten the tax and raise the exemptions. By
1867, they raised the exemption to $1000, and fixed a 5 per cent rate. Profits
from real estate transactions and the value of sales from livestock were added
to the definitions of income. They also exempted the salaries from mechanics
or laborers employed on public works. 'In a republican form of government the
true theory is to make no distinctions as to the persons in the rates of taxation',
stated Morrill in favouring a uniform rate for the income tax.[107]

The income tax received less attention in the immediate post-war discussion
than other measures, another irony given the focus it received in the late nineteenth century. In his opening remarks on the readjustment of the tax legislation,

Morrill suggested leaving it place. The healthy returns from the tax, Morrill stated, provided evidence of the 'strict integrity of character' of the wealthy citizens who paid the tax. 'The law left it almost to the conscience of each man as to how much he should pay, and all seemed to vie with each other as to who should pay the most'.[108] While recognizing the 'inquisitorial' nature of the tax, Morrill also believed that the large revenue it drew 'from a free people, imposed upon themselves', favoured retaining, rather than terminating the tax. Few disagreed. Whether or not to continue graduating the rates instead became the focus of the discussion. While favouring the retention of the income tax, Wells argued that the 'discrimination' in the tax, in the form of graduated rates, seemed 'unjust'. The income tax fell on the 'results of successful industry and business enterprise', thus should the rates be set to 'equalize' the burden at 5 per cent.[109]

Set to expire in 1870, the real contest over the income tax began that year. On 1 June 1870, the Ways and Means Committee released its latest proposal on winnowing the tax receipts, they advocated renewing the income tax, but abolishing the tax on inheritances, gas and other selected articles. The coalition opposed to continuing the income tax centered geographically on the three states that contributed most of the revenue, rather than politically on the divide between Republicans and Democrats. Because the citizens of New York, Pennsylvania and Massachusetts paid over 60 per cent of the income tax, the opposition to it came from congressional leaders from those states. Beginning in 1870, Dennis McCarthy (R. NY), Benjamin Butler (R. MA), William D. Kelley (R. PA), and Roscoe Conkling (R. NY), spoke forcefully for the removing the income tax.[110] Kelley, who emerged as a fervent protectionist after the war, consistently advocated removing most of the internal revenue measures in order to reassert the dependence of the federal government on tariff revenue. McCarthy declared, 'It has no moral force. This tax is unequal, perjury provoking and crime encouraging because it is at war with the right of a person to keep private and regulate his business affairs and financial matters. It makes the tax-gatherer a spy'.[111]

John Sherman emerged as the most ardent defender of the income tax in Congress. In England, Sherman noted, the income tax provided the only means for reducing the taxes on consumption:

> [The] only discrimination in our tax laws that will reach wealthy men as against the poorer classes...If I had my way, I would retain the income tax at five percent on all incomes above $1,000...then throw off these taxes upon consumption that oppress the poor and take coppers out of the dollars of the people who earn them by their daily work...We tax the tea, the coffee, the sugar, the spices the poor man uses. We tax every little thing that is imported from abroad together with the whiskey that makes him drunk and the beer that cheers him and the tobacco that consoles him. Everything that he consumes we call a luxury and tax it; yet we are afraid to touch the income of Mr. Astor. Is there any justice in that?[112]

Robert Stanley suggested cynically that Sherman supported the income tax 'certainly not to challenge the protective and regressive system' which he had helped to build by replacing it with income taxation. Rather the object was to avoid placing the 'entire tax load upon consumption'.[113] The indirect taxes on liquor and imports affected Sherman's constituents more than an income tax. Trying the keep the burden of taxation off his constituents played a more significant role.

Columbus Delano, the Commissioner of Internal Revenue during the postwar tax debates, advocated retaining the tax in his *Annual Report*. 'My opinion is that, so long as a large internal revenue is required by the financial necessities of the government, a portion of that revenue should be collected from incomes ... After all, it is but a tax upon the increased wealth of the nation; and when it is understood that government securities are exempted from taxation, and that the interest on these securities produces a large amount of the income of taxpayers'.[114] Wells, who now held a more permanent position as Special Commissioner of Internal Revenue assigned to continue reporting on the revenue system, expressed his support for the tax, noting that only 'about a million of the population are interested in having the tax removed', while the remaining 38.5 million were interested in having it maintained.[115] Ironically, Wells would come forth in the 1890s as a leading opponent of the income tax, equating it with socialism.[116]

The Forty-first Congress kept the income tax, but raised the exemption to $2,000 and limited its duration to two more years. When considered again in 1872, the tax failed to win support, but the votes were close in both the House and Senate.[117] Although all his subordinates favored retaining the income tax, President Ulysses S. Grant opposed continuing it beyond 1872. Fearing his prospects in the upcoming election, President Grant decided he needed the support of the great moneyed interests who did not wish to see the income tax renewed. In an example of these moneyed interests, John C. Hamilton, one of the 'wealthier men of New York', wrote Grant's Secretary of State, Hamilton Fish, prior to the 1872 election, explaining that 'I wish the income tax could yet be repealed. Our Union League has denounced it unanimously'. Grant's Treasury secretary George Boutwell 'warmly denounce[d] the repeal of the income tax', fearing 'the substitution or continuance of the other taxes which affect a larger number of persons will be unpopular'. However, Boutwell's diffident and difficult personality gave him little credence.[118]

Ironically, southern delegates, who began participating in Congress again in 1868, remained 'ambivalent' about the income tax. Seip noted that 'members from more heavily agricultural districts tended to favor retaining the income tax', but their support for the bill held little of the passion that would surface twenty years later.[119] 'The chief reason the income tax did not continue', Seligman explained, 'is not because of objections raised by its opponents as the simple fact that it was not necessary for revenue purposes'.[120] The prosperity of the country continued apace. Government surpluses had reached $101 million by 1870. Opponents of the income tax waged a more serious and prolonged attack against it than its defenders fought to retain it. The income tax died a natural death – the House allowed it to expire. Only after the downturn in 1873 did levying an income tax become the central goal of tax reformers and part of the class conflict of the late nineteenth century.

Conclusion

After a visit to England in 1870, Hugh McCulloch, in language reminiscent of that used by delegates to the Constitutional Conventions and subsequent ratification conventions, described the tax structure developed after the war:

> The national taxes are indirect, and although heavy, they are not complained of and do not seem to be felt, because they are taxes upon consumption, and are paid by the consumers in the increased prices of the taxed articles which are consumed...Taxes upon imports are easily and cheaply collected, and always have been, and probably always will be, the most popular taxes; but they are, nevertheless, the most unequal and consequently the most unjust of all, because the very rich people rarely pay more than those in moderate circumstances.[121]

When faced with the decision to reduce the debt or the government revenues, Congress followed precedent: they compromised. The Republicans leaders in both Congress and the Treasury managed to reduce both internal taxes and the debt, slowly, but steadily. This system became the pragmatic juncture between two different and conflicting directions in policy. However, the price for this pragmatism emerged in the form of increased tariff duties and a more regressive tax structure than originally envisioned during the war. Fiscal leaders believed that winnowing the tax system to garner revenue almost exclusively from excise taxes on liquor and tobacco represented a success in taxation and not a failure. These articles provided substantial and consistent revenue. Further, the public accepted this programme. 'From the storm of Civil War the North moved into the sunshine of an unrestrained economic boom'.[122] While basking in this sunshine, the tax system seemed to have accomplished what its authors wished. Americans accepted this post-war adjustment before the Panic of 1873. 'The majority of Americans would appear disposed to endure any amount of sacrifice rather than bequeath a portion of their debt to future generations', noted economist Francis A. Walker in 1869 in a popular magazine article.[123]

Wells remained disappointed throughout his public career that Congress could not move on his recommendations regarding the tariff. Fat and happy, with coffers bulging, the debt going down, and memorials flooding Congress in support of the tariff policy, the leaders did not see any reason to act on lowering import duties. Only after the prosperity slowed and the country plunged into depression did tariff revision become a hot political issue.

CONCLUSION

After James Bryce toured the United States in 1887, he described the persistence of James Madison's vision of federalism. The central government, he wrote, directed the 'national common purpose', including 'foreign relations, internal commerce, weights and measures, and the post office'. 'State governments', Bryce continued, assumed responsibility for the 'maintenance of [local] law and order, the creation of local institutions, the provision of education, and the relief of the poor'.[1] The states continued in their responsibility for all the functions of government that touched citizens 'individually'.

Federalism persisted through the nineteenth century as law as well as tradition. Not until 1941, in the Supreme Court case of *Edwards* v. *California*, did the Court declare the 'Elizabethan poor laws' asserting that 'relief is solely the responsibility of local government' no longer applied in the United States. In overturning California's 'Okie law' forbidding residents from aiding 'paupers' from entering the state, the Court declared, 'the duty to share the burden, if not wholly to assume it, has been recognized ... by the federal government'.[2] In lamenting the forsaken aspirations for racial and economic justice in the years after the Civil War, historians have rarely considered the continuity of federalism as a strong impediment to fulfilling the ideals espoused by the Radical Republicans.

Immediately after the Civil War, surpluses accumulated in the Treasury that gave the government more financial flexibility than at any time in its history. Rather than using these funds to assist the freedmen, the Treasury, under Hugh McCulloch, initiated an aggressive debt reduction plan. However, the government did launch a politically popular Civil War veteran's pension system that, by 1890, expended $109 million a year. Instead of assisting indigent freedmen, these funds were 'lavished on a selected subset of the working and middle-class people of both races, who by their own choices and efforts as young men had *earned aid*...[by] participat[ing] victoriously in the morally fundamental moment of national preservation'.[3]

Americans had provided pensions to veterans since the American Revolution. These payments not only rewarded valour, but also served as a practical means of overcoming the problem of how to pay soldiers. Granting land, bonds, or long-term payments over time compensated for delivering pay inconsistently during the conflict, a constant problem for the early military. Throughout the American Civil War, soldiers received their pay in a variety of dubious paper 'heresies': Treasury bills, bonds that did not sell on the market and Greenbacks. Thus the pensions awarded to soldiers, and eventually their widows, seemed appropriate and hardly inconsistent with the past. However, the increase in federal receipts and new fiscal power of the government facilitated the expansion of this traditional programme into the prototype of the twentieth-century welfare system.

Despite the growth in the federal budget, and largesse to veterans and their families, giving assistance to the indigent remained a local, not a national, concern. We now interpret the use of the financial power attained during the war as woefully inadequate, however those applying that power thought they had done well. When James Blaine reviewed the 'progress' of the United States from 1861 to 1881, he exulted that, 'No period of history has been more marked by generous expenditure for worthy ends. The provision made for those who suffered in the Civil War has perhaps no parallel at home or abroad'.[4] This reticence to use national funds for 'individual' relief, coupled with persistent racial prejudice, the desire for national reconciliation, frustrations with the continued violence in the South, impatience with the freedmen's 'inability' to become self-supporting free labourers, and the salve of economic prosperity, makes the failure to direct more social spending to the emancipated slaves seem inevitable. When the Panic of 1873 struck the nation, John Sherman noted with some disgust that, 'the wildest schemes for relief to the people were proposed'. Most of these 'wild schemes' involved manipulating the currency supply, not providing assistance to those impoverished by the downturn.[5] However, individual concerns became national concerns after the Civil War. During the Forty-third Congress, Margaret Thompson related, 441 of the 833 bills enacted gave private relief to petitioning individuals and organizations, including 'reparations to businesses, churches and schools, and other properties sustaining military damage during the war'.[6]

The increase in the national budgets did not result in a corresponding concern for spending public funds with care. Authorities could not sustain the antebellum ideal of keeping an 'unsleeping watchfulness' over national expenditures. Mark W. Summers explained that corruption seeped into the federal system because, 'the government had more work to do, more responsibilities to oversee, and more money to spend'.[7] Douglas Bowers noted that in the antebellum era, lobbying and political influence peddling occurred primarily at the state level since that's where most public funds were expended.[8]

However, the expense of the war permanently altered the role of the national government in the public and private economy. Per capita receipts rose from $1.78 in 1860 to $8.00 in 1873 then steadied at $5.75 by 1886.[9] George Boutwell related that when first appointed commissioner of internal revenue, he and three clerks tabulated the early returns. However, by March 1863, the Bureau of Internal Revenue 'exceeded in magnitude the entire Treasury Department. It was in fact the largest government department ever organized in historical times. By its machinery, it became so vast that $350 million were assessed and collected in a single year'.[10]

The ideal of trying to keep public revenue close to the scrutiny of 'the people' continued, however the size of the organization defied this commitment. 'It is well to keep the power over public funds and public expenses as close to the people as possible', Supreme Court Justice David J. Brewer recommended to law school students in 1897. He lamented the 'growing tendency in government' towards 'extravagance' in the late nineteenth century. He expressed this worthy sentiment in a speech he delivered defending his participation in striking down the constitutionality of the income tax. In declaring the tax a 'direct' rather than an indirect tax, the Court attempted to reassert the antebellum mores of fiscal federalism in an era where all such restraints had disappeared.[11]

Before the war, citizens paid their taxes primarily as tariffs fixed to 'luxuries' entering the country. After the war, American citizens paid taxes on all types of articles and transactions. Besides the excise taxes on liquor and tobacco that became the staples of the new internal revenue system, the government continued to collect duties on matches, patent medicines, licences and most bank transactions. In order to cure a malady, warm or illuminate your house, legally open a shop or provide a service, or complete any type of financial transaction besides local barter, the citizen interacted with the national government. Tax collectors during the antebellum era stayed confined to distant ports, but during the post-war era, over 3,500 revenue officers dotted the country. Erected hastily as a wartime expedient, it became clear after the war that the structure would not be dismantled. The government would continue to collect internal taxes, Sherman noted in 1895, 'as a part of the organized machinery of the government ... as long as our public debt remains, and until the list of pensioners will be obliterated by the hand of time'.[12]

No longer stationed only at distant ports, Treasury officials now roamed the land, assessing, collecting and punishing when they detected fraud. Federal tax officials in the 'mountain South' chased down small-scale 'moonshiners' to collect the whiskey excise, the single largest source of internal revenue. Wilbur Miller related that in enforcing this system, 'the government presented itself as both powerful and conciliatory;' arresting offenders, then issuing only small fines rather than jail time.[13] The whiskey excise taxes resulted in the grandest scandal that beset the Treasury in the post-war era. Although unveiled during the Grant administration, the corruption in collecting the whiskey excise began early. Fernando Wood (D, NY) speculated on the House floor in 1864 that some members took too vigorous a stand against applying increased excise rates to manufactured whiskey, and insisted that any new tax should apply solely to future production.[14] Distillers paid tax officials to miscount the number of gallons they produced, thus lowering their tax payments. The revenue officers reaped enormous profits. The supervisor of revenue in upstate New York would habitually collect $500,000 annually in graft. Orville E. Babcock, President Grant's 'confidential advisor' kept a close watch over the executive branch to alert his co-conspirators in the 'Whiskey Ring' of any pending investigations. The opportunity to profit from skimming the distilled liquor excise collections became pervasive. New Orleans officials alone skimmed well over $1.5 million from the tax system.

Congress did not become officially involved in regulating business until the establishment of the Interstate Commerce Commission in 1887. However, lawmakers had experience in manipulating consumer preferences through taxation. Protective tariffs purposefully raised prices on imported goods in order to make American products more competitive. Congress passed the 10 per cent tax on state bank notes in 1865 specifically to make their use prohibitively expensive so they would fall out of circulation. Excise taxes on liquor and tobacco, the backbone of the new internal revenue system, taxed 'superfluities' that all could avoid, if desired. Government power could now be used to modify individual behavior. Congressmen Lott Morrill (R. ME) spoke often of taxing liquor into 'extinction'. He hoped that by raising the tax high enough, those without moral fibre could no longer afford to indulge.[15] By 1895, the excise tax on margarine became the fifth-largest source of internal revenue. Enacted solely for the purpose of discouraging the use of this product at the behest of dairy farmers, this tax did not produce needed revenue, but simply raised the price on this product to make butter the preferred commodity.

The character of government changed during the post-war era, not only because of the swell of revenue within, but also the new opportunities in the private sector. Over 1,500 members served in the House between 1861 and 1881. 'Rapidity of change in elective officers' characterized the post-war chamber. Each succeeding session in those ten Congresses contained a majority of new members. Only William D. Kelley kept his seat during this entire period. Many members, such as Justin S. Morrill, John Sherman and Roscoe Conkling advanced to the Senate, but the House during this period remained singularly inexperienced.[16] Thompson described the House during the 'Gilded Age' as having 'high turnover, no formal leadership, largely inexperienced membership, and little or no professional staff'.[17] 'The House of Representatives [in December

1873] is best understood as one suffering acutely from time-lag. The House was a fundamentally antebellum institution endeavoring with limited success to cope with the enlarged federal purview of postwar America.'[18] Yet, this inexperienced body now controlled far more 'power of the purse' than the early congresses. This in part explains why Congress during the Gilded Age 'subsidized but did not supervise'.[19] Government now had the 'power to choose favorites and alter the market', yet most of the members of the body did not have the experience to do this wisely.[20] 'Teaching the American people that government could legitimately spend on a grand scale – in the billion dollar range for the first time', proved decisive in redefining government power after the Civil War.[21] Justin S. Morrill gave an explanation of these new powers during the tax debates in 1862:

> The government of the United States – the most parental and benign of all earthly governments – in its hour of need has the right to *demand* whatever may be the measure of its necessities to sustain the public credit ... That the government is the property of the people is not more true than that the property of the people for public use belongs to the Government. If the power of taxation gives the right to take three percent, it gives to the extent of ninety-nine percent, just as much; but it would be an abuse of power justifying a revolution if it exacted *anything* beyond it reasonable and urgent necessities.[22]

Yet, the war changed the character of what constituted 'reasonable and urgent necessities'. In trying to redefine these new parameters, the only restraint became that of the democratic forces garnering their strength and 'justifying a revolution' against the newly vested powers of government. These changes resulted from pressure created by the exigencies of war and the need to overcome the limitations of the antebellum government to meet those challenges. Because the developments happened quickly, without a preconceived agenda, the resulting policies left the government with uncertainty about how to set a course within the new financial framework.

NOTES

Introduction

1. These works are prevalent in current historiography: H. C. Richardson, *The Greatest Nation of the Earth: Republican Economic Policies during the Civil War* (Cambridge, MA: Harvard University Press, 1997); C. A. Beard and M. R. Beard, *The Rise of American Civilization*, 4 vols (New York: Macmillan, 1934), vol. 2; R. F. Bensel, *Yankee Leviathan: The Origins of Central State Authority in American, 1859-1877* (New York: Cambridge University Press, 1995).

2. J. Williamson, 'Watersheds and Turning Points; Conjectures on the Long Term Impact of Civil War Financing', *Journal of Economic History*, 34 (1974), pp. 631–61.

3. N. Ferguson, *The Cash Nexus: Money and Power in the Modern World, 1700–2000* (New York: Basic Books, 2001), p. 50.

4. Quote in R. L. Einhorn, 'Slavery and the Politics of Taxation in the Early United States', *Studies in American Political Development*, 14 (Autumn 2000), p. 182; Einhorn expands on this thesis in her most recent book, *American Taxation, American Slavery* (Chicago, IL: University of Chicago Press, 2006); E. R. Seligman, *The Income Tax: A Study of the History, Theory, and Practice of Income Taxation* (New York: Macmillan and Co., 1914), 548–55; C. J. Bullock, 'The Origin, Purpose, and Effect of the Direct Tax Clause of the Federal Constitution', *Political Science Quarterly*, 15 (September 1900), pp. 217–39; C. Dunbar, 'The Direct Tax of 1861', *Quarterly Journal of Economics*, 3 (July 1889), pp. 436–61; B. Ackerman, 'Taxation and the Constitution', *Columbia Law Review*, 99 (January 1999), pp. 1–58; Beard and Beard, *Rise of American Civilization*, vol. 2, p. 45.

5. C. Webber and A. Wildvasky, *A History of Taxation and Expenditure in the Western World* (New York: Simon and Schuster, 1986), p. 151.

6. D. Elazar, *American Federalism: A View from the States* (New York: Crowell Press, 1966), p. 24; Two classics include: B. Bailyn, *The Ideological Origins of the American Revolution* (Cambridge, MA: Harvard University Press, 1967); E. Foner, *Free Soil, Free Labor, Free Men: The Ideology of the Republican Party Before the Civil War* (New York: Oxford University Press, 1970).

7. John Niven, *Salmon P. Chase: A Biography* (New York: Oxford University Press, 1995), p. 330.

8. W. B. Parker, *The Life and Public Services of Justin Smith Morrill* (Boston, MA: Houghton Mifflin, 1924), p. 144; H. McCulloch, *Men and Measures of Half a Century: Sketches and Comments.* (New York: Charles Scribner's Sons, 1888), p. 164.

9. Gavin Wright, Review of Richardson, *Greatest Nation of the Earth*, www.h-net.msu.edu, accessed 19 January 1998.

10. Beard and Beard, *The Rise of American Civilization*, vol. 2, p. 54.

11. L. Hacker, *The Triumph of American Capitalism: The Development of Forces in American History to the End of the Nineteenth Century.* 2nd edn (New York: Simon, Schuster, 1947), pp. 340, 373, 361; For the historiography of the Beard–Hacker thesis, see R. Ransom, 'Fact and Counterfact: The Second American Revolution Revisited', *Civil War History,* 45 (March, 1999), pp. 28–60; also, P. S. Paludan, 'What Did the Winners Win? The Social and Economic History of the North During the Civil War', in , J. M. McPherson and W. J. Cooper, Jr (eds), *Writing the Civil War: The Quest to Understand* (Columbia, SC: University of South Carolina Press, 1998), pp. 174–200.

12. D. F. Weiman, 'Introduction to the Special Issue on the Formation of an American Monetary Union', *Financial History Review*, 13 (April 2006), pp. 11–17. Although this issue of *Financial History Review* addresses earlier American history, the papers, and most notably, Weiman's introduction, give a thorough review of the 'economic interpretation'.

13. Bensel, *Yankee Leviathan*, p. 419, n. 7; p. 10.

14. Ibid., pp. 236–7, 416.

15. J. M. McPherson, *For Cause and Comrades: Why Men Fought in the Civil War* (New York: Oxford University Press, 1997); J. M. McPherson, *Abraham Lincoln and the Second American Revolution* (New York: Oxford University Press, 1990); in 1862, Thaddeus Stevens lamented that too few had 'sufficient grasp of mind and sufficient moral courage to treat [the war] as a radical revolution and remodel our institutions', H. L. Trefousse, *Thaddeus Stevens: Nineteenth Century Egalitarian* (Chapel Hill, NC: University of North Carolina Press, 1997), p. 126.

16. E. Foner, *Reconstruction: America's Unfinished Revolution, 1863–1877* (New York: Harper & Row, 1988), p. xxiv; see also R. Ransom and R. L. Sutch, *One Kind of Freedom: The Economic Consequences of Emancipation* (New York: Cambridge University Press, 1977).

17. Beard and Beard, *Rise of American Civilization*, vol. 2, p. 53.

18. S. J. Engerman and J. M. Gallman, 'The Civil War Economy: A Modern View', in Stig Forster and Jorg Nagler (eds) *On the Road to Total War: The American Civil War and the German Wars of Unification, 1861–1871* (New York: Cambridge University Press, 1997), p. 233.

19. T. C. Cochran, 'Did the Civil War Retard Industrialization?', *Mississippi Valley Historical Review*, 48 (September 1961), pp. 197–210.

20. G. R. Taylor, 'The National Economy Before and After the Civil War', in D. T. Gilchrist and W. D. Lewis (eds), *Economic Change in the Civil War Era* (Greenville, DE: Eleutherian Mills-Hagley Foundation, 1965), p. 22.

21. D. C. North, *The Economic Growth of the United States, 1790–1860* (New York: W.W. Norton, 1966), p. v.

22. J. M. Gallman, *Mastering Wartime: A Social History of Philadelphia during the Civil War* (New York: Cambridge University Press, 1990), p. 256.

23. R. L. Ransom, *Conflict and Compromise: The Political Economy of Slavery, Emancipation, and the American Civil War* (New York: Cambridge University Press, 1989), is the best of this scholarship. By 'Stevensian' I refer to Thaddeus Stevens, who, unlike the Beards, never lost sight of the economic importance of emancipation or the impact it would have on southern society.

24. J. Majewski, *A House Dividing: Economic Development in Pennsylvania and Virginia Before the Civil War* (New York: Cambridge University Press, 200); J. L. Huston, *Cal-*

culating the Value of the Union: Slavery, Property Rights, and the Economic Origins of the Civil War (Chapel Hill, NC: University of North Carolina Press, 2003); E. L. Ayers, *In the Presence of Mine Enemies: War in the Heart of America, 1859–1863* (New York: W. W. Norton, 2003).

25. S. D. Brandes, *Warhogs: A History of War Profits in America* (Lexington, KY: University Press of Kentucky), pp. 103, 105; M. R. Wilson, *The Business of Civil War: Military Mobilization and the State, 1861–1865* (Baltimore, MD: Johns Hopkins University Press, 2006), p. 35.

26. E. L. Thompson, *The Reconstruction of Southern Debtors: Bankruptcy after the Civil War* (Athens, GA: University of Georgia Press, 2004), pp. 141–2.

27. M. Egnal, 'The Beards Were Right: Parties in the North, 1840-1860', *Civil War History*, 47 (March 2001), pp. 30–56.

28. Beard and Beard, *The Rise of American Civilization*, vol. 2, pp. 105, 54.

29. Richardson, *The Greatest Nation of the Earth*, p. 255. Emphasis added.

30. M. Green, *Freedom, Union, and Power: Lincoln and His Party during the Civil War* (New York: Fordham University Press, 2004), p. 9.

31. Egnal, 'The Beards Were Right', p. 45.

32. D. R. Dewey, *Financial History of the United States*, 12th edn (New York: Longmans, Green and Co., 1939), p. 300.

33. P. Studenski and H. E. Krooss, *Financial History of the United States: Fiscal, Monetary, Banking and Tariff* (New York: McGraw-Hill, 1952), p. 159.

34. Ibid.

35. M. Thornton and R. B. Ekelund, *Tariffs, Blockades, and Inflation: The Economics of the Civil War* (Wilmington, DE: SR Books, 2004).

36. W. C. Mitchell, *A History of the Greenbacks* (Chicago, IL: University of Chicago Press, 1903), p. 135.

37. Sidney Ratner, *American Taxation: It's History as a Social Force in Democracy* (New York: W.W. Norton, 1942), p. 63.

38. J. Flaherty, 'Incidental Protection: An Examination of the Morrill Tariff', *Essays in Economic and Business History*, 19 (2001), pp. 103–18. This paper refutes the standard interpretation of the Morrill tariff.

39. R. F. Sharkey, *Money, Class, and Party: An Economic Study of Civil War and Reconstruction* (Baltimore, MD: Johns Hopkins University Press, 1959), p. 14.

40. R. T. Patterson, 'Government Finance on the Eve of the Civil War', *Journal of Economic History*, 12 (1956), p. 36.

41. W. E. Brownlee, 'Reflections on the History of Taxation', in *Funding the American State, 1941–1995* (New York: Cambridge University Press, 1996), pp. 20–2.

42. Bensel, *Yankee Leviathan*, p. 237.

43. Albert S. Bolles, *The Financial History of the United States from 1865 to 1885* (New York: D. Appleton and Co., 1886), p. 116.

44. Richardson, *The Greatest Nation of the Earth*, 255.

45. Beard and Beard, *The Rise of American Civilization*, vol. 2, p. 105; Richardson, *The Greatest Nation of the Earth*, p. 250.

46. J. G. Blaine, *Twenty Years of Congress: From Lincoln to Garfield*, 2 vols (Norwich: Henry Bill Publishing Co., 1884), vol. 1, p. 399.

1 Fiscal Federalism

1.   The term 'fiscal federalism' is found in C. Hamilton and D. T. Wells, *Federalism, Power, and Political Economy: A New Theory of Federalism's Impact on American Life* (Englewood Cliffs, NJ: Prentice Hall, 1990), p. 81.

2.   These terms come from the Constitution, the Preamble and Article I, Section VIII; J. Madison, *Notes of the Debates on the Federal Convention of 1787*, ed. A. Koch (Athens, OH: Ohio University Press, 1960), p. 140.

3.   Madison, 'Federalist 45', in *Federalist*, 307, 310.

4.   K. R. Gutzman, 'A Troublesome Legacy: James Madison and the 'The Principles of '98', *Journal of the Early Republic*, 15 (Winter 1995), p. 572.

5.   J. J. Wallis, 'Constitutions, Corporations, and Corruption: American States and Constitutional Change, 1842–1852', *Journal of Economic History*, 65 (March 2005), pp. 211–56.

6.   R. A. Becker, *Revolution, Reform, and Politics of American Taxation, 1763–1783* (Baton Rouge, LA: Louisiana State University Press, 1980), p. 6.

7.   J. N. Rakove, 'The Articles of Confederation', in J. P. Greene and J. R. Pole (eds), *The Blackwell Encyclopedia of the American Revolution* (Cambridge, MA: Basil Blackwell, Inc., 1991), pp. 289–95, p. 116.

8.   R. Chernow, *Alexander Hamilton* (New York: Penguin Press, 2004), pp. 107–8.

9.   John Fiske coined the term 'critical period' in *The Critical Period of American History: 1783–1789* (Boston, MA: Houghton Mifflin, 1888). A good review of the work on this scholarship is R. B. Morris, 'The Confederation Period and the American Historian', *William and Mary Quarterly*, 3:13 (April 1956), pp. 139–56.

10. E. J. Ferguson, *The Power of the Purse: A History of American Public Finance, 1776–1790* (Chapel Hill, NC: University of North Carolina Press, 1961).

11. Becker, *Revolution, Reform, and the Politics of American Taxation*, p. 6.

12. R. H. Brown, *Redeeming the Republic: Federalists, Taxation, and the Origins of the Constitution* (Baltimore, MD: Johns Hopkins University Press, 1993).

13. Rakove, 'The Articles of Confederation', p. 294.

14. Alexander Hamilton to George Washington, *Documentary History of the Ratification of the Constitution*, ed. M. Jensen, 20 vols (Madison, WI: State Historical Society of Wisconsin, 1976), vol. 13, p. 9 Referred to hence as Jensen (ed.), *Documentary History*.

15. A. H. Jones, 'Wealth Estimates for the American Middle Colonies, 1774', *Economic Development and Cultural Change*, 18 (1970), pp. 1–172, p. 130.

16. J. J. McCusker and R. R. Menard, *The Economy of British America, 1607–1789* (Chapel Hill, NC: University of North Carolina Press, 1985), pp. 373–4.

17. M. Schweitzer, 'State-Issued Currency and the Ratification of the US Constitution', *Journal of Economic History*, 49 (June 1989), p. 315; J. J. McCusker, *Money and Exchange in Europe and America, 1660–1775* (Chapel Hill, NC: University of North Carolina Press, 1978).

18. Ferguson, *The Power of the Purse*, pp. 250, 112–113.

19. Jensen (ed.), *Documentary History*, vol. 13, p. 414.

20. P. L. Rousseau, 'A Common Currency: Early US Monetary Policy and the Transition to the Dollar', *Financial History Review*, 13:1 (2006), pp. 97–8.

21. Jensen (ed.), *Documentary History*, vol. 15: 21.

22. J. Elliot (ed.), *Debates on the Adoption of the Federal Constitution*, 5 vols (1888; Salem, NH: Ayer Publishers, 1987), vol. 3, p. 115.

23. Hamilton, 'Federalist 21', *Federalist 21,* p. 129.
24. J. Wilson in, Elliot (ed.), *Debates,* vol. 2, p. 467.
25. D. McCoy, *The Elusive Republic: Political Economy in Jeffersonian America,* 2nd edn (New York: Oxford University Press, 1982), pp. 90–104.
26. Madison, *Notes,* p. 498.
27. E. K. Browning and J. M. Browning, *Public Finance and the Price System,* 4th edn (Englewood Cliffs, NJ: Prentice Hall, inc., 1994), p. 346.
28. 'Luther Martin's Letter on the Federal Convention', in Elliot, *Debates,* vol. 1, p. 364.
29. 'Petition on the Whiskey Excise,' 28 January 1791, in T. C. Cochran, *New American State Papers, Finance,* 32 vols (Wilmington, DE: Scholarly Resources Inc., 1973), vol. 32, p. 13.
30. Hamilton, *Federalist 12,* p. 74.
31. Elliott, *Debates,* vol. 2, p. 60.
32. T. P. Slaughter, 'The Tax Man Cometh: Ideological Opposition to Internal Taxes, 1760–1790', *William and Mary Quarterly,* 3:41 (October 1984), pp. 566–91, p. 575.
33. Hamilton, *Federalist 21,* p. 130.
34. Charles Bullock, 'Direct and Indirect Taxes in Economic Literature', *Political Science Quarterly,* 13 (September 1898), pp. 442–76. The passage of the Sixteenth Amendment made defining the income tax as direct or indirect a moot question. However this concern meant the various tax schemes proposed to eliminate the income tax, such as the 'fair' tax or the 'flat tax' could refocus attention on the limitations inherent in the direct tax.
35. Madison *Notes,* p. 494.
36. Elliot, *Debates,* vol. 2, p. 36. (See note 91 below).
37. Most Americans associate 'poll' taxes with the post-Civil War and twentieth-century efforts to limit the right to vote, and therefore think of them as taxes paid at the voting booth. Historically, poll taxes are defined as capitation, or per person taxes levied on individuals, as explained in greater detail below.
38. For two examples of how historians have misused the term, see C. Kenyon (ed.), *The Anti-Federalists* (New York: Bobbs-Merrill, Co., 1966), p. civ; *Greatest Nation of the Earth,* p. 116.
39. H. A. Ohline, 'Republicanism and Slavery: Origins of the Three-Fifths Clause in the United States Constitution', *William and Mary Quarterly,* 3:28 (October 1971), pp. 563–84.
40. Madison *Notes,* pp. 272—3.
41. Ibid., p. 277.
42. Ibid., p. 362.
43. Ibid., p. 507. This argument re-emerges during the American Civil War. See page 000.
44. Elliot, *Debates,* vol. 3, p. 453.
45. Elliot, *Debates,* vol. 2, p. 37.
46. Bullock, 'The Direct Tax Clause', p. 462. A poll tax is a type of capitation tax, often with different amounts levied on individuals based on race, class or gender. It is not a tax paid when going to vote, although in the post-Reconstruction era, not paying the high poll taxes levied on African-Americans became a means for preventing them from voting.
47. Elliot, *Debates,* vol. 2, p. 467.
48. Hamilton, *Federalist 36,* p. 227.

49. S. Benson, 'A History of the General Property Tax', in *The American Property Tax: Its History, Administration, and Economic Impact* (Claremont, CA: Claremont Men's College, 1965), p. 24.
50. Elliot, *Debates*, vol. 2, p. 29.
51. Kenyon (ed.), *The Anti-Federalists*, pp. cii–civ.
52. Jensen (ed.) *Documentary History*, vol. 15, p. 112.
53. Elliot, *Debates*, vol. 2, p. 341.
54. Elliot, *Debates*, vol. 2, p. 339.
55. M. Edling, *A Revolution in Favor of Government: Origins of the United States Constitution and the Making of the American State* (New York: Oxford University Press, 2003), p. 42.
56. Slaughter, 'The Tax Man Cometh', pp. 583–4.
57. Becker, *Revolution, Reform and Politics of American Taxation, 1763–1783*, p. 226.
58. Brown, *Redeeming the Republic*, pp. 32–40; Perkins gives a thorough description of the tax schemes in the different states. E. J. Perkins, *American Public Finance and Financial Services, 1700–1815* (Columbus, OH: Ohio State University Press, 1994), pp. 137–74.
59. Jensen (ed.), *Documentary History*, vol. 13, pp. 414–15.
60. Jensen, (ed.), *Documentary History*, vol. 15, p. 378.
61. Ibid., p. 22.
62. The suggested amendments are reprinted in P. L. Ford (ed.), *The Federalist*, pp. 632–51.
63. E. J. Perkins, *The Economy of Colonial America*, 2nd edn (New York: Columbia University Press, 1988), pp. 196–7.
64. Jensen (ed.), *Documentary History,* vol. 13, pp. 414–15.
65. Ferguson, *Power of the Purse*, p. 290; Slaughter, 'The Tax Man Cometh', p. 584.
66. D. Forsythe, *Taxation and Political Change in the Young Nation, 1781–1883* (New York: Columbia University Press, 1977), p. 53; Edling, *Revolution in Favor of Government*, p. 42.
67. Jensen (ed.), *Documentary History*, vol. 15, p. 280.
68. Hamilton, *Federalist 36*, p. 227.
69. Jensen (ed.), *Documentary History*, 15, p. 277.
70. E. Stanwood, *American Tariff Controversies in the Nineteenth Century*, 2 vols (New York: Russell and Russell, 1967), pp. 114–18. *Ad valorem* tariffs, duties 'according to value', levy a fixed percentage (40 per cent on shelled almonds, for example) upon an imported good. When the value of the merchandise changes, so does the actual import. Conversely, a specific duty affixes a set amount collected on the imported good (.04 per pound on shelled almonds, for instance). The amount collected does not fluctuate with the changing value of the imported article.
71. Hamilton, *Federalist 12*, p. 77.
72. Hamilton, *Federalist 32*, p. 197.
73. *Hamilton's Papers*, September–December, 1789, vol. 5, p. 218.
74. Chernow, *Alexander Hamilton*, p. 347.
75. T. P. Slaughter, *The Whiskey Rebellion: Frontier Epilogue to the American Revolution* (New York: Oxford University Press, 1986), p. 226.
76. Rousseau, 'A Common Currency', p. 117.
77. F. C. Howe, *Taxation and Taxes in the United States under the Internal Revenue System, 1791–1895* (New York: Thomas Y. Crowell, 1896), pp. 18–20. With a progressive tax, the average rate rises with the tax base; the wealthy pay a higher percentage of their

income as taxes than the less fortunate. Browning and Browning, *Public Finance and the Price System*, p. 346.

78. B. Ackerman, 'Taxation and the Constitution', p. 20.
79. J. N. Rakove, 'The Origins of Judicial Review: A Place for New Contexts', *Stanford Law Review*, 49 (May, 1997), pp. 1031–64, p. 1039.
80. Ackerman, 'Taxation and the Constitution', p. 23.
81. I elaborate on this on p. 000.
82. C. L. Ver Steeg, *Robert Morris: Revolutionary Financier* (Philadelphia, PA: University of Pennsylvania Press, 1954). This provides the best overview of the Superintendent's policies; also M. G. Myers, *A Financial History of the United States* (New York: Columbia University Press, 1970), pp. 33–43.
83. H. C. Adams, 'Taxation in the United States', *Johns Hopkins University Studies in Historical and Political Science*, 2nd series (May–June 1884), pp. 1–79, p. 54; Forsythe, *Taxation and Political Change*, p. 53.
84. P. D. Newman, *Fries Rebellion: The Enduring Struggle for the American Revolution* (Philadelphia, PA: University of Pennsylvania, 2004), p. 141; also W. W. H. Davis, *The Fries Rebellion, 1798–1799* (New York: Arno Press, 1969).
85. A. M. Joseph, 'The Cheerful Taxpayer: An Early Modern Political Idiom in the Early American Republic' (unpublished paper read at the 2000 SHEAR Conference).
86. A. Lenner, 'A Tale of Two Constitutions: Nationalism in the Federalist Era', *American Journal of Legal History*, 40 (January 1996), p. 105.
87. Albert Gallatin to Thomas Jefferson, 16 November 1801 in H. Adams, *The Life of Albert Gallatin*, 2nd edn (New York: Peter Smith, 1943), p. 270.
88. Studenski and Kross, *Financial History of the United States*, p. 68.
89. Adams, 'Taxation in the United States', p. 58.
90. A. Gallatin, 'Increase of Revenue', Twelfth congress, first session, in T. C. Cochran (ed.), *The New American State Papers, Finance*, vol. 3, pp. 34–44. Taxes included: carriage duty, sugar tax, licences for professionals and sellers of liquor, stamp duties and auction proceeds.
91. D. R. Adams, Jr, *Finance and Enterprise in Early America: A Study of Stephen Girard's Bank, 1812–1831* (Philadelphia, PA: University of Pennsylvania Press, 1978), pp. 25–44; J. D. Haeger, *John Jacob Astor: Business and Finance in the Early Republic* (Detroit, MI: Wayne State University Press, 1991), pp. 139–42; D. R. Hickey, *The War of 1812: The Forgotten Conflict* (Urbana, IL: University of Illinois press, 1989), pp. 166–7, pp. 100–25.
92. Adams, 'Taxation in the United States', p. 59; C. F. Dunbar, 'The Direct Tax of 1861', *Quarterly Journal of Economics*, 3 (July 1889), p. 443.
93. Howe, *The Internal Revenue System*, p. 46.
94. Gallatin, *Increase of Revenue*, p. 35.
95. J. W. Cummings, 'Financing the Mexican American War' (PhD thesis, Oklahoma State University, 2003); H. M. Larson, *Jay Cooke: Private Banker* (Cambridge, MA: Harvard University Press, 1936), pp. 70–1.
96. M. Clawson, *The Land System of the United States: An Introduction to the History and Practice of Lane Use and Land Tenure* (Lincoln, NE: University of Nebraska Press, 1968).
97. H. U. Faulkner, *American Economic History* (New York: Harper Brothers, 1924), pp. 216–17.

98. B. H. Hibbard, *A History of Public Land Policies* (Madison: University of Wisconsin Press, 1965), p. 5. Clawson, *The Land System of the United States*; P. W. Gates, 'Charts of Public Land Sales and Entries', *Journal of Economic History*, 24 (March 1964), pp. 22–38.

99. Dewey, *Financial History of the United States*, p. 168.

100. Ibid., p. 246.

101. *Debow's Review* strongly promoted this idea during the 1850s. See *Debow's Review*, 'Direct Taxation and Free Trade', 25 (July 1858), pp. 1–25;

102. *Debow's Review*, 'Report of the Southern Commercial Convention', 22 (January 1857), pp. 92–3.

103. *Debow's Review*, 'Report on the Savannah Convention', 22 (March 1857), pp. 307–9.

104. P. Wallenstein, *From Slave to New South: Public Policy in Nineteenth Century Georgia* (Chapel Hill, NC: University of North Carolina Press, 1987), pp. 23–32; John Wallis adopts this term as well. J. J. Wallis, 'Constitutions, Corporations, and Corruption: American States and Constitutional Change, 1842—1852', *Journal of Economic History*, 65 (March 2005), pp. 211–56.

105. D. Elazar, *The American Partnership: Intergovernmental Cooperation in Nineteenth Century United States* (Chicago, IL: University of Chicago Press, 1962), pp. 131–3.

106. P. Wallenstein, *From Slave South to New South: Public Policy in Nineteenth Century Georgia* (Chapel Hill, NC: University of North Carolina Press, 1987), p. 27.

107. S. Bruchey, *The Roots of American Economic Growth, 1607–1861* (New York: Harper Row, 1965), p. 128.

108. R. Sylla, J. B. Legler, and J. J. Wallis, 'Banks and State Finance in the New Republic: The United States, 1790–1860', *Journal of Economic History*, 47 (June 1987), pp. 391–403, quote on p. 400. The decision in *McCulloch* v. *Maryland* only barred the state from taxing the notes of the Bank of the United States, not any other banks.

109. Wallis, 'Constitutions, Corporations, and Corruption', p. 246.

110. J. Majewski, 'The Political Impact of Great Commercial Cities: State Investment in Antebellum Pennsylvania and Virginia', *Journal of Interdisciplinary History*, 28 (Summer 1997), pp. 1–26.

111. Wallis, 'Constitutions, Corporations, and Corruption', p. 226.

112. D> E. Bowers, 'From Logrolling to Corruption: The Development of Lobbying in Pennsylvania, 1815–1861', *Journal of the Early Republic*, 3 (Winter 1983), p. 443.

113. C. H. Brough, 'Taxation in Mississippi', in *Studies in State Taxation with Particular Reference to the Southern States* (Baltimore, MD: Johns Hopkins Press, 1900), pp. 177–8.

114. G. S. Callender, 'The Early Transporation and Banking Enterprises of the States in Relation to the Growth of the Corporations', *Quarterly Journal of Economics*, 17 (November 1902), p. 142.

115. R. C. McGrane, *Foreign Bondholders and American State Debts* (New York: Macmillan Co., 1935), pp. 204–6.

116. Ibid., pp. 280–1.

117. B. U. Ratchford, *American State Debts* (Durham, NC: Duke University Press, 1941), pp. 98–106.

118. A. de Tocqueville, *Democracy in America* 2 vols (New York: Vintage Books, 1954), vol. 1, pp. 91–2.

119. R. L. Einhorn, 'Species of Property: The American Property Tax Uniformity Clauses Reconsidered', *Journal of Economic History*, 61 (December 2001), pp. 974–1008.

120. US Department of Commerce, Bureau of the Census, *Statistics of the United States in 1860, compiled from the Eighth Census* (Washington, DC: GPO, 1866), p. 511; Dewey, *Financial History of the United States*, p. 267.

121. J. S. Ezell, *Fortune's Merry Wheel: The Lottery in America* (Cambridge, MA: Harvard University Press, 1960), pp. 120, 135.

122. G. R. Blakey, 'State Conducted Lotteries: History, Problems, and Promises', *Journal of Social Issues*, 35 (December 1952), p. 68.

2 The 'Exhausted Condition of the Treasury'

1. M.Dix (ed.), *Memoirs of John A. Dix*, 2 vols (New York: Harper Brothers, 1883), vol. 1, p. 364.

2. L. D. White, *The Jacksonians: A Study in Administrative History, 1829–1861* (New York: Macmillan Co., 1954), p. 163.

3. John A. Dix to John Sherman, *Congressional Globe*, Thirty-sixth Congress, Second session, 12 February 1861, p. 871.

4. J. Sherman, *Congressional Globe*, Thirty-sixth Congress Second session, 18 December 1861, p. 42.

5. J. A. Dix, *Condition of the Treasury*, Thirty-sixth Congress, Second session, House Ex. Doc. 20, serial set 1103, 18 January 1861, p. 2.

6. J. Sherman, *Recollections of Forty Years in the House, Senate, and Cabinet: An Autobiography*, 2 vols (Chicago, IL: Werner Co., 1895), vol. 1, p. 251.

7. For example, L. P. Curry, *Blueprint for Modern America: Nonmilitary legislation of the First Civil War Congress* (Nashville, TN: Vanderbilt University Press, 1968).

8. D. R. Dewey, *Financial History of the United States*, p. 272.

9. R. N. Current, 'God and the Strongest Battalions', in D. Donald (ed.), *Why the North Won the Civil War* (New York: Collier Books, 1960), p. 15.

10. P. Foner, *Business and Slavery: The New York Merchants and the Irrepressible Conflict* (Chapel Hill, NC: University of North Carolina Press, 1941), p. 218.

11. E. D. Fite, *Social and Industrial Conditions in the North During the Civil War* (New York: Peter Smith, 1930), p. 106. These figures count only businesses with over $5,000 in capital.

12. R. G. Albion, *The Rise of New York Port* (New York: Charles Scribner's Sons, 1939), p. 400.

13. J. Sherman, *Recollections of Forty Years in the House, Senate and Cabinet: An Autobiography*, 2 vols (Chicago, IL: Werner, Co., 1895), vol. 1, p. 259.

14. A common term used when the government ran a deficit.

15. de Tocqueville, *Democracy in America*, vol. 1, pp. 89–90.

16. M. R. Wilson, *The Business of Civil War*, p. 35.

17. Best demonstrated in Egnal, 'The Beards Were Right'.

18. J. M. McPherson, *What They Fought For, 1861–1865* (Baton Rouge, LA: Louisiana State University Press, 1994).

19. For the Civil War as the 'first modern war', see J. G. Dawson, 'First of the Modern Wars', in S. M. Grant and B. H. Reid (eds), *The American Civil War: Explorations and Reconsiderations*, (New York: Longman, Green, Co., 2000), pp. 121–141.

20. Beard and Beard, *The Rise of American Civilization*.

21. Beard, *The Rise of American Civilization*, vol. 2, p. 105.

22. Richardson, *The Greatest Nation of the Earth*, p. 250.

23. J. G. Blaine, *Twenty Years of Congress*, p. 399.
24. John A. Dix to Buchanan quoted in George T. Curtis, *Life of James Buchanan*, 2 vols (New York: Harper & Bros., 1883), vol. 1, p. 537.
25. Studenski and Krooss, *Financial History of the United States*, pp. 125, 152; J. W. Schuckers, *The Life and Public Services of Salmon Portland Chase* (1874; New York: Dacapo Press, 1970), p. 274; Dewey R. Dewey, *Financial History of the United States*, 12th edn (New York: Longmans, Green and Co, 1939), p. 255.
26. J. Huston, *The Panic of 1857 and the Coming of the Civil War* (Baton Rouge, LA: Louisiana State University Press, 1987), pp. 14–34.
27. *Harper's Weekly* (19 December 1857), p. 802.
28. *Commerce and Navigation Report, 1857*, House Ex. Doc., 145, ser. set 960, p. 21; *Commerce and Navigation Report, 1858*, Thirty-fifth Congress, Second session, House Ex. Doc., 120, ser. set 1015, p. 49.
29. C. W. Calomiris and Larry Schweikart, 'The Panic of 1857: Origins, transmission, and Containment', *Journal of Economic History*, 51 (December 1991), pp. 807–34.
30. Dewey, *Financial History*, p. 267.
31. P. S. Klein, *President James Buchanan: A Biography* (University Park, PA: Pennsylvania State University Press, 1978), p. 327.
32. A. Nevins, *The Emergence of Lincoln*, (New York: Charles Scribner's Sons, 1950), vol. 2, pp. 476–87; J. B. McMaster, *History of the People of the United States*, 9 vols (New York: D. Appleton, Co., 1916), vol. 8, pp. 358–60; C. H. Scheele, *A Short History of the Mail Service* (Washington, DC: Smithsonian Institution Press, 1970).
33. J. H. Baker, *James Buchanan* (New York: Henry Holt, 2004), pp. 113–16.
34. The historical importance of this phenomenon is best explained in Ferguson, *The Cash Nexus*, pp. 163–85.
35. R. Sylla, 'Political Economy and Financial Development: Canada and the United States in the Mirror of the Other, 1790–1840', *Enterprise and Society*, 7 (December 2006), p. 657; also P. L. Rousseau and R. Sylla, 'Emerging Financial Markets and Early US Growth', *Explorations in Economic History*, 42 (January 2005), pp. 1–26.
36. R. H. Timberlake, Jr 'The Independent Treasury and Monetary Policy before the Civil War', *Southern Economic Journal*, 27 (October, 1960), p. 95; F. Noll, 'The United States Public Debt, 1861–1975', *EH.NET Encyclopedia*, Robert Whaples, ed. http://eh.net/encyclopedia/articke/noll.publicdebt.
37. Studenski and Krooss, *Financial History of the United States*, pp. 139–40; also, Dewey, *Financial History of the United States*, pp. 317–18.
38. J. D. Richardson (ed.), *Compilation of the Message of the Presidents, Buchanan's Third Annual Message*, 19 December 1859 (New York: Bureau of National Literature, 1925), p. 3105; J. Flaherty, 'The Revenue Imperative' (MA thesis, Texas A&M University, 2000), pp. 36–47.
39. R. Bayley, *Public Indebtedness: A Report in the Tenth Census* (Washington: GPO, 1884), p. 269.
40. S. Homer and R. Sylla, *A History of Interest Rates*, 3rd edn (New Brunswick, NJ: Rutgers Univerity Press, 1991), p. 2867.
41. Dewey, *Financial History of the United States*, pp. 124–6; J. J. Knox, *United States Notes*, 2nd edn (New York: Sanford J. Durst, 1978), pp. 21–3, pp. 60–2.
42. J. Sexton, *Debtor Diplomacy: Finance and American Foreign Relations in the Civil War Era, 1837–1873* (Oxford: Clarendon Press, 2005), p. 78.

43. M. G. Myers, *A Financial History of the United States* (New York: Columbia University Press, 1970), pp. 117–19; *New York Tribune*, 4 April 1857, p. 2.

44. Quoted in P. G. Auchampaugh, *James Buchanan and His Cabinet on the Eve of Secession*, (Lancaster, PA: Lancaster Press, 1926), p. 68.

45. Dix, *Memoirs*, vol. 1 pp. 362–3; Biographical information in J. F. Rhodes, *History of the United States From the Compromise of 1850 to the Final Restoration of Home Rule at the South in 1877*, 9 vols (New York: Macmillan Co., 1919), vol. 1: pp. 386–7, 395, vol. 3, pp. 251–2. Philip Foner questions the veracity of the Dix memoirs regarding the bankers' meeting. P. Foner, *Business and Slavery*, p. 246.

46. Dix, *Memoirs*, vol. 1, pp. 362–4. Note that 'finance capitalists' wield this extraordinary influence on the Buchanan, not the Lincoln, administration.

47. Dix, *Memoirs*, vol. 1, p. 366.

48. *Annual Report of the Secretary of the Treasury*, House Ex. Doc. 3, Thirty-fifth Congress, Second session, ser set 996, pp. 240–59.

49. 'Collection of Duties in the Seceding States', House Ex. Doc. 73, Thirty-sixth Congress, Second session, ser set 1100, pp. 3–8.

50. Ibid.; Sampling from Dix, *Memoirs*, vol. 1: pp. 366–72.

51. *New York Times*, (1 February 1861) p. 1. Now we refer to these revenue cutters as the Coast Guard.

52. Dix, *Memoirs*, vol. 1, p. 371.

53. Ibid., p. 374.

54. J. D. Winters, *The Civil War in Louisiana*, (Baton Rouge: Louisiana State University Press, 1963), pp. 12–14.

55. J. A. Dix, 'Collection of Duties in the Seceding States', p. 5.

56. W. T. Sherman to John Sherman in Sherman, *Recollections*, vol. 1, p. 241.

57. Egnal, 'The Beards Were Right', p. 52.

58. *Hunt's Merchant Magazine*, 44 (May 1861), pp. 668–9. Critics of the Morrill Tariff claim that it caused a reduction of import duties however revenue declined before its enactment.

59. *New York Times*, 3 March 1861, p. 1.

60. Patterson, 'Government Finances', p. 35.

61. J. D. Richardson (ed.) *Compilation of the Messages of the Presidents*, 11 vols (New York: Bureau of National Literature and Art,1925), p. 3105.

62. Regarding the Congresses: D. Potter, *The Impending Crisis, 1848–1861* (New York: Harper Row, 1976); M. J. Stegmaier, 'Intensifying the Sectional Conflict', *Civil War History*, 31 (September 1985), pp. 197–221; Huston described the situation in Congress as a logjam in J. L. Huston, *The Panic of 1857*, p. 193.

63. Dix, *Memoirs*, vol. 1, p. 364.

64. J. Flaherty, 'Incidental Protection: An Examination of the Morrill Tariff', *Essays in Economic and Business History*, 19 (2001), pp. 103–18.

65. Quoted in J. W. Schuckers, *Life and Public Services*, pp. 225–6.

66. K. C. Martis, *The Historical Atlas of Political Parties in the United States Congress, 1789–1989* (New York: Macmillan Co., 1989), pp. 113–18.

67. R. F. Nichols, *The Disruption of American Democracy* (New York: Macmillan, Co., 1948), 509—510.

68. K. H. Porter and D. B. Johnson (eds), *National Party Platforms, 1840–1964* (Urbana, IL: University of Illinois Press, 1966), p. 32.

69. R. Hofstadter, *American Political Tradition and the Men Who Made It* (New York: Alfred A. Knopf, 1949), p. 116.

70. A. G. Guelzo, 'Houses Divided: Lincoln, Douglas, and the Political Landscape of 1858', *Journal of American History*, 94 (September 2007), p. 411.

71. W. E. Gienapp, *The Origins of the Republican Party, 1852–1856* (New York: Oxford University Press, 1987).

72. M. F. Holt, *The Rise and Fall of the American Whig Party: Jacksonian Politics and the Onset of the Civil War* (New York: Oxford University Press, 1999), pp. 951–2.

73. Porter and Johnson (eds), *National Party Platforms*, pp. 9, 20.

74. J. H. Baker, *Affairs of Party: The Political Culture of Northern Democrats in Mid-Nineteenth Century* (Ithaca, NY: Cornell University Press, 1983), p. 109.

75. P. Temin, *The Jacksonian Economy* (New York: W.W. Norton, 1969), p. 37.

76. W. M. Gouge, *The Curse of Paper-Money and Banking or A Short History of Banking in the United States of America* (1833; New York: Greenwood Press, 1968), p. 191.

77. J. M. McFaul, *The Politics of Jacksonian Finance* (Ithaca, NY: Cornell University Press, 1972), pp. 58–106. McFaul provides a more critical analysis of Jackson's policies than does Temin.

78. Porter and Johnson (eds), *National Party Platforms*, pp. 9–21. One is struck by the consistency of the Democratic platforms throughout the antebellum era.

79. Quoted in J. H. Baker, *Affairs of the Party: The Political Culture of Northern Democrats in the Mid-Nineteenth Century* (Ithaca, NY: Cornell University Press, 1983), p. 143.

80. D. Donald (ed.), *Inside Lincoln's Cabinet: The Wartime Diaries of Salmon P. Chase* (New York: Longmans, Green and Co., 1954), p. 36.

81. Many biographies of Chase have been written. The most comprehensive are: J. Niven, *Salmon P. Chase: A Biography* (New York: Oxford University Press, 1995); Frederick Blue contributed a political biography of Chase. F. J. Blue, *Salmon P. Chase: A Life in Politics* (Kent, OH: Kent State University Press, 1987); Schuckers, *Life and Public Services of Salmon Portland Chase*, contains invaluable insight into Chase's actions throughout his professional life.

82. Schuckers, *Life and Public Services of Salmon Portland Chase*, p. 52.

83. *Ibid*, 52.

84. Chase to Charles Miller, 11 September 1851 in J. Niven (ed.), *Salmon P. Chase Papers*, 5 vols (Kent, OH: Kent State University Press, 1994), vol. 2, pp. 323–5.

85. Niven, *Salmon P. Chase: A Biography*, p. 427.

86. Such as Jay Cooke, John A. Stevens, president of the Bank of Commerce who became instrumental in the development of the national banking system, and August Belmont.

87. *Report of the Secretary of the Treasury*, Thirty-seventh Congres, First session, 4 July 1861, S. Ex. Doc. 2, ser set 1112, p. 12.

88. Gideon Welles quoted in D. Donald (ed.), *Inside Lincoln's Cabinet*, p. 5; Blue, *Chase, Life in Politics*, p. 322; E. P. Oberholtzer, *Jay Cooke: Financier of the Civil War* (Philadelphia, PA: George W. Jacobs, Co., 1907), p. 128.

89. E. Whipple to Jacob Schuckers, 29 June 1873, in Schuckers, *Life and Public Services*, pp. 629–30.

90. Justin S. Morrill to Henry C. Carey, 6 July 1861. *H.C. Carey papers*, HSP.

91. Blue, *Chase, Life in Politics*, p. 322.

92. Oberholtzer, *Jay Cooke*, vol. 1, p. 129.

93. *Diary of Gideon Welles*, 3 vols (Boston, MA: Houghton Mifflin, Co., 1911), vol. 1, p. 203.

94. Foner, *Free Soil*, p. 176.

95. Clifford Arick to Abraham Lincoln, 22 January 1861 in *Abraham Lincoln papers*, LC (available online.)
96. Niven, *Salmon P. Chase: A Biography*, p. 238; Schuckers, *Life and Public Services*, p. 202
97. Schuckers, *Life and Public Services*, p. 203.
98. D. V. Smith, 'Chase and Civil War Politics', *Ohio Archaeological and Historical Quarterly*, 3 (July–October 1930), p. 25.
99. R. H. Luthin, 'Salmon P. Chase's Political Career Before the Civil War,' *Mississippi Valley Historical Review*, 29 (March 1943), p. 536.
100. *Diary of GW*, vol. 1, p. 224.
101. *Report of the Secretary of the Treasury*, Thirty-seventh Congress, First session, Senate Ex. Doc. 2, ser. Set 1112, July 4, 1861, pp. 15–16.
102. William Pitt Fessenden to 'His Dear Lizzy', 12 January 1861, *Fessenden Papers*, Bowdoin College.
103. Peter Temin, *The Jacksonian Economy*.
104. H. N. Scheiber, 'The Pet Banks in Jacksonian Politics and Finance, 1833–1841,' *Journal of Economic History*, 23 (June 1963), p. 213.
105. S. Rezneck, 'The Social History of an American Depression, 1837–1843', *American Historical Review*, 40 (July 1935), p. 673.
106. M. F. Holt, *Political Parties and American Political Development from the Age of Jackson to the Age of Lincoln* (Baton Rouge, LA: Louisiana State University Press, 1992), p. 36.
107. D. Kinley, *The History, Organization and Influence of the Independent Treasury of the United States* (1893; New York: Greenwood Press, 1968), p. 57.
108. Ibid., p. 29.
109. *Report on the Constitutional Treasury System*, Thirty-fourth Congress, First session, Senate Ex. Doc. 2, ser. set 814, p. 212.
110. *Treasury Report*, 1858, House Ex. Doc., Thirty-fifth Congress, Second sess., ser. set 996, p. 16.
111. *Debow's Review*, 26 (February 1859), p. 193.
112. Howard Bodenhorn, *State Banking in Early America* (New York: Oxford University Press, 2003), p. 206.
113. J. B. Phillips, 'Methods of Keeping the Public Money of the United States', *Publications of the Michigan Political Science Association*, 4 (1900–2), p. 129.
114. *Report on Depositories*, House Ex. Doc., 5 Thirty-third Congress, Second session, ser set 780, p. 261–2.
115. B. Hammond, *Banks and Politics in the Civil War*, (Princeton, NJ: Princeton University Press, 1970), p. 545.
116. *Report on Depositories*, pp. 256–7; Phillips, 'Methods of Keeping Public Money', pp. 131–3.
117. Kinley, *Independent Treasury*, p. 58.
118. Hammond, *Banks and Politics in America*, p. 545.
119. Kinley, *Independent Treasury*, pp. 284–6.
120. *Treasury Report*, 1862, Sen. Ex. Doc, 1, Thirty-seventh Congress, Third sess., ser. set 1149, p. 14.
121. Hammond, *Banks and Politics*, p. 721.
122. Richardson, *The Greatest Nation of the Earth*, p. 28.
123. Routine practice before 1846, and an important reason for instituting the 1863 National Banking Act. The famous 'bond drives' of World Wars I and II also went through banks.

124. F. Noll, 'The Start of a Government Monopoly: Civil War Finance, the Rise of the Bureau of Engraving and Printing, and the Decline of Bank Note companies, 1863', (Paper read at the 2005 *Economic and Business Historical Society Conference*, April, 2005). This limitation necessitated the creation of the Bureau of Printing and Engraving.

125. T. H. Benton, *Thirty Years' View*, 2 vols. (New York: D. Appleton and Co., 1856): I, 726.

126. J. W. Cummings, 'Financing the Mexican War', p. 190.

127. Chase knew Jay Cooke's brother, Henry, a newspaper publisher in Ohio during the 1850s. Chase contracted 148 loan agents to sell the first war loan in August 1861. Jay Cooke sold one-fifth of this issue himself, which brought him to the attention of the Treasury secretary. See, Schuckers, *Life and Public Services*, p. 229.

128. B. Hammond, *Sovereignty and an Empty Purse: Banks and Politics in the Civil War* (Princeton, NJ: Princeton University Press, 1970).

129. Knox, *US Notes*, pp. 89–90.

130. S. Mihm, *A Nation of Counterfeiters: Capitalists, Con Men, and the Making of the United States* (Cambridge, MA: Harvard University Press, 2007), p. 309.

131. J. J. Knox, *History of Banking* (1900; New York: A.M. Kelley, 1969), pp. 305–28; P. Trescott, *Financing American Enterprise: The Story of Commercial Banking* (New York: Harper Row, 1963).

132. H. Rockoff, *Free Banking Era: A Re-examination* (New York: Arno Press, 1975). Contrary to my argument, Rockoff posits that the currency craziness created by free banking was not harmful.

133. As noted earlier, Bodenham praises the economic stimulus inherent in the free banking system.

134. A. J. Rolnick and W. E. Weber, 'The Causes of Free Bank Failures: A Detailed Examination', *Journal of Monetary Economics*, 14 (1984), pp. 267–91, p. 271.

135. J. A. Dix, 'Condition of the Banks', Thirty-sixth Congress, Second session, House Ex. Doc. 77, ser set 1101, 46.

136. Hammond, *Banks and Politics*, pp. 6–9.

137. E. J. Stevens, 'Composition of the Money Stock Prior to the Civil War', *Journal of Money, Credit, and Banking*, 3 (February 1971), pp. 84–101, p. 87.

138. Schuckers, *Life and Public Services*, pp. 282–4; the figures are on p. 284.

139. D. R. Johnson, *Illegal Tender: Counterfeiting and the Secret Service in Nineteenth Century America* (Washington, DC: Smithsonian Institution, 1995), 37; Mihm, *Nation of Counterfeiters*.

140. Beard and Beard, *Rise of American Civilization*, vol. 2, p. 12.

141. Knox, *History of Banking*, p. 312.

142. Schultz and Caine, *Financial Developments of the United States*, pp. 244–6; Trescott, *Financing American Enterprise* (New York: Prentice Hall, Inc., 1937), p. 18.

143. Schuckers, *Life and Public Services*, p. 283.

144. L. P. Doti and L. Schweikart, *Banking in the American West: From Gold rush to Deregulation* (Norman, OK: University of Oklahoma Press, 1991), p. 7

145. P. Glenn Porter and Harold C. Livesay, *Merchants and Manufacturers* (Baltimore, MD: John Hopkins University Press, 1971), p. 125.

146. Mihm, *Nation of Counterfeiters*, pp. 209–59 gives a thorough explanation of the counterfeit 'passing and detection' industry; A. B. Hepburn, *A History of Currency in the United States*, pp. 164–5.

147. Knox, *History of Banking*, 315.

148. S. Hooper to H. C. Carey, 16 May 1866, *Edwin Carey Gardner* papers, HSP, Box 69, F–34.

149. Hepburn, '*A History of Currency in the U.S.*', p. 176; Stevens, 'Composition of Money Stock', 86–7.

150. John Sherman, *Recollections*, I: 251; Knox, *United States*, 72.

151. *New York Times*, 23 April 1861.

152. *Congressional Globe*, Thirty-seventh Congress, First session, 17 July 1861, pp. 171–3.

3 The Magnitude of the Contest

1. Dewey, *Financial History*, pp. 267, 398.

2. P. P. Van Riper and K. A. Sutherland, 'The Northern Civil Service: 1861–1865', *Civil War History*, 11 (December 1965), pp. 351–69; Schuckers put the number of Treasury employees at the end of the war, 'both direct and indirect', at 15,000. Schuckers, *Life and Public Services of Salmon Porter Chase*, p. 481.

3. McPherson, *Battle Cry of Freedom*, p. 264.

4. Schuckers, *Life and Public Services*, p. 282.

5. Oberholtzer, *Jay Cooke*, vol. 1, p. 135

6. *Treasury Report*, 4 July, 1861, p. 4.

7. Patterson, 'Government Finance', pp. 42–3; Niven, *Salmon P. Chase*, p. 248.

8. McCulloch, *Men and Measures of Half a Century*, p. 184.

9. J. Sexton, *Debtor Diplomacy: Finance and American Foreign Relations in the Civil War Era, 1837–1873* (Oxford: Clarendon Press, 2005), 92.

10. D. R. Stabile and J. A. Cantor, *The Public Debt of the United States: An Historical Perspective, 1775–1990* (New York: Praeger, 1991), pp. 60–1.

11. Schuckers, *Life and Public Services*, pp. 282–4.

12. J. Sherman, *Selected Speeches of John Sherman* (New York: D. Appleton and Co., 1879), pp. 81–2. By 1815 and 1837 Sherman refers to the great depreciation of currency nationally during the War of 1812 and the Depression of 1837.

13. Dewey, *Financial History*, 354–5.

14. *Message of the President to the Special Session of Congress*, Thirty-seventh Congress, First session, 4 July 1861, p. 10.

15. J. Brewer, *Sinews of Power: War, Money, and the English State* (New York: Alfred A. Knopf, 1998), 133; P. G. M. Dickson, *The Financial Revolution in England* (London: Melbourne Pub., 1967). Both Brewer and Dickson observe that the English based their financial system on the earlier Dutch model, extending even deeper the historic roots of this mode of financing. However, for the unique aspects of the resulting English finance system during this period, see D. R. Weir, 'Tontines, Public Finance, and the Revolution in France and England, 1688-1789', *Journal of Economic History*, 49 (March, 1989), pp. 95–124.

16. Flaherty, *Perceived Power*, p. 102; J. G. Blaine, *Twenty Years of Congress from Lincoln to Garfield*. 2 vols. (Norwich, CT: Henry Bill Publishing Co., 1884), vol. 1, pp. 404–5.

17. WPF to William Fessenden, 1 July 1861, *Fessenden Papers*, Bowdoin College.

18. Most famously attacked in J. G. Randall, *Constitutional Problems Under Lincoln* (Urbana, IL: University of Illinois Press, 1951); a more nuanced approach appears in M. E. Neely, *Fate of Liberty: Abraham Lincoln and Civil Liberties* (New York: Oxford University Press, 1991).

19. G. Welles, *Diary of Gideon Welles*, 3 vols (Boston, MA: Houghton Mifflin Co., 1911) vol. 1, p. 525.
20. *Report of the Secretary of the Treasury to the Special Session of Congress*, Thirty-seventh Congress, First session, Senate Ex. Doc. 2, 4 July 1861, pp. 6–9
21. Ibid., pp. 10–11.
22. Donald (ed.), *Inside Lincoln's Cabinet*, p. 36.
23. Sherman, *Selected Speeches of John Sherman*, pp. 81–2.
24. J. McPherson, *Battle Cry of Freedom*, pp. 308–38.
25. *Congressional Globe*, Thirty-seventh Congress, First session, 23 July 1861, p. 307.
26. *Congressional Globe*, Thirty-seventh Congress, First session, 24 July 1861, pp. 247, 252.
27. Act of 22 July 1813, p. 3 *United States Statutes at Large*, 26.
28. *Congressional Globe*, Thirty-seventh Congress, First session, 24 July 1861, p. 246.
29. Ibid., p. 247.
30. Ibid., pp. 248–9. The word 'odious', originally pegged to taxes by Adam Smith, is used frequently in the tax debates to describe different types of taxes.
31. Quoted in Seligman, *The Income Tax*, pp. 430–5. This book provides the best concise description of the nineteenth century income tax measures.
32. Ibid., pp. 247–9.
33. Ibid., p. 283.
34. Ibid., p. 279.
35. Seligman, *The Income Tax*, p. 435.
36. Ibid., 559–60.
37. *Congressional Globe*, Thirty-seventh Congress, First session, p. 272.
38. Ibid., p. 254.
39. Ibid., p. 315.
40. J. L. Waltham, *Copying Other Nations Policies: Two American Case Studies* (Cambridge: Schenkman Publishing Co., 1980), pp. 14–15.
41. Appendix to the *Congressional Globe* – Laws of the United States, Thirty-seventh Congress, First session, 5 August 1861, 39; 'The Income Tax Act', Vict. C. 35, 2nd edn London, 1842 in Gale, *Making of the Modern World*.
42. Waltman, *Copying Other Nation's Policies*, pp. 15–17. Full exploration on pp. 3–20.
43. A. Hope-Jones, *Income Tax in the Napoleonic Wars* (Cambridge: Cambridge University Press, 1939), pp. 112–13.
44. *Congressional Globe*, Thirty-seventh Congress, First session, 29 July 1861, p. 330.
45. D. M. Jordan, *Roscoe Conkling of New York: Voice in the Senate* (Ithaca, NY: Cornell University Press, 1971), p. 142.
46. S. D. Cashman, *America in the Gilded Age: From the Death of Lincoln to the Rise of Theodore Roosevelt* (New York: New York University Press, 1984), p. 217; D. B. Eaton, *The Spoils System and Civil Service Reform in the Custom-House and Post Office at New York* (1881; New York: Arno Press, 1974), pp. 12–14, 21–2.
47. P. A. Lamphier, *Kate Chase and William Sprague: Politics and Gender in a Civil War Marriage* (Lincoln, NE: University of Nebraska Press, 2003.)
48. Cashman, *America in the Gilded Age*, pp. 220–5.
49. *Congressional Globe*, Thirty-seventh Congress, First session, 24 July 1861, pp. 247–8.
50. Ibid., 25 July 1861, p. 269.
51. New York Chamber of Commerce to Chase, *S.P Chase Papers*, LC, August 1861, reel 13, no. 364.
52. Mitchell, *A History of the Greenbacks*, pp. 23–8.

53. Hammond, *Sovereignty and an Empty* Purse, p. 87.
54. H. M. Larson, *Jay Cooke, Private Banker* (Cambridge, MA: Harvard University Press, 1936).
55. Niven (ed.), *Chase Papers*, vol. 3, pp. 266–7.
56. Mitchell, *History of the Greenbacks*, p. 33.
57. Sharkey, *Money, Class and Party*, p. 24.
58. Sexton, *Debtor Diplomacy*, p. 96.
59. McPherson, *Battle Cry of Freedom*, pp. 389–91 for an overview of the *Trent* Affair.
60. *Report of the Secretary of the Treasury*, 9 December 1861, Thirty-seventh Congress, Second sessions, House Ex. Doc, 28, ser Set 1121, pp. 13–15.
61. Ibid., pp. 16–19.
62. Both Hammond, *Sovereignty and the Empty Purse*, pp. 109–163 and Sharkey, *Money, Class and Party*, pp. 22–8 recount these events; D. M. Gische, 'The New York City Banks and the Development of the National Banking System, 1860–1870', *American Journal of Legal History*, 23 (January 1979), pp. 31–4.
63. *Report of the Secretary of the Treasury*, Thirty-seventh Congress, First session, Senate Ex. Doc. 2, 4 July1861, p. 12.
64. Dawes to Mrs Dawes quoted in B. P. Thomas and H. M. Hyman, *Stanton: The Life and Times of Lincoln's Secretary of War* (New York: Alfred A. Knopf, 1962), p. 135.
65. McPherson, *Battlecry of Freedom*, p. 368.
66. *Hepburn v. Griswold*, 8 Wall 603 (1870).

4 The Poverty of the Treasury

1. McPherson, *Battle Cry of Freedom,* p. 367.
2. Donald (ed.), *Inside Lincoln's Cabinet*, p. 14.
3. Larson, *Jay Cooke*, p. 112.
4. D. M. Gische, 'The New York City Banks', p. 1
5. H. M. Larson, *Jay Cooke*, pp. 112–13.
6. Sexton, *Debtor Diplomacy*, pp. 98–100.
7. *Report of the Secretary of the Treasury*, 9 December 1861, pp. 13–15.
8. *Congressional Globe*, Thirty-seventh Congress, Second session, 15 January 1862, p. 345.
9. *Annual Report, 1861*, p. 19.
10. Ibid., pp. 18–20.
11. E. G. Spaulding, *A Resource of War – the Credit of the Government Made Immediately Available: A History of the Legal Tender* (Buffalo, NY: Express Printing Co., 1869), p. 30.
12. Ibid, 15–16; Sharkey, *Money, Class and Party*, pp. 15–55. Sharkey most cogently, although critically, argues for the 'necessity' of printing the Greenbacks.
13. Larson, *Jay Cooke*, pp. 116–17
14. Mitchell, *History of the Greenbacks*, p. 71.
15. *Spaulding, A History of the Legal Tender*, pp. 59–60.
16. Sharkey, *Money, Class, and Party*, pp. 42–4.
17. Ibid., 91–2.
18. Niven, *Salmon P. Chase: A Biography*, p. 293.
19. Sharkey, *Money, Class and Party*, p. 52.
20. Mitchell, *History of the Greenbacks*, p. 162.

21. A. Nussbaum, *A History of the Dollar* (New York: Columbia University Press, 1957), p. 113.
22. Mitchell, *History of the Greenbacks*, p. 181.
23. M. D. Weidenmeir, 'Financial Aspects of the American Civil War: War News, Price Risk, and the Processing of Information' (PhD theis, 1999); Mihm, *Nation of Counterfeiters*, pp. 323–7.
24. Nussbaum, *History of the Dollar*, pp. 109–10.
25. Mitchell, *History of the Greenbacks*, p. 179.
26. *Internal Revenue Record*, 29 July 1865, p. 25.
27. Both quotes in Hammond, *Sovereignty and an Empty Purse: Banks and Politics in the Civil War* (Princeton, NJ: Princeton University Press, 1970), p. 347.
28. K. L. Willard, T. W. Guinnanc, H. S. Rosen, 'Turning Point in the Civil War: Views from the Greenback Market', *American Economic Review*, 86 (September 1996), pp. 1001–18.
29. D. B. Ball, *Financial Failure and Confederate Defeat* (Urbana, IL: University of Illinois Press, 1991), pp. 161–99.
30. Parker, *Life and Public Services of Justin Smith Morrill*, p. 144.
31. *Report of the Secretary of the Treasury*, 1862, quoted in Mitchell, *History of the Greenbacks*, pp. 91–2.
32. Niven 9ed.), *The Salmon P. Chase Papers*, vol. 1, p. 381.
33. *Economist* (20 October 1862), pp. 1149–50.
34. Irwin Unger and Robert Sharkey have written the standard accounts of this turmoil. Although I am more inclined toward Sharkey's interpretation, both are very good resources. I. Unger, *The Greenback Era: A Social and Political History of American Finance, 1865–1879* (Princeton, NJ: Princeton University Press, 1964); Sharkey, *Money, Class, and Party*.
35. Larson, *Jay Cooke*, p. 109.
36. Gordon, *Hamilton's Blessing*, p. 78; Larson, *Jay Cooke*, p. 121; E. Vidal, *The History and Methods of the Paris Bourse* (Washington: GPO, 1918), p. 173.
37. Larson, *Jay Cooke*, p. 121.
38. Mitchell, *History of the Greenbacks*, p. 178.
39. Larson, *Jay Cooke*, pp. 143–51.
40. G. S. Callender, 'The Early Transportation and Banking Enterprises of the States in Relation to the Growth of Corporations', *Quarterly Journal of Economics*, 17 (November 1902), p. 142.
41. McGrane, *Foreign Bondholders*, pp. 204—206.
42. Sexton, *Debtor Diplomacy*, pp. 123–7.
43. Chase to W. T. Sherman, 13 October 1861 in Niven (ed.), *The Salmon P. Chase Papers*, vol. 3, pp. 101–2,
44. J. L. Bertolet, 'Justin S. Morrill', in *Encyclopedia of the American Civil War*, D. Heilder and J. Heilder (eds) 5 vols (Santa Barbara, CA: ABC–CLIO, 2000), vol. 3, pp. 1364–5; although folksy, Parker's biography of Morrill remains the most comprehensive, and contains many important letters and portions of speeches (alas, without footnotes). Parker, *Life and Public Services*. The students and professors at Texas A&M University, and other land grant institutions, owe Morrill a nod of gratitude.
45. This remains an under-explored aspect of the protection vs. free trade policy debates. Protectionists prefer specific duties, while free trade advocates prefer *ad valorem* duties.

46. R. Hofstadter, 'The Tariff Issue on the Eve of the Civil War', *American Historical Review*, 44 (October 1938), pp. 50–5; see also, J. Flaherty, 'Incidental Protection'.

47. *Congressional Globe*, Thirty-seventh Congress, Second session, 12 March 1862, p. 1196.

48. Ibid., p. 1195.

49. *Congressional Globe*, Thirty-seventh Congress, Second session, 12 March 1862, p. 1197; see also, pp. 1199–200, 1294–5.

50. *Congressional Globe*, Thirty-seventh Congress, Second session, March 19 1862, p. 1287. The irony here, of course, is that Bingham thought of the way to circumvent the Constitution in order to enact the income tax.

51. F. C. Howe, *Taxation and Taxes in the United States Under the Internal Revenue System 1791–1895* (New York: Thomas Y. Crowell, Co., 1896), p. 57.

52. *Congressional Globe*, Thirty-seventh Congress, Second session, 12 March 1862, p.1194.

53. Ibid., 1196.

54. Ibid., p. 1195. Text of statute: 12 *Statutes at Large*, Thirty-seventh Congress, Second session, 1 July 1862, pp. 432–89.

55. *Congressional Globe*, Thirty-seventh Congress, Second session, 13 March 1862, p. 1225.

56. *Congressional Globe*, Thirty-seventh Congress, Second session, 8 April 1862, 1577.

57. A more detailed discussion of the incidence of these taxes follows in the next chapter.

58. *Congressional Globe*, Thirty-seventh Congress, Second session, 23 May 1862, p. 2310.

59. For summaries of this bill, G. Boutwell, *The Taxpayer's Manual* (Boston, MA: Little Brown and Co., 1866); H. E. Smith, *The United States Federal Internal Tax History from 1861 to 1871* (Boston, MA: Houghton Mifflin Co., 1914).

60. *Congressional Globe*, Thirty-seventh Congress, Second session, 27 March 1862, p. 1406.

61. L. P. Curry, *Blueprint for Modern America: Non-Military Legislation of the First Civil War Congress* (Nashville, TN: Vanderbilt University Press, 1968), 164.

62. D. E. Bowers, 'From Logrolling to Corruption: The Development of Lobbying in Pennsylvania, 1815–1861', *Journal of the Early Republic*, 3 (Winter 1983), pp. 439–74.

63. J. J. Pincus, 'Pressure Groups and the Pattern of Tariffs', *Journal of Political Economy*, 83 (August, 1975), 775.

64. *Congressional Globe*, Thirty-seventh Congress, Second session, 21 March 1862, p. 1325.

65. *Congressional Globe*, Thirty-seventh Congress, Second session, 23 May 1862, p. 2317; also pp. 2400–8.

66. Curry, *Blueprint for Modern America*, p. 168.

67. *Congressional Globe*, Thirty-seventh Congress, Second session, 19 March 1862, p. 1287.

68. Debates on this matter, Thirty-seventh Congress, Second session, 13 March 1862, pp. 1217–26; 14 March, pp. 1238–42.

69. Thirty-seventh Congress, Second session, 12 March 1862, p. 1194.

70. Richardson, *Greatest Nation*, p. 121.

71. Curry, *Blueprint for Modern America*, p. 174.

72. William Pitt Fessenden to [unknown], 25 April 1862 in Francis Fessenden, *Life and Public Services of William Pitt Fessenden*, 2 vols (Boston, MA: Houghton, Mifflin and Co., 1907), I; 190.

73. This changed with the passage of the Seventeenth Amendment in 1913 which allowed direct election of Senators.

74. Blaine, *Twenty Years of Congress*, vol. 1, 326.

75. *New York Times* (3 May 1862), p. 2.

76. Quoted in Curry, *Blueprint for Modern America*, p. 172

77. Henderson and Wilson from Missouri, Powell, Kentucky. Senators from Virginia, Maryland, Missouri, and Connecticut supported this effort. Curry, *Blueprint for Modern America,* p. 173.
78. *Congressional Globe,* Thirty-seventh Congress, Second session, 12 March 1862, p. 1196.
79. According to Schuckers, Chase and policy makers were greatly offended when US citizens moved their assets abroad after the firing at Fort Sumter. 'Many persons of large wealth, in apprehension of war, had, even before the breaking out of hostilities, transferred their property to foreign countries ... it was to escape not only the pressure of war taxes, but also to preserve their opulence should the result of the war prove unfavorable to the national cause'. Schuckers, *Life and Public Services,* 330 (footnote).
80. Smith, *The United States Federal Internal Tax,* p. 55.
81. G. B. Boutwell, *Reminiscences of Sixty Years in Public Affairs,* 2 vols (New York: Greenwood Press, 1968), vol. 1, p. 303.
82. Dewey, *Financial History of the United States,* p. 302.
83. *Report of the Secretary of the Treasury,* Thirty-seventh Congress, Second session, S. Ex. Doc 2, ser. set 1121, pp. 18–20.
84. *Report of the Secretary of the Treasury,* Thirty-seventh Congress, Second session, S. Ex. Doc 2, ser. set 1149, p. 15.
85. Hammond, *Sovereignty and an Empty Purse,* p. 289.
86. Ibid., p. 290.
87. Gische, 'Development of the National Banking System', p. 37.
88. Ibid., p. 37.
89. Flaherty, *The Perceived Power,* ch. 5.
90. Ransom, *Conflict and Compromise,* pp. 272–3.
91. Gische, 'Development of the National Banking System, 1860–1870', p. 65.
92. *Report of the Secretary of the Treasury,* Thirty-seventh Congress, Second session, S. Ex. Doc 2, ser. set 1121, pp. 18–20.

5 Sparing the Necessaries of Life

1. Brewer, *Sinews of Power,* p. 133; Dickson, *The Financial Revolution in England.* Both Brewer and Dickson observe that the English based their financial system on the earlier Dutch model, extending even deeper the historic roots of this mode of financing. However for the unique aspects of the resulting English finance system during this period, see D. R. Weir, 'Tontines, Public Finance, and the Revolution in France and England, 1688–1789', *Journal of Economic History,* 49 (March 1989), pp. 95–124.
2. Robin L. Eihnorn, *American Taxation, American Slavery,* pp. 21–2; Richardson, *The Greatest Nation of the Earth,* pp. 67–103.
3. Maxims refers to Adam Smith's four 'Maxims of Taxation'. A. Smith, *An Inquiry into the Nature and Causes of the Wealth of Nations* 5th edn (1776; New York: Modern Library, 1937), pp. 777–9.
4. Throughout this section, I employ the definition of regressive, progressive and proportional taxes suggested by Edgar K. and Jacquelene M. Browning: 'If the average tax rate is the same at all levels of the tax base, the tax is proportional; if the average tax rate rises with the tax base, the tax is progressive; if the average tax rate falls as the tax base increases, the tax is regressive.' Browning and Browning, *Public Finance and the Price System,* pp. 346–8. W. E. Brownlee, 'Reflections on the History of Taxation', in *Funding the Modern American State, 1941–1995* (New York: Cambridge University Press,

1996); Bensel, *Yankee Leviathan*, p. 237; J. Atack and P. Passell, *A New Economic View of American History*, 2nd edn (New York: W.W. Norton, 1994), p. 370; P. S. Paludan, '*A People's Contest': The Union and Civil War, 1861–1865* (New York: Harper, Row Pub., 1988), p. 121 emphasizes the primacy of excise taxes during the war.

5. R. A. Becker, *Revolution, Reform, and the Politics of American Taxation, 1763–1783* (Baton Rouge, LA: Louisiana State University Press, 1980), p. 6.

6. G. L. Harriss, *The King, Parliament, and Public Finance in Medieval England to 1369* (Oxford: Clarendon Press, 1975), p. 26.

7. S. A. Morgan, *History of Parliamentary Taxation in England* (New York: Moffat, Bard and Co., 1911), p. 36.

8. J. Sherman, *Recollections of Forty Years in the House, Senate, and Cabinet: An Autobiography*, 2 vols (Chicago: Werner Co., 1895), I: 155.

9. Paul S. Boyer, 'Borrowed Rhetoric: The Massachusetts Excise Controversy of 1754', *William and Mary Quarterly*, 3:21 (July 1964), p. 341.

10. D. M. Palliser, *The Age of Elizabeth: England Under the Later Tudors: 1547–1603*. (New York: Longman Group, 1983), p. 303.

11. O'Brien and Hunt, 'Rise of the Fiscal State in England 1485–1815', *Historical Research: The Bulletin of the Institute of Historical Research*, 66 (June 1993), pp. 129–76, p. 139.

12. Adams, 'Taxation in the United States', p. 53.

13. E. R. A. Seligman, *The Shifting and Incidence of Taxation* (New York: Columbia University Press, 1927), p. 87.

14. W. Kennedy, *English Taxation, 1640–1799: An Essay on Policy and Opinion* (London: G. Bell and Sons, Ltd., 1913), p. 38.

15. A. E. Bland, P. A. Brown and R. H. Tawney (eds) *English Economic History: Selected Documents* (London: G. Bell and Sons, Ltd., 1914), pp. 204–5.

16. Kennedy, *English Taxation*, p. 66.

17. S. Dowell, *A History of Taxation and Taxes in England, from Earliest Times to the Present Day*, 4 vols (London: Longman, Green and Co., 1884) vol. 3, p. 9; Kennedy, *English Taxation*, p. 54; J. V. Beckett, 'Land Tax or Excise: The Levying of Taxation in Seventeenth-and Eighteenth-Century England', *English Historical Review*, (April 1985), pp. 285–308, p. 305.

18. B. Coward, *The Stuart Age: England: 1603–1714* 2nd edn (New York: Longman Press, 1994), p. 211; C.D. Chandaman, *The English Public Revenue, 1660–1668*. (Oxford: Oxford University Press, 1975), p. 40.

19. E. Hughes, *Studies in Administration and Finance, 1558–1825* (Manchester: University of Manchester, 1934), p. 118.

20. Dowell, *History of Taxation*, vol. 2, p. 11; Chandaman, *The English Public Revenue* (Oxford: Oxford University Press, 1975), p. 40.

21. J. E. D. Binney, *British Public Finance and Administration* (Oxford: Clarendon Press, 1958), p. 34.

22. Kennedy, *English Taxation*, p. 83.

23. J. V. Beckett, 'Land or Excise', p. 305.

24. Lois F. Schwoerer, *The Declaration of Rights, 1689* (Baltimore, MD: Johns Hopkins Press, 1981), p. 291.

25. J. Locke, 'Of Civil Government', in *The Works of John Locke*, 10 vols (London, Thomas Tegg, 1823), vol. 5, pp. 422–3.

26. Smith, *Wealth of Nations*, p. 777.

27. Seligman provides a comprehensive summary of the acceptance of this idea. Seligman, *Shifting and Incidence of Taxation*, pp. 23–88.

28. Ibid., 111–12. I have paraphrased portions of this quote.
29. 'An Ordinance...for the Leavying of moneys, by way of Excise', 1643. Reprinted in Gale, *The Making of the Modern World*.
30. James Walvin, *Fruits of Empire: Exotic Produce and British Taste, 1660–1800* (New York: New York University Press, 1997), pp. ix, 193–9.
31. Smith, *Wealth of Nations*, pp. 821–2.
32. R. Cooper, 'William Pitt, Taxation, and the Needs of War', *Journal of British Studies*, 22 (Autumn 1982), pp. 94–103; R. A. Cooper, *British Government Finance 1793–1807: The Development of a Policy Based on War Taxes* (PhD thesis, University of North Carolina, Chapel Hill, 1976).
33. Smith, *Wealth of Nations*, p. 828.
34. A. Hamilton, 'Federalist 12', in *The Federalist*, p. 77.
35. *Letters of Delegates to Congress*, 2 (14 November 1775).
36. Flaherty, 'The Perceived Power: Government and Taxation during the Civil War' (PhD dissertation, Texas A&M University, 2005).
37. Howe, *Taxation and Taxes*, p. 37.
38. R. T. Ely, *Taxation in American States and Cities* (New York: Thomas Crowell, 1888), p. 11.
39. The arrival of easily searchable, digital collections has given scholars the ability to make bold assertions like this with actual data, rather than just hubris. In the US Congressional Serial Set Digital Collection, which includes the Congressional Serial Set, vols. 1–1543 and 1817–72, (infoweb.newsbank.com) one finds 656 'hits' on the search term 'necess* NEAR life'. In the Early American Newspaper series (1690–1879) one finds 'over 1,000' hits on a search of 'poor' and 'necessities'. In Making of America, University of Michigan (moa.umdl.umich.edu) the search 'neces* near poor' renders 1,130 references; a request for 'neces* near life' hits 5,457 citations. In Making of America, Cornell University (cdl. lbrary.cornell.edu/moa), searching for 'neces* near life' returns 2,957 citations and 487 for 'neces* near poor'. These searches are not foolproof, but certainly a strong indication of the ubiquity of the terms. I thank Joel Kitchens of the Sterling C. Evans Library at Texas A&M University for assistance in compiling this information.
40. A. Hamilton, *Papers on Public Credit, Credit, Commerce, and Finance*, ed. Samuel McKee (New York: Liberal Arts Press, 1957), pp. 37–8; A. Gallatin, 'Expenses of the War', in *Pamphlets in American History* (New York: John T. Towers, 1848), p. 12;
41. *Congressional Globe*, Twenty-ninth Congress, First session, 17 January 1846, p. 216.
42. 'Message from the President, 18 January 1833', Ser Set 230, Twenty-second Congress, Second session, Senate Doc. 30, 32.
43. 'Report from Sec. of the Treasury', Twenty-sixth Congress, Second session, Sen. Ex. Doc 93, ser. Set 377, p. 6.
44. J. L. Huston, *Securing the Fruits of Labor: The American Concept of Wealth Distribution, 1765–1900* (Baton Rouge, LA: Louisiana State University Press, 1998), p. 201.
45. J. Iceland, *Poverty in America: A Handbook* (Berkeley, CA: University of California Press, 2003); Michael B. Katz, *Poverty and Policy in American History* (New York: Academic Press, 1983).
46. 'Birkbeck's Letters from Illinois', *North American Review*, 8 (March 1819), pp. 351–2.
47. W. Kirkland, 'The West, The Paradise of the Poor', *The United States Democratic Review*, 15 (August 1844), pp. 189–90.
48. 'Report on the State of the Finances', Ninetheenth Congress, First sess., 22 December 1825, ser. Set 131, pp. 21–2.

49. 'Petition from Residents of Westmoreland, PA', Twenty-second Congress, Second session, House Doc. 144, 25 February 1833, Serial Set 235.

50. 'Reciprocal Trade', Thirty-second Congress, Second session, House Report 4, 11 February 1853, Ser. Set 687.

51. 'Bread and breadstuff' is listed as one of the exempt items in the Civil War revenue measures.

52. 'Recommendations on the Salt Duty', Senate Ex. Doc. 84, Fifteenth Congress, First session, ser. Set 2, 17 January 1818, p. 1.

53. Colin Brooks, 'Public Finance and Political Stability: The Administration of the Land Tax, 1688–1720', *The Historical Journal*, 2 (June 1974), pp. 283–4.

54. Beckett, 'Land Tax or Excise', p. 287.

55. Dickson, *The Financial Revolution in England*; H. V. Bowen, *War and British Society: 1688–1815* (Cambridge: Cambridge University Press, 1998), pp. 20–40.

56. Brewer provides the best examination of this transformation. Brewer, *The Sinews of Power*, pp. 22.

57. Beckett, 'Land or Excise', p. 307.

58. O'Brien, 'Political Economy of British Taxation', pp. 5–7.

59. Brewer, *Sinews of Power*, pp. 128–9.

60. *Congressional Globe*, Thirty-seventh Congress, First session, 29 July 1861, p. 315.

61. *Congressional Globe*, Thirty-seventh Congress, Second session, 12 March 1862, p. 1196.

62. *Congressional Globe*, Thirty-seventh Congress, Second session, 12 March 1862. The speech appears on p. 1194–7.

63. *Congressional Globe*, Thirty-seventh Congress, Second session, 8 April 1862, p. 1577.

64. *Report of the Commissioner of Internal Revenue*, 30 November 1863, p. 8.

65. Ibid., p. 11.

66. 'Report on Finances', House Ex. Doc 3, Thirty-eighth Congress, First sess., 10 December 1863, p. 67.

67. 'Report of the Secretary of the Treasury', House Ex. Doc 3, Thirty-eighth Congress, Second session, ser. Set 1222, p. 54.

68. 'Revenue System of the United States,' House Ex. Doc 34, Thirty-ninth Congress, First session, 29 January 1866, p. 39.

69. *Congressional Globe*, Thirty-seventh Cong., First sess., 29 July 1861, pp. 313–15.

70. Waltham, *Copying Other Nations Policies*, pp. 14–15.

71. Appendix to the *Congressional* – Laws of the United States, Thirty-seventh Congress, First session, 5 August 1861, p. 39; 'The Income Tax Act', 5&^, Vict. C. 35 with a practical and explanatory introduction and index, 2nd edn London, 1842 in, Gale *Making of the Modern World*.

72. *Congressional Globe*, Thirty-seventh Congress, Second session, see pp. 2283, 2368, 2370.

73. *Congressional Globe*, Thirty-seventh Congress, Second session, 27 May 1862, p. 2337; *Congressional Globe*, Forty-first Congress, 2nd session, Appendix, pp. 377–80. For Adam Smith's four maxims of taxation, Smith, *Wealth of Nations*, pp. 777–9.

74. K. Marx and F. Engels, *The Civil War in the United States*, ed. Richard Enmale, (New York: International Publishers, 1937), p. 253.

75. Chase to Cyrus W. Field, 17 February 1864, Niven (ed.) *Salmon P. Chase* Papers, vol. 4: pp. 293–5.

76. *Annual Report of the Secretary of the Treasury*, 1863, p. 13.

77. *Annual Report of the Commissioner of Internal Revenue*, 1863, p. 5.

78. *Congressional Globe*, Thirty-seventh Congress, Second session, 12 March 1862, p. 1194.
79. *Congressional Globe*, Thirty-seventh Congress, Second session, 20 March 1862, p. 1312.
80. *Congressional Globe*, Thirty-eighth Congress, First session, 21 April 1864, 1786.
81. Quoted in Smith, *United States Federal Tax History*, pp. 195–6.
82. Smith, *Taxation in the United States*, pp. 64–5; Seligman, *The Income Tax*, pp. 443–5.
83. *Annual Report of the Secretary of the Treasury*, 1864, p. 15.
84. *Congressional Globe*, Thirty-seventh Congress, Second session, 23 May 1862, p. 2310.
85. Curry, *Blueprint for Modern America*, p. 180.
86. Thaddeus Stevens, *Congressional Globe*, Thirty-seventh Congress, Second session, 8 April 1862, p. 1577.
87. *Congressional Globe*, Thirty-eighth Congress, Second session, 17 February 1865, p. 878.
88. *Congressional Goble*, Thirty-eighth Congress, Second session, 14 January 1864, p. 218.
89. D. N. McCloskey, 'The Incidence in Taxation in England and France: A Reply to Mathias and O'Brien', *Journal of European Economic History*, 7 (Spring 1978), p. 210.
90. Palludan, *A People's Contest*, p. 118.
91. N. G. Mankiw, *Principles of Microeconomics* (New York: Dryden Press, 1997), pp. 12–27.
92. Senator King, *Congressional Globe*, Thirty-seventh Congress, Second session, 27 May 1862, p. 2375.
93. *Congressional Globe*, Thirty-ninth Congress, First sess., 7 May 1865, p. 2438.
94. *Report of the Commissioner for Internal Revenue*, 1863, Thirty-eighth Congress, First session, House Ex. Doc. 3, Serial Set 1186, p. 1.
95. *Congressional Globe*, Thirty-eighth Congress, Second session, 11 February 1865, p. 757.
96. *Internal Revenue Recorder* (16 February 1867), p. 50.
97. *Report of the Assessors and Collectors Convention*, p. 14.
98. Smith, *United States Federal Tax History*, pp. 54–55.
99. Webber and Wildavsky, *A History of Taxation and Expenditure in the Western World* (New York: Simon and Schuster, 1986), p. 273.
100. H. E. Smith, *The United States Federal Internal Tax History from 1861–1871* (Boston, MA: Houghton Mifflin, Co., 1914), Table 29.
101. This tax represents the 3, then 5, per cent duty levied on all manufactured products, plus the specific duties on selected manufactures (iron, if example).
102. 'Articles and Occupations' covers a broad set of specific taxes including: receipts from infrastructure (bridges, canals, express companies, railroads); sales taxes (apothecaries, auctions, brokers, confectioners); licences (dealers, including liquor retailers, manufacturers (who had to purchase a license as well as the duties noted in footnote 7), brokers, butchers, peddlers, and plumbers; *ad valorem* tax on items from 'Schedule A', the list of luxury goods (gold watches, yachts, billiard tables); legacies; finally, entertainment (theater, museums, circuses).
103. 'Message from the President', January 18, 1833', Twenty-second Congress, Second session, Senate Doc 30, Serial Set 230, p. 32. See also J. Flaherty, 'The English Origins of American Civil War Taxation' (unpublished manuscript, 2004).
104. The Beards have been most closely identified with this interpretation. Beard and Beard, *The Rise of American Civilization*, vol. 2 in particular. Also, Sidney Ratner follows a Beardian argument in this study of tariffs. S. Ratner, *The Tariff in American History* (New York: D. Van Nostrand Co., 1972).
105. E. Stanwood, *American Tariff Controversies in the Nineteenth Century*, 2 vols (Boston: Houghton Mifflin and Co., 1903), vol. 1, p. 62.

106. F. W. Taussig, *The Tariff History of the United States: A Series of Essays* (New York: G. P. Putnam's Sons, 1888).

107. Articulated best in W. W. Freehling, *Prelude to Civil War: The Nullification Controversy in South Carolina, 1816–1836* (New York: Oxford University Press, 1966).

108. J. R. Commons, 'Tariff Revision and Protection for American Labor', *Annals of the American Academy of Political and Social Science*, 32 (September 1908), pp. 51–6; J. L. Huston, 'A Political Response to Industrialism: the Republican Embrace of Protectionist Labor Doctrines', *Journal of American History*, 70 (June 1983), pp. 35–57.

109. J. J. Pincus, *Pressure Groups and Politics in Antebellum Tariffs* (New York: Columbia University Press, 1977).

110. I. M. Tarbell, *The Tariff in Our Times* (New York: Macmillan Co., 1912), 11; R. H. Luthin, 'Abraham Lincoln and the Tariff', *American Historical Review* 35 (July, 1944), 627; Heather Cox Richardson, *The Greatest Nation of the Earth: Republican Economic Policies During the Civil War* (Cambridge: Harvard University Press, 1997), 105.

111. Stanwood, *American Tariff Controversies*: II, 129-130.

112. See for example S. Ratner, *American Taxation: Its History as a Social Force in Democracy* (New York: W.W. Norton, 1942), p. 63; R. F. Sharkey, *Money, Class, and Party: An Economic Study of Civil War and Reconstruction* (Baltimore, MD: Johns Hopkins University Press, 1959), p. 14; Patterson, 'Government Finance on the Eve of the Civil War', p. 36; Brownlee, 'Reflections on the History of Taxation', in *Funding the American State*.

113. *Congressional Globe*, Thirty-seventh Congress, Second session, 8 April 1862, p. 1225.

114. Flaherty, 'The Perceived Power', pp. 226–73.

115. *Rates of Duties on Imports into the United States*, Fifty-first Congress, Second session, S. Misc. Report 2130, ser. set 2827, p. 506. In the historical literature, an interesting array of figures appears for average tariff rates. This report, the only 'official' comprehensive study of nineteenth-century tariffs, provides a standard method of calculating tariff rates from 1802 to 1889. The figure above gives the average *ad valorem* rate for free and dutiable goods. Most figures reported rely only on the average for dutiable goods. By incorporating both figures, the average rate is lower, but I believe, more accurately affects the 'tax burden' assumed by the population.

116. *Congressional Globe,* Thirty-eighth Congress, Second session, 17 February 1865, p. 878.

117. Ibid., p. 506. These figures do not include goods imported than re-exported to other countries.

118. *Report of the Commissioner of Internal Revenue*, 30 November 1863, p. 8.

119. *Digest of Statutes of the United States Prescribing the Rates of Duties,* Thirty-ninth Congress, Second session, Senate Misc. Doc 8, 12.

120. *Ad valorem* duties 'according to value' levied a fixed percentage (40 per cent on shelled almonds, for example) upon an imported good. When the value of the merchandise changes, so does the actual import. Conversely, a specific duty affixes a set amount collected on the imported good (.04 per pound on shelled almonds, for instance.) The amount collected does not fluctuate

121. Flaherty, 'Incidental Protection', pp. 103–18.

122. Douglas A. Irwin argued recently that this was a deliberate action of the Republicans to invoke a form of protectionism. See, D. A. Irwin, 'Changes in US Tariffs: The Role of Import Prices and Commercial Policies', *American Economic Review* 88 (September 1998), pp. 1015–26.

123. Act of 14 July 1862, *Statutes at Large* 12, p. 549.

124. *Digest of Statutes*, p. 37.

125. Flaherty, 'Incidental Protection', pp. 115–17.
126. Hofstadter, 'The Tariff Issue on the Eve of the Civil War', pp. 50–5. Also, note the number of agricultural products listed on the spreadsheet showing the movement of goods from the free to the dutiable list.
127. *Congressional Globe*, 37ᵗʰ Cong., 2ⁿᵈ sess., May 23, 1862, p. 2310.
128. P. G. Porter and Harold C. Livesay, *Merchants and Manufacturers: Studies in the Changing Structure of Nineteenth-Century Marketing* (Chicago, IL: Ivan R. Dee, Inc., 1989), p. 8.
129. L. E. Atherton, 'The Services of the Frontier Merchant', *Mississippi Valley Historical Review*, 24 (September 1937), p. 160
130. Porter and Livesay, *Merchants and Manufacturers*, p. 126.
131. *Congressional Globe*, Thirty-seventh Congress, Second session, 27 March 1862, p. 1404.
132. Arthur M. Lee, *The Development of an Economic Policy in the Early Republican Party* (PhD thesis, Syracuse University, 1953. One of Lee's main theses).
133. O. van Mering, *The Shifting and Incidence of Taxation* (Philadelphia, PA: Blakiston Co, 1942), pp. 173–8.
134. Smith, *United States Federal Internal Tax History*, pp. 257–8.
135. *Congressional Globe*, Thirty-seventh Congress, Second session (27 March 1862), p. 1403.
136. Ibid., p. 1404.
137. Ibid., p. 1404–6.
138. *Finance Report for 1864*, Thirty-eighth Congress, Second session, House Ex. Doc. 3, ser. set 1222, 6 Dec. 1864, p. 60–1.
139. *Congressional Globe*, Thirty-eighth Congress, Second session, 17 February 1865, p. 874.
140. Ibid., p. 874.
141. Ibid., p. 875.
142. J. H. Silbey, *A Respectable Minority: The Democratic Party in the Civil War Era, 1860–1868* (New York: W. W. Norton, Co, 1977), p. 100.
143. *Congressional Globe*, Thirty-eighth Congress, Second session, p. 875.
144. Ibid., p. 876.
145. Ibid., p. 873.
146. Ibid., 17 February 1865, p. 877.
147. Ibid., p. 875.
148. *Congressional Globe*, Thirty-eighth Congress, Second session, 17 February 1865, p. 878.
149. Ibid., p. 1457.
150. Richardson, *Greatest Nation of the Earth*, p. 137.
151. Hacker, *The Triumph of American Capitalism*, p. 340.
152. Bensel, *Yankee Leviathan*, p. 169.
153. *Congressional Globe*, Thirty-eighth Congress, Second session, 17 February 1865, p. 878.
154. Niven (ed.), *Salmon P. Chase Papers*, vol. 4, p.154.
155. Chase to Horace Greeley, 6 April 1864, Niven (ed.), *Salmon P. Chase Papers*, vol. 4, pp. 366–7. See also, Chase to Thaddeus Stevens, 12 April 1864; Chase to William Pitt Fessenden, 12 April 1864; Chase to Joseph Medill, 30 January 1864, Chase to John Hamilton 13 May 1864.
156. Events related in Flaherty, 'The Revenue Imperative'; D. K. Goodwin, *Team of Rivals: The Political Genius of Abraham Lincoln* (New York: Simon and Schuster Paperback, 2005), pp. 631–9.

157. *Revenue System of the United States*, Thirty-ninth Congress, First session, House Ex. Doc., 34, 29 January 1866, p. 2.

158. Seligman, *The Income Tax*, p. 130.

159. *Congressional Globe*, Thirty-seventh Congress, First session, 25 July 1861, p. 272.

6 The Most Burdened of Them All

1. These events are best related in J. Winik, *April 1865: The Month That Saved America* (New York: Harper Perennial, 2001), p. 322.

2. This refers to the open letter President Lincoln sent Horace Greeley on 22 August 1862 in which he stated his commitment to save the Union, with or without emancipating the slaves. A. Lincoln, *The Collected Works of Abraham Lincoln*, ed. R. B. Basler (New Brunswick, NJ: Rutgers University Press, 1953–7), vol. 5, pp. 388–9.

3. Foner, *Reconstruction*, p. 6.

4. *New York Tribune*, (26 December 1861), p. 4.

5. *Chicago Tribune*, 7 March 1862, p. 1.

6. Thaddeus Stevens Papers, *Library of Congress*, 8 February 8 1862; see also Milo A. Holcomb to Thaddeus Stevens, 28 January 1864.

7. *Report of the Commissioner of Internal Revenue*, in Annual Report of the Secretary of the Treasury, Thirty-eighth Congress, First session, 6 December, 1863, Ser. Set 1186, p. 1.

8. Chase to John C. Fremont, 16 August 1861, *Salmon P. Chase Papers*, Niven (ed.), vol. 3, pp. 85–6.

9. *Diary of Gideon Welles*, vol. 2, p. 16.

10. *Congressional Globe*, Thirty-seventh Congress, Second session, 24 May 1862, 2330.

11. J. M. Gallman, *The North Fights the Civil War: The Homefront* (Chicago: Ivan R. Dee, 1994), p. 149.

12. Sherman, *Recollections*, vol. 1, pp. 329–30.

13. Chase in A. B. Hart, *Salmon Portland Chase* (Boston: Houghton Mifflin, 1899), p. 237.

14. Mitchell, *History of the Greenbacks*, p. 179.

15. M. Friedman, 'Price, Income, and Monetary Changes in Three Wartime Periods', *American Economic Review*, 42 (May 1952), pp. 613–25.

16. H. A. Ferleger, *David A. Wells and the Revenue System, 1865–1870* (Ann Arbor, MI: Edward Borthers, 1942), p. 44.

17. *Congressional Globe*, Thirty-ninth Congress First session, 7 May 1866, p. 2438.

18. W. H. Barnes, *History of the Thirty-Ninth Congress of the United States*. Reprint. (1868; New York: Negro Universities Press, 1969), p. 20.

19. Foner, *Reconstruction*, 176–238.

20. R. Cook, 'The Grave of all My Comforts: William Pitt Fessenden as Secretary of the Treasury, 1864–1865', *Civil War History*, 61 (Fall 1983), pp. 208–26.

21. Larson, *Jay Cooke*, pp. 165–75.

22. McCulloch, *Men and Measures*.

23. Mitchell, *History of the Greenbacks,* p. 202.

24. Chronicled fully in Sharkey, *Money, Class, and Party*; Irwin Unger, *The Greenback Era* (Princeton, NJ: Princeton University Press, 1964).

25. C. K. Yearly, *The Money Machines: The Breakdown and Reform of Governmental and Party Finance in the North, 1860–1920* (Albany, NY: State University of New York Press, 1970), p. 13.

26. *Commercial and Financial Chronicle*, 13, quoted in R. T. Patterson, *Federal Debt Management Policies, 1865–1879* (Durham, NC: Duke University Press, 1954), p. 117.

27. McCulloch, *Men and Measures*, p. 202

28. *Report of the Secretary of the Treasury*, 5 December 5 1865, Thirty-ninth Congress, First session, House Ex. Doc. 3, ser set 1254, p. 16.

29. Patterson, *Federal Debt Management*, 118 (both quotes).

30. *Congressional Globe*, Thirty-ninth Congress, First session, 7 May 1866, p. 2436.

31. Patterson, *Federal Debt Management Policies, 1865-1879* (Durham, NC: Duke University Press, 1954), p. 123.

32. Ferguson, *Cash Nexus*; J. Macdonald, A Free Nation Deep in Debt: The Financial Roots of Democracy (New York: Farrar, Straus and Giroux, 2003), pp. 6–7

33. R. E. Wright, 'Born in Debt: America's First National Debt and Its Lessons for Today' (pre-print draft, 2007), 229–30. I thank the author sharing the final, pre-publication draft with me.

34. F. Wheen, *Karl Marx: A Life* (New York: W.W. Norton, 1999), p. 268.

35. Macdonald, *Free Nation*, pp. 398–9; M. Lawson, *Patriotic Fires: Forging a New American Nationalism in the Civil War North* (Lawrence, KS: University Press of Kansas, 2002).

36. Jon Sturges to John Sherman, 29 December 1866, in Sharkey, *Money, Class and Party*, pp. 172–3.

37. Foner, *Reconstruction*, p. 233; *Congressional Globe*, Thirty-eighth Congress, Second session, 11 February 1865, p. 761.

38. R. Kanigel, *The One Best Way: Frederick Winslow Taylor and the Enigma of Efficiency* (New York: Viking Press, 1997).

39. H. R. Ferleger, *David A. Wells and the American Revenue System, 1865–1870* (Philadelphia, PA: Porcupine Press, 1977), p. 19.

40. F. B. Joyner, *David Ames Wells: Champion of Free Trade* (Cedar Rapids, IA: Torch Press, 1939), p. 3.

41. Ferleger, *David A. Wells*, pp. 1–8.

42. Information culled from Joyner and Ferleger.

43. Sherman, *Recollections*, vol. 1, pp. 334–6.

44. D. A. Wells, 'Our Burden and Our Strength', in F. Freidel, (ed.) *Union Pamphlets of the Civil War, 1861–1865*, 2 vols (Cambridge, MA: Harvard University Press, 1967), vol. 2, pp. 940–75.

45. Ibid., p. 974.

46. Ibid., p. 943.

47. Ferleger, *David A. Wells*, 12–13.

48. Wells recounted these events in D. A. Wells, *The Theory and Practice of Taxation*, ed. W. C. Ford (New York: D. Appleton Co., 1900), pp. 19–20. Although this account suggests that Wells first thought of the commission, the idea of soliciting help to 'legislate wisely on the subject of taxation', had been raised in Congress before the Lincoln–Wells meeting.

49. Ferleger, *David A. Wells*, pp. 19.

50. Ferleger, *David A. Wells*, pp. 25–6.

51. *Harper's Weekly*, 12 August 1865, p. 499.

52. *Revenue System of the United States*, Thirty-ninth Congress, First session, House Ex. Doc 34, January 29, 1866, p. 13. Hence, *Revenue Commission Report*.

53. Ibid., p. 17.

54. Ibid., p. 24.

55. Ibid., p. 27.
56. Ibid., pp. 16–18.
57. Ibid., pp. 36–7.
58. Ibid., p. 12.
59. Ibid., p. 51.
60. Ferleger, *David A. Wells*, p. 135.
61. T. E. Terrill, 'David A. Wells, the Democracy, and Tariff Reduction, 1877–1894', *Journal of American History*, 56 (December, 1969), p. 546.
62. D. M. Tucker, *Mugwumps: Public Moralists of the Gilded Age* (Columbia, MO: University of Missouri Press, 1998), p. 14. For a more comprehensive, but less sympathetic examination of these politicos, G. W. McFarland, *Mugwumps, Morals, and Politics, 1884–1920* (Amherst, MA: University of Massachusetts Press, 1975).
63. Joyner, *David Ames Wells*, p. 44.
64. *Congressional Globe,* Thirty-eighth Congress, First session, 14 January 1864, p. 216.
65. *Congressional Globe*, Thirty-ninth Congress, First session, 7 May 1866, p. 2436.
66. Ibid., p. 32.
67. Ibid., p. 2439.
68. *Congressional Globe*, Thirty-ninth Congress, First session, 21 May 1866, p. 2729.
69. Sherman, *Recollections*, vol. 1, pp. 305–6.
70. Smith, *United States Federal Internal Tax History* (Boston, MA: Houghton, Mifflin Co., 1914), p. 226; *U.S. Statutes at Large*, p. 465.
71. *Congressional Globe*, Thirty-seventh Congress, Second session, 27 March 1862, p. 1412.
72. Ibid., pp. 2478–9.
73. Senator Cowan, *Congressional Globe*, Thirty-seventh Congress, Second session, 23 May 1862, p. 2320.
74. Ibid., 8 May 1866, pp. 2473–7,
75. *Congressional Globe*, Thirty-ninth Congress, First session, 8 May 1866, p. 2473.
76. *Congressional Globe*, Thirty-ninth Congress, First session, 21 May 1866, p. 2728.
77. *Internal Revenue Recorder*, 30 December 1865, p. 208.
78. It was classified under this section of the revenue laws. Smith, *Internal Tax History*, 226–42 gives a good overview of the tax's progress.
79. Wells, *Special Report of the Commissioner of Internal Revenue*, Ex. Doc 34, Thirty-ninth Congress, First session, 1865–6, 40–4; H. C. Richardson, 'A Marshall Plan for the South? The Failure of Republican and Democratic Ideology during Reconstruction', *Civil War History*, 51 (December 2005), pp. 378–87.
80. Taussig, *Tariff History*, p. 177; also, Ferleger, *David A. Wells*, pp. 143–82.
81. Patterson, *Federal Debt Management*, p. 114.
82. Taussig, *Tariff History*, pp. 171–90; Stanwood, *American Tariff Controversies*, pp. 173–4.
83. Sharkey, *Money, Class, and Party*, p. 151.
84. O'Brien, 'Political Economy of British Taxation, 1660–1815', *Economic History Review*, 2:41 (February 1988), pp. 1–32, p. 12.
85. Patterson, *Federal Debt Management*, p. 127.
86. McCulloch, *Men and Measures*, p. 473.
87. Taussig, *Tariff History*, p. 174.
88. T. Skocpol, *Protecting Soldiers and Mothers: The Political Origins of Social Policy in the United States* (Cambridge, MA: Harvard University Press, 1992), pp. xx, 525.
89. Dewey, *Financial History of the United States*, p. 428.

90. C. Dunbar, 'The Direct Tax of 1861', p. 447.
91. Ibid., p. 448.
92. Smith, *Tax History*, p. 20.
93. Quoted in 'Liability of the States for the Direct Tax,' Forty-sixth Congress, First session, Senate Ex. Doc. 24, May 24, 1879, Ser. Set 1869, p. 41.
94. Ibid., p. 14.
95. J. G. Randall, *Constitutional Problems Under Lincoln* (Gloucester, MA: Peter Smith, Publisher, 1963), pp. 317–19.
96. Curry, *Blueprint for Modern America: Nonmilitary Legislation of the First Civil War*, pp. 96–7.
97. 'Liability of the States for the Direct Tax', pp. 1–9.
98. *Internal Revenue Recorder*, 16 December 1865, p. 191.
99. Smith, *Tax History*, 42–3; 'Liability of the States for the Direct Tax', pp. 13–14.
100. *Revenue Commission Report*, 1866, p. 27.
101. 13 *United States Statutes at Large*, 30 June 1864, pp. 480–2.
102. *Congressional Globe*, Thirty-eighth Congress, First session, 2 July 1864, p. 3528; Howe, *Taxation and Taxes*, p. 93.
103. R. Stanley, *Dimensions of Law in the Service of Order: Origins of the Federal Income Tax, 1861–1913* (New York: Oxford University Press, 1993), pp. 40–1.
104. *Report of the Secretary of the Treasury*, Thirty-eighth Congress, Second session, House Ex. Doc., 3, 6 December1864, p. 15.
105. Quoted in, Barnes, p. 555.
106. C. B. Swisher, *American Constitutional Development* (Boston, MA: Houghton Mifflin, Co., 1943), p. 437.
107. *Congressional Globe*, Thirty-ninth Congress, First session, 25 April1866, p. 2437.
108. *Congressional Globe*, Thirty-ninth Congress, First session, 7 May 1866, p. 2437.
109. *1866 Report of the Special Commission*, p. 27.
110. For these debates, see *Congressional Globe*, Forty-first Congress, Second session, pp. 3993–5, 4023.
111. *Congressional Globe*, Forty-first Congress, Second session, 1870 quoted in Seligman, *Income Tax*, p. 458.
112. *Congressional Globe*, Forty-first Congress, Second session, 23 May 1870, p. 4715. Sherman's speeches on the income tax are also reprinted in Sherman, *Selected Speeches*. Also, Appendix, pp. 707–14.
113. Stanley, *Dimensions of Law*, p. 21.
114. *Report of the Commissioner of Internal Revenue*, Forty-first Congress, Second session, House Ex. Doc. 4, 6 December 1869, p. 14. Later in his career, Wells would denounce the income tax.
115. *Report of the Special Commissioner of Revenue*, Forty-first Congress, Second session, House Ex. Doc 27, 20 December 1869, pp. 68–70.
116. D. A. Wells, 'An Income Tax: Is It Desirable?', *The Forum* (March 1894), pp. 12–13.
117. Seligman, *Income Tax*, p. 467. The vote in the House was 105 to 104, while the vote in the Senate was 26 to 25.
118. A. Nevins, *Hamilton Fish: The Inner History of the Grant Administration*, 2 vols (New York: Frederick Ungar Publishing Co., 1957), vol. 2, pp. 600, 606.
119. T. L. Seip, *The South Returns to Congress: Men, Economic Measures, and Intersectional Relationships, 1868–1879* (Baton Rouge, LA: Louisiana State University Press, 1983), pp. 158–59.

120. Seligman, *The Income Tax,* p. 468.

121. McCulloch, *Men and Measures of Half a Century: Sketches and Comments* (New York: Charles Scribner's Sons, 1888), pp. 462–3.

122. Nevins, *Hamilton Fish,* vol. 1, p. ix.

123. F. A. Walker in *Lippincott's Monthly Magazine,* September 1869 quoted in Patterson, *Federal Debt Management,* p. 56.

Conclusion

1. James Bryce, *The American Commonwealth,* 2 vols (New York: Macmillan Co., 1904), vol. 1, p. 316.

2. *Edwards* v. *California,* 314 US 160 (1941).

3. Skocpol, *Protecting,* p. 151. Emphasis in original.

4. Blaine, *Twenty Years of,* vol. 2, p. 674.

5. Sherman, *Recollections,* vol. 1, p. 490.

6. M. S. Thompson, *The Spider Web: Congress and Lobbying in the Age of Grant* (Ithaca, NY: Cornell University Press, 1985), 42.

7. M. W. Summers, *The Era of Good Stealings* (New York: Oxford University Press, 1993), p. 108.

8. Bowers, 'From Logrolling to Corruption', pp. 439–74.

9. *Annual Report of the Secretary of the Treasury,* 1886, p. 242.

10. Boutwell, *Reminiscences,* vol. 1, p. 313.

11. D. J. Brewer, *The Income Tax Cases: An Address at the University of Iowa* (Iowa City, IA: University of Iowa Press, 1898), pp. 19–20.

12. Sherman, *Recollections,* vol. 1, p. 309.

13. W. K. Miller, 'The Revenue: Federal Enforcement in the Mountain South, 1870–1900', *Journal of Southern History,* 55 (May 1989), pp. 195–216, p. 213.

14. *Congressional Globe,* Thirty-eighth Congress, First session, 14 January 1864, pp. 216–18.

15. *Congressional Globe,* Thirty-seventh Congress, Second session, 14 March 1862, p. 1346.

16. Blaine, *Twenty Years,* vol. 2, pp. 675–6.

17. Thompson, *Spider Web,* p. 19.

18. Thompson, *Spider Web,* p. 73.

19. H. M. Hyman, *A More Perfect Union: The Impact of the Civil War and Reconstruction on the Constitution* (New York: Knopf, 1973), 382.

20. Hurst, *Law and the Conditions of Freedom in Nineteenth Century United States* (Madison, WI: University of Wisconsin Press, 1967), p. 79.

21. Elazar, *American Partnership,* p. 105.

22. *Congressional Globe,* Thirty-seventh Congress, Second session, 12 March 1862, p. 1194. This quote is often taken out of context by citing only Morrill's statement that the government has the right to demand the property of the people.

WORKS CITED

Primary Sources

Edited Collections of Documents

Belz, H. (ed.), *The Webster-Hayne Debate on the Nature of the Union: Selected Documents* (Indianapolis, IN: Liberty Fund, 2000).

Benton, W. E. (ed.), *1787: Drafting the Constitution*. 2 vols (College Station, TX: Texas A&M University Press, 1986).

Bland, A. E., P. A. Brown and R. H. Tawney (eds) *English Economic History: Selected Documents* (London: G. Bell and Sons, 1914).

Elliot, J. (ed.), *Debates on the Adoption of the Federal Constitution*, 5 vols (1888; Salem, NH: Ayer Publishers, 1987).

Gunter, G. (ed.), *John Marshall's Defense of McCulloch v. Maryland* (Stanford, CA: Stanford University Press, 1966).

Jensen, M. (ed.) *Documentary History of the Ratification of the Constitution* 20 vols (Madison, WI: University of Wisconsin Press, 1976).

Lincoln, A., *The Collected Works of Abraham Lincoln*, ed. R. B. Basler (New Brunswick, NJ: Rutgers University Press, 1953–7).

Madison, J., *Notes of the Debates on the Federal Convention of 1787*, ed. A. Koch (Athens, OH: Ohio University Press, 1960).

Porter, K. H., and Johnson, D. B. (eds), *National Party Platforms, 1840–1956* (Urbana, IL: University of Illinois Press, 1956).

Sherman, J., *Selected Speeches of John Sherman* (New York: D. Appleton and Co., 1879).

Edited Collections of Papers and Pamphlets

Brewer, D. J., *The Income Tax Cases: An Address at the University of Iowa* (Iowa City, IA: University of Iowa Press, 1898).

Crall, R. K. (ed.) *Works of John C. Calhoun*, 6 vols (New York: D. Appleton, 1860).

Gallatin, Albert, 'Expenses of the War' in *Pamphlets in American History* (New York: John T. Towers, 1848).

Hamilton, A., *Papers on Public Credit, Commerce, and Finance*, ed. Samuel McKee (New York: Liberal Arts Press, 1957).

—, *Writings*, ed. J. B. Freeman (New York: Penguin Books, 2001).

—, Madison, James, Jay, John. *The Federalist*, ed. P. L. Ford (New York: Henry Holt, Co., 1898).

Hunt, G. (ed.), *The Writings of James Madison*, 9 vols (New York: G. P. Putnam Sons, 1901).

Locke, J., *The Works of John Locke*, 10 vols (London: Thomas Tegg, 1823).

Moore, J. B., (ed.) *The Works of James Buchanan*, 12 vols (New York: Antiquarian Press, 1960).

Niven, J., (ed.) *Salmon P. Chase Papers*. 5 vols (Kent, OH: Kent State University Press, 1994).

Richardson, James D. (ed.), *A Compilation of the Messages and Papers of the Presidents*, 11 vols (New York: Bureau of National Literature and Art, 1925).

Syrett, H. C. (ed.), *The Papers of Alexander Hamilton*, 18 vols (New York: Columbia University Press, 1972).

Wells, D. A., 'Our Burden and Our Strength', in Frank Freidel (ed.), *Union Pamphlets of the Civil War, 1861–1865*, 2 vols (Cambridge, MA: Harvard University Press, 1967).

Reminiscences, Diaries, and Autobiographies

Benton, T. H., *Thirty Years, or the History of the Working of the American Government for Thirty Years, from 1820–1850* (New York: D. Appleton and Co., 1856).

Blaine, J. G., *Twenty Years of Congress from Lincoln to Garfield*, 2 vols (Norwich, CT: Henry Bill Publishing Co., 1884).

Boutwell, G. S. *Reminiscences of Sixty Years in Public Affairs*, 2 vols (1902; New York: Greenwood Press, 1968).

Chittenden, L. E., *Personal Reminiscences, 1840–1890* (New York: Richmond, Croscup and Co., 1893).

Dix, M. (ed.), *Memoirs of John A. Dix*, 2 vols (New York: Harper Brothers, 1883).

Donald, D. (ed.), *Inside Lincoln's Cabinet: The Civil War Diaries of Salmon P. Chase*. (New York: Longman's Green and Co., 1954).

McCulloch, H., *Men and Measures of Half a Century: Sketches and Comments* (New York: Charles Scribner's Sons, 1888).

Sherman, J., *Recollections of Forty Years in the House, Senate, and Cabinet: An Autobiography*, 2 vols (Chicago, IL: Werner, Co., 1895).

de Tocqueville, A., *Democracy in America*, 2 vols (New York: Vintage Books, 1954).

Welles, G., *Diary of Gideon Welles*, 3 vols (Boston: Houghton Mifflin, Co., 1911).

Manuscript Collections

Brunswick, ME. Bowdoin College Library. Special Collections. William Pitt Fessenden Papers, Fessenden Family Papers.

Ithaca, NY. Cornell University Libraries. Justin S. Morrill Papers, #1146. Division of Rare and Manuscript Collections.

Philadelphia, PA. Historical Society of Pennsylvania. Henry C. Carey Papers, Edwin Carey Gardiner Papers.

Washington, DC Library of Congress. Papers of Salmon P. Chase. Manuscript Reading Room.

Washington, DC Library of Congress. Papers of Abraham Lincoln. Manuscript Reading Room.

Washington, DC Library of Congress. Papers of Justin S. Morrill. Manuscript Reading Room.

Washington, DC Library of Congress. Papers of Thaddeus Stevens. Manuscript Reading Room.

Government Documents

Bayley, R., *Report on Public Indebtedness*. 10th Census (Washington, DC: GPO, 1884), vol. 7.

Cochran, T. C. (ed.), *The New American State Papers. Finance*, 32 vols (Wilmington, DE: Scholarly Resources, Inc., 1973).

Dix, J. A., 'Condition of the Treasury', *Congressional Globe*, Thirty-sixth Congress, Second session H. Doc., 20, Serial Set 1103.

—, John A. 'Condition of the Banks', *Congressional Globe*, Thirty-Sixth Congress, Second session, H. ExDoc. 77, serial set 1101.

US Congress. House. *Annual Report of the Secretary of the Treasury, 1857*. Report prepared by Howell Cobb. Thirty-fifth Congress, Second session, H. ExDoc. 4, serial set 996.

Annual Report of the Secretary of Treasury, 1860. Report prepared by Howell Cobb. Thirty-sixth Congress, Second session, H. ExDoc. 2, serial set 996.

—, *Annual Report of the Secretary of Treasury, 1863*. Report prepared by Salmon P. Chase, Thirty-eighth Congress, First session, H. ExDoc. 3, serial set 1186.

—, *Annual Report of the Secretary of Treasury, 1864*. Report prepared by W. P. Fessenden, Thirty-eighth Congress, Second session, H. ExDoc. 3, Serial Set 1222.

—, *Annual Report of the Secretary of Treasury, 1865*. Report prepared by Hugh McCulloch. Thirty-ninth Congress, First session, H. ExDoc. 3, Serial Set 1254.

—, *Annual Report of the Secretary of Treasury, 1866*. Report prepared by Hugh McCulloch. Thirty-ninth Congress, Second session, H. ExDoc. 12, Serial Set 1288.

—, 'Collection of Duties in the Seceding States', Report prepared by John A. Dix. 36th Cong., 2nd sess., H. ExDoc. 4, Serial Set 1100.

—, *Commerce and Navigation Report, 1857.* Report prepared by the Department of Treasury, Thirty-fifth Congress, First session, H. ExDoc. 145, Serial Set 960.

—, *Commerce and Navigation Report, 1858.* Report prepared by the Department of Treasury. Thirty-fifth Congress, Second session, H. ExDoc. 120. Serial Set 1015.

—, *Revenue System of the United States.* Report prepared by David A. Wells, Thirty-ninth Congress, First session, H. ExDoc 34, Serial Set 1255.

US Congress. Senate. *Annual Report of the Secretary of Treasury, 1861.* Report prepared by Salmon P. Chase, Thirty-seventh Congress, Second session, S. ExDoc. 2, Serial Set 1121.

—, *Annual Report of the Secretary of Treasury, 1862.* Report prepared by Salmon P. Chase, Thirty-seventh Congress, third session, S. ExDoc. 1, Serial Set 1149.

—, *Report on the Constitutional Treasury System.* Report prepared by William M. Gouge, thirty-fourth Congress, 1st session, S. ExDoc. 2, Serial Set 814.

—, *Report of the Secretary of the Treasury to the Special Session of Congress, 1861.* Report prepared by Salmon P. Chase. Thirty-seventh Congress, First session, S. ExDoc. 2, 4 July 1861.

US Department of Commerce, Bureau of the Census, *Statistics of the United States in 1860, compiled from the Eighth Census* (Washington, DC: GPO, 1866).

Newspapers and Magazines

Chicago Tribune

Congressional Globe

Debow's Review

Economist (London)

Harper's Weekly

Merchant's Magazine and Commercial Review (Hunt's Merchant Magazine)

Internal Revenue Recorder

Times (London)

New York Times

New York Herald Tribune

North American Review

United States Democratic Review

Secondary Sources

Books

Adams, D. R., Jr, *Finance and Enterprise in Early America: A Study of Stephen Girard's Bank, 1812-1831* (Philadelphia, PA: University of Pennsylvania Press, 1978).

Adams, Henry. *History of the United States During the Administration of Thomas Jefferson*, 2 vols (New York: Albert and Charles Boni Publishers, 1930).

—, *The Life of Albert Gallatin* (1879; New York: Peter Smith, 1943).

—, *The Great Secession Winter and Other Essays*, ed. George Hatfield (New York: Sagamore Press, 1958).

Albion, R. G., *The Rise of New York Port* (New York: Charles Scribner's Sons, 1939).

Andreano, R. (ed.), *The Economic Impact of the American Civil War* (Cambridge, MA: Schenkmen Publishing Co., 1962).

Ashworth, J., *Agrarians and Aristocrats: Party Political Ideology in the United States, 1837–1846* (New Jersey: Humanities Press, 1983).

Atack, J., and P. Passell, *A New Economic View of American History*, 2nd edn (New York: W.W. Norton, 1994).

Atton, Henry and Henry Hurst Holland. *The King's Custom: An Account of Maritime Revenue and Contraband Traffic in England, Scotland and Ireland, From the Earliest Times to the Year 1800* (1908; New York: August M. Kelley, 1967).

Auchampaugh, P. G., *James Buchanan and His Cabinet on the Eve of Secession* (Lancester, PA: Lancester Press, 1926).

Ayers, E. L., *In the Presence of Mine Enemies: War in the Heart of America, 1859–1863* (New York: W.W. Norton, 2003).

Bailyn, B., *The Ideological Origins of the Americans Revolution* (Cambridge, MA: Harvard University Press, 1967).

Baker, J. H., *Affairs of the Party: The Political Culture of Northern Democrats in the Mid-Nineteenth Century* (Ithaca, NY: Cornell University Press, 1983).

—, *James Buchanan* (New York: Henry Holt, 2004).

Ball, D. B., *Financial Failure and Confederate Defeat* (Urbana, IL: University of Illinois Press, 1991).

Banner, J. M., *To the Hartford Convention: The Federalists and the Origins of Party Politics in Massachusetts, 1789–1815* (New York: Knopf, 1970).

Banning, L., *The Jeffersonian Persuasion: Evolution of a Party Ideology* (Ithaca, NY: Cornell University Press, 1978).

Barnes, W. H., *History of the Thirty-Ninth Congress of the United States* (1868; New York: Negro Universities Press, 1969).

Barrow, T., *Trade and Empire: The British Customs Service in Colonial America, 1660–1775* (Cambridge, MA: Harvard University Press, 1967).

Beard, C. A. and M. R. Beard, *The Rise of American Civilization*, 4 vols (New York: Macmillan, Co, 1927).

Beckett, J.V., *Local Taxation: National Legislation and the Problems of Enforcement* (London: Bedford Square Press, 1980.

Becker, R. A. *Revolution, Reform, and the Politics of American Taxation, 1763–1783.* (Baton Rouge, LA: Louisiana State University Press, 1980).

Bensel, R. F., *Yankee Leviathan: The Origins of Central State Authority in America, 1859–1877* (New York: Cambridge University Press, 1990).

Benton, T. H., *Thirty Years' View*, 2 vols (New York: D. Appleton and Co., 1856).

Binney, J. E. D., *British Public Finance and Administration* (Oxford: Clarendon Press, 1958).

Blue, F. J., *Salmon P. Chase: A Life in Politics* (Kent, OH: Kent State University Press, 1987).

Bodenhorn, H., *State Banking in Early America* (New York: Oxford University Press, 2003).

Bogue, A. G., *The Earnest Men: Republicans of the Civil War Senate* (Ithaca, NY: Cornell University Press, 1981).

Bolles, A. S., *The Financial History of the United States from 1861–1885* (New York: A. M. Kelley, 1969).

Borritt, G., *Lincoln and the Economics of the American Dream* (Memphis, TN: Memphis State University Press, 1978).

Boutwell, G., *The Taxpayer's Manual* (Boston, MA: Little Brown and Co., 1866).

Bowen, H. V. *War and British Society, 1688–1815* (Cambridge: Cambridge University Press, 1998).

Braddick, M. J., *The Nerves of State: Taxation and the Financing of the English State, 1558–1714* (Manchester: Manchester University Press, 1996).

Brandes, S. D., *Warhogs: A History of War Profits in America* (Lexington, KY: University Press of Kentucky, 2006).

Brewer, J., *The Sinews of Power: War, Money, and the English State* (New York: Alfred A. Knopf, 1988).

Brown, R. H., *Redeeming the Republic: Federalists, Taxation, and the Origins of the Constitution* (Baltimore, MD: Johns Hopkins University Press, 1993).

Brownlee, W. E., *Funding the Modern American State, 1941–1995* (New York: Cambridge University Press, 1996).

—, *Federal Taxation in America, A Short History* (New York: Cambridge University Press, 2004).

Browning, E. K. and J. M. Browning, *Public Finance and the Price System*, 4th edn (Englewood Cliffs, NJ: Prentice Hall, Inc., 1994).

Bruchey, S., *The Roots of American Economic Growth, 1607–1861* (New York: Harper Row, 1965).

—, *The Wealth of the Nation: An Economic History of the United States* (New York: Harper Row, 1988).

Bryce, J., *The American Commonwealth*, 2 vols (New York: Macmillan Co., 1904).

Carey, H. C., *Principles of Political Economy* (1837; New York: A. M. Kelley, 1965).

—, *Harmony of Interests: Agricultural, Manufacturing, and Commercial* (Philadelphia, PA: J. S. Skinner, 1851).

Carson, E., *The Ancient and Rightful Customs: A History of the English Customs Service* (Hamden, CT: Archon Books, 1972).

Cashman, S. D., *America in the Gilded Age: From the Death of Lincoln to the Rise of Theodore Roosevelt* (New York: New York University Press, 1984).

Chandaman, C. D. *The English Public Revenue, 1660–1668* (Oxford: Oxford University Press, 1975).

Chernow, R., *Alexander Hamilton* (New York: Penguin Press, 2004).

Clarkson, L. A., *The Pre-Industrial Economy in England, 1500–1750* (New York: Schocken Books, 1972).

Clawson, M., *The Land System of the United States: An Introduction to the History and Practice of Lane Use and Land Tenure* (Lincoln, NE: University of Nebraska Press, 1968).

Clay, C. G. A., *Economic Expansion and Social Change: England 1500–1700*, 2 vols (New York: Cambridge University Press, 1984).

Cooley, T. J., *The Law of Taxation*, 4 vols (Chicago, IL: Callahan Publishers, 1924).

Coward, B., *The Stuart Age: England: 1603–1714* 2nd edn (New York: Longman Press, 1994).

Curry, L. P., *Blueprint for Modern America: Non-Military Legislation for the First Civil War Congress* (Nashville, TN: Vanderbilt University Press, 1968).

Curtis, G. T., *Life of James Buchanan*, 2 vols (New York: Harper & Bros, 1883).

Daunton, M. J., *Progress and Poverty: An Economic and Social History of Britain, 1700–1850* (Oxford: Oxford University Press, 1995).

Davis, W. W. H., *The Fries Rebellion, 1798–1799* (New York: Arno Press, 1969).

Dewey, D. R., *Financial History of the United States,* 12th edn (New York: Longmans, Green and Co., 1939).

Dickson, P. G. M., *The Financial Revolution in England* (London: Melbourne Publishers, 1967).

Donald, D. H., *Lincoln* (New York: Simon and Schuster, 1995).

Dorfman, J., *The Economic Mind in American Civilization, 1606–1865* (New York: Viking Press, 1966).

Doti, L. P., and L. Schweikart. *Banking in the American West: From Gold Rush to Deregulation* (Norman, OK: University of Oklahoma Press, 1991).

Dowell, S., *A History of Taxation and Taxes in England, from Earliest Times to the Present Day*, 4 vols (London: Longman, Green and Co., 1884).

Eaton, D. B., *The Spoils System and Civil Service Reform in the Custom-House and Post Office at New York* (1881; Reprint. New York: Arno Press, 1974).

Edling, M., A *Revolution in Favor of Government: Origins of the United States Constitution and the Making of the American State* (New York: Oxford University Press, 2003).

Einhorn, R. L. *American Taxation, American Slavery* (Chicago, IL: University of Chicago Press, 2006).

Elazar, D., *The American Partnership: Intergovernmental Cooperation in Nineteenth Century United States* (Chicago, IL: University of Chicago Press, 1962).

—, *American Federalism: A View from the States*. New York: Crowell Press, 1966.

Ely, R. T., *Taxation in American States and Cities* (New York: Thomas Crowell, 1888).

Ezell, J. S., *Fortune's Merry Wheel: The Lottery in America* (Cambridge, MA: Harvard University Press, 1960).

Faulkner, H. U., *American Economic History* (New York: Harper Brothers, 1924).

Fehrenbacher, D., *Slavery, Law, Politics: The Dred Scott Case in Historical Perspective* (New York: Oxford University Press, 1981).

Feldberg, M., *The Turbulent Era: Riot and Disorder in Jacksonian America* (New York: Oxford University Press, 1980).

Ferguson, N., *The Cash Nexus: Money and Power in the Modern World, 1700–2000* (New York: Basic Books, 2001)

Fessenden, F., *Life and Public Services of William Pitt Fessenden* 2 vols (Boston, MA: Houghton, Mifflin and Co., 1907).

Ferguson, E. J., *The Power of the Purse: A History of American Public Finance, 1776–1790* (Chapel Hill, NC: University of North Carolina Press, 1961).

Ferguson, N., *The Cash Nexus: Money and Power in the Modern World, 1700-2000* (New York: Basic Books, 2001).

Ferleger, H. R., *David A. Wells and the American Revenue System, 1865-1870* (Philadelphia, PA: Porcupine Press, 1977).

Fine, S., *Laissez-Faire and the General Welfare States: A Study of Conflict in American Thought, 1865–1901* (Ann Arbor, MI: University of Michigan Press, 1956).

Fiske, J., *The Critical Period of American History: 1783–1789* (Boston, MA: Houghton Mifflin, 1888).

Fite, E. D., *Social and Industrial Conditions in the North During the Civil War* (New York: Peter Smith, 1930).

Fogel, R.W., *The Union Pacific Railroad: A Case in Premature Enterprise* (Baltimore, MD: Johns Hopkins University Press, 1960).

Foner, E., *Free Soil, Free Labor, Free Men: The Ideology of the Republican Party before the Civil War* (New York: Oxford University Press, 1970).

—, *Reconstruction: America's Unfinished Revolution, 1863-1877* (New York: Harper Row, 1988).

Foner, P., *Business and Slavery: The New York Merchants and the Irrepressible Conflict* (Chapel Hill, NC: University of North Carolina Press, 1941).

Forsythe, D., *Taxation and Political Change in the Young Nation, 1781–1883* (New York: Columbia University Press, 1977).

Fox-Genovese, E., *The Origins of Physiocracy: Economic Revolution and Social Order in Eighteenth Century France* (Ithaca, NY: Cornell University Press, 1976).

Freehling, W. H. *Prelude to Civil War: The Nullification Controversy in South Carolina, 1816-1836* (New York: Harper Row, 1965).

Galbraith, J. K., *Economics in Perspective: A Critical History* (Boston, MA: Houghton-Mifflin, 1987).

Gale, T., *Making of the Modern World*, (College Station, TX: Texas A&M University Press, 2006).

Gallman, J. M., *The North Fights the Civil War: The Homefront* (Chicago, IL: I.R. Dee Publishers, 1994).

—, *Mastering Wartime: A Social History of Philadelphia during the Civil War* (New York: Cambridge University Press, 1990).

Gates, P. W., *Frontier Landlords and Pioneer Tenants* (Ithaca, NY: Cornell University Press, 1945).

Gilchrist, D. T. and W. D. Lewis (eds), *Economic Change in the Civil War Era:* Proceedings of a Conference on American Institutional Change, 1850-1873 and the Impact of the Civil War (Greenville, DE: Eleutherian Mills-Hagley Foundation, 1965).

Gienapp, W. E., *The Origins of the Republican Party, 1852–1856* (New York: Oxford University Press, 1987).

Goodrich, C., *Government Promotion of American Canals and Railroads, 1800–1890* (New York: Columbia University Press, 1960).

—, *Government and the Economy, 1783-1861* (Indianapolis, IN: Bobbs-Merrill, 1967).

Goodrich, C. B., *The Science of Government as Exhibited in the Institutions of the United States* (Boston, MA: Little, Brown and Co., 1853).

Goodwin, D. K., *Team of Rivals: The Political Genius of Abraham Lincoln* (New York: Simon and Schuster Paperback, 2005), pp. 631–9.

Gouge, W. M., *The Curse of Paper-Money and Banking or A Short History of Banking in the United States of America* (1833; New York: Greenwood Press, 1968).

Gras, N. S. B., *The Early English Customs System: A Documentary Study of the Institutional and Economic History of the Customs from the Thirteenth to the Sixteenth Century* (Cambridge, MA: Harvard University Press, 1918).

Green, M., *Freedom, Union, and Power: Lincoln and His Party during the Civil War* (New York: Fordham University Press, 2004).

Gross, Robert A., *The Minutemen and Their World* (New York: Hill and Wang, 2001).

Hacker, L. M. *The Triumph of American Capitalism: The Development of Forces in American History to the End of the Nineteenth Century*, 2nd edn (New York: Simon and Schuster, 1940).

Haeger, J. D., *John Jacob Astor: Business and Finance in the Early Republic* (Detroit: Wayne State University Press, 1991).

Hall, H., *A History of the Custom-Revenue in England from the Earliest Times to the Year 1827*, 2 vols (1885; New York: Burt Franklin, 1970).

Hamilton, C., and D. T. Wells. *Federalism, Power, and Political Economy: A New Theory on Federalism's Impact on American Life* (Englewood Cliffs, NJ: Prentice Hall, 1990).

Hammond, B., *Banks and Politics in America: From the Revolution to the Civil War* (Princeton, NJ: Princeton University Press, 1957).

—, *Sovereignty and an Empty Purse: Banks and Politics in the Civil War* (Princeton, NJ: Princeton University Press, 1970).

Handlin, O., and M. Handlin, *Commonwealth: A Study of the Role of Government in the American Economy: Massachusetts, 1774–1861* (New York: New York University Press, 1947).

Harriss, G. L., *King, Parliament, and Public Finance in Medieval England to 1369* (Oxford, UK: Clarendon Press, 1975).

Hart, A. B., *Salmon Portland Chase* (Boston, MA: Houghton Mifflin, 1899).

Hartz, L., *Economic Policy and Democratic Thought: Pennsylvania, 1776–1860* (Cambridge, MA: Harvard University Press, 1948).

Heath, M. S., *Constructive Liberalism: The Role of the State in Economic Development in Georgia to 1860* (Cambridge, MA: Harvard University Press, 1954).

Hepburn, A. B., *A History of Currency in the United States* (New York: Macmillan Co., 1924).

Hibbard, B. H., *A History of Public Land Policies* (Lincoln, NE: University of Nebraska Press, 1968).

Hickey, D. R., *The War of 1812: The Forgotten Conflict* (Urbana, IL: University of Illinois Press, 1989).

Hofstadter, R., *American Political Tradition and the Men Who Made It* (New York: Oxford University Press, 1999).

Holt, M. F., *Political Parties and American Political Development for the Age of Jackson to the Age of Lincoln* (Baton Rouge, LA: Louisiana State University Press, 1992).

—, *The Rise and Fall of the American Whig Party: Jacksonian Politics and the Onset of the Civil War* (New York: Oxford University Press, 1999).

—, *The Fate of the Country: Politicians, Slavery Extension, and the Coming of the Civil War* (New York: Hill and Wang, 2004).

Homer, S., and R. Sylla, *A History of Interest Rates*, 3rd edn (New Brunswick, NJ: Rutgers University Pres, 1991).

Hope-Jones, A., *Income Tax in the Napoleonic Wars* (Cambridge, UK: Cambridge University Press, 1939).

Howe, F. C., *Taxation and Taxes in the United States Under the Internal Revenue System, 1791–1895* (New York: Thomas Y. Crowell, Co., 1896).

Hoyt, R. S., *The Royal Demesne in English Constitutional History: 1066-1272* (Ithaca, NY: Cornell University Press, 1950).

Hughes, E., *Studies in Administration and Finance, 1558–1825* (Manchester: Manchester University Press, 1934).

Hurst, J. W., *Law and the Conditions of Freedom in Nineteenth Century United States* (Madison, WI: University of Wisconsin Press, 1967).

Huston, J. L., *The Panic of 1857 and the Coming of the Civil War* (Baton Rouge, LA: Louisiana State University Press, 1987).

—, *Securing the Fruits of Labor: The American Concept of Wealth Distribution, 1765–1900* (Baton Rouge, LA: Louisiana State University Press, 1998).

—, *Calculating the Value of the Union: Slavery, Property Rights, and the Economic Origins of the Civil War* (Chapel Hill, NC: University of North Carolina Press, 2003).

Hyman, H. M., *A More Perfect Union: The Impact of the Civil War and Reconstruction on the Constitution* (New York: Knopf, 1973).

Iceland, J., *Poverty in America: A Handbook* (Berkeley, CA: University of California Press, 2003).

Jellison, C. A., *Fessenden of Maine: Civil War Senator* (Syracuse, NY: Syracuse University Press, 1962).

Jensen, M., *The Articles of Confederation: An Interpretation of the Social-Constitutional History of the American Revolution, 1774–1781*, 20 vols (Madison, WI: University of Wisconsin Press, 1940).

Johnson, D. R., *Illegal Tender: Counterfeiting and the Secret Service in Nineteenth Century America* (Washington, DC: Smithsonian Institution, 1995).

Jordan, D. M., *Roscoe Conkling of New York: Voice in the Senate* (Ithaca, NY: Cornell University Press, 1971).

Josephson, M., *The Robber Barons: The Great American Capitalists, 1861–1901* (New York: Harcourt, Brace, Co., 1934).

Joyner, F. B., *David Ames Wells: Champion of Free Trade* (Cedar Rapids, IA: Torch Press, 1939).

Kanigel, R., *The One Best Way: Frederick Winslow Taylor and the Enigma of Efficiency* (New York: Viking, 1997).

Katz, M. B., *Poverty and Policy in American History* (New York: Academic Press, 1983).

Kennedy, W., *English Taxation, 1640–1799: An Essay on Policy and Opinion* (London: G. Bellard and Sons, 1913).

Kenyon, C. (ed.), *The Anti-Federalists* (New York: Bobbs-Merrill, Co., 1966).

Kinley, D., *The History, Organization and Influence of the Independent Treasury of the United States* (1893; New York: Greenwood Press, 1968).

Kirk, R., *John Randolph of Roanoke* (Chicago, IL: University of Chicago Press, 1951).

Klein, P. S., *President James Buchanan: A Biography* (University Park, PA: Pennsylvania State University Press, 1978).

Knox, J. J. *United States Notes: A History of the Various Issues of Paper Money by the Government of the United States*, 3rd edn (New York: Charles Scribner's Sons, 1888).

—, *History of Banking* (1900; New York: A.M. Kelley, 1969).

Kohl, L. F. *The Politics of Individualism: Parties and the American Character in Jacksonian Era* (Englewood Cliffs, NJ: Prentice Hall, 1961).

Lamphier, P. A., *Kate Chase and William Sprague: Politics and Gender in a Civil War Marriage* (Lincoln: University of Nebraska Press, 2003).

Larson, H. M., *Jay Cooke, Private Banker* (Cambridge, MA: Harvard University Press, 1936).

Lawson, M., *Patriotic Fires: Forging a New American Nationalism in the Civil War North* (Lawrence: University Press of Kansas, 2002).

Leonard, E. M., *The Early History of English Poor Relief* (1900; London: Frank Cass & Co, 1965).

Lyon, B. D., and A. E. Verhulst, *Medieval Finance: A Comparison of Financial Institutions in Northwestern Europe* (Providence, RI: Brown University Press, 1967).

Macdonald, J., *A Free Nation Deep in Debt: The Financial Roots of Democracy* (New York: Farrar, Straus and Giroux, 2003).

Main, J. T., *The Anti-Federalists: Critics of the Constitution, 1781–1788* (Chapel Hill, NC: University of North Carolina Press, 1961).

Majewski, J., *A House Dividing: Economic Development in Pennsylvania and Virginia Before the Civil War* (New York: Cambridge University Press, 2006).

Mankiw, N. G., *Principles of Microeconomics* (New York: Dryden Press, 1997).

Martis, K. C. *The Historical Atlas of Political Parties in the United States Congress, 1789–1989* (New York: Macmillan Co., 1989).

Marx, K., and E., Frederick. *The Civil War in the United States*, 3rd edn Edited by R. Enmale (New York: International Publishers, 1937).

McCoy, D., *The Elusive Republic: Political Economy in Jeffersonian America*, 2nd edn (New York: Oxford University Press, 1982).

McCusker, J. J., *Money and Exchange in Europe and America, 1660-1775* (Chapel Hill, NC: University of North Carolina Press, 1978).

McCusker, J. J., and R. R. Menard, *The Economy of British America, 1607–1789.* (Chapel Hill, NC: University of North Carolina Press, 1985).

McFarland, G. W., *Mugwumps, Morals, and Politics, 1884–1920* (Amherst, MA: University of Massachusetts Press, 1975).

McFaul, J. M., *The Politics of Jacksonian Finance* (Ithaca, NY: Cornell University Press, 1972).

McGrane, R. C., *Foreign Bondholders and American State Debts* (New York: Macmillan Co., 1935).

McMaster, J. B., *History of the People of the United States*, 9 vols (New York: D. Appleton, Co., 1916).

McPherson, J. M., *Battle Cry of Freedom* (New York: Oxford University Press, 1988).

—, *Abraham Lincoln and the Second American Revolution* (New York: Oxford University Press, 1990

—, *What They Fought For, 1861–1865* (Baton Rouge, LA: Louisiana State University Press, 1994).

McPherson, J. M., *For Cause and Comrades: Why Men Fought in the Civil War* (New York: Oxford University Press, 1997)

Meek, R. L., *The Economics of Physiocracy: Essays and Translations* (Cambridge, MA: Harvard University Press, 1963).

Mihm, S., *A Nation of Counterfeiters: Capitalists, Con Men, and the Making of the United States* (Cambridge, MA: Harvard University Press, 2007).

Mitchell, W. C., *A History of the Greenbacks, with Special Reference to the Economic Consequences of Their Issue* (Chicago, IL: University of Chicago Press, 1903).

Morgan, S. A., *The History of Parliamentary Taxation in England* (New York: Moffat, Bard and Co., 1911).

Morison, Samuel Eliot and Henry Steele Commager. *The Growth of the American Republic*, 2 vols (New York: Oxford University Pres, 1950).

Morriss, T. D. *Free Men All: The Personal Liberty Laws of the North, 1780–1861* (Baltimore, MD: Johns Hopkins University Press, 1974).

Myers, M. G., *A Financial History of the United States* (New York: Columbia University Press, 1970).

Neeley, Mark E., *Fate of Liberty: Abraham Lincoln and Civil Liberties* (New York: Oxford University Press, 1991).

Nettels, C. P., *The Emergence of a National Economy* (New York: Holt, Rinehart, and Winston, 1962).

Nevins, A., *The Emergence of Lincoln*, 2 vols (New York: Charles Scribner's Sons, 1950).

—, *Hamilton Fish: The Inner History of the Grant Administration*, 2 vols (New York: Frederick Unger Publishing Co., 1957).

Newman, P. D., *Fries Rebellion: The Enduring Struggle for the American Revolution* (Philadelphia, PA: University of Pennsylvania, 2004).

Nichols, R. F., *The Disruption of American Democracy* (New York: Macmillan Co., 1948).

Niven, J., *Salmon P. Chase: A Biography* (New York: Oxford University Press, 1995).

North, D. C., *The Economic Growth of the United States, 1790–1860* (New York: W. W. Norton, 1966).

Novak, W. J., *The People's Welfare: Law and Regulation in Nineteenth Century America* (Chapel Hill, NC: University of North Carolina Press, 1996).

Nussbaum, A., *A History of the Dollar* (New York: Columbia University Press, 1957).

Oberholtzer, E. P., *Jay Cooke: Financier of the Civil War*. 2 vols (Philadelphia, PA: George W. Jacobs, Co., 1907).

O'Brien, P., *The Economic Effects of the American Civil War* (Atlantic Highlands, NJ: Humanities Press International, 1988).

Ostrum, V., *The Meaning of American Federalism: Constitution a Self-Governing Society* (San Francisco: Institute of Contemporary Studies, 1991).

Palliser, D. M. *The Age of Elizabeth: England Under the Later Tudors: 1547–1603* (New York: Longman Group, 1983).

Paludan, P. S., *A People's Contest: The Union and Civil War, 1861–1865* (Lawrence: University Press of Kansas, 1996).

Parker, W. B., *The Life and Public Services of Justin Smith Morrill* (Boston: Houghton Mifflin, 1924).

Patterson, R. T., *Federal Debt Management Policies* (Durham, NC: Duke University Press, 1954).

Perkins, E. J., *The Economy of Colonial America* (New York: Columbia University Press, 1988).

—, *American Public Finance and Financial Services, 1700–1815* (Columbus: Ohio State University Press, 1994).

Porter, P. G., and H. C. Livesay, *Merchants and Manufacturers* (Baltimore, MD: Johns Hopkins University Press, 1971).

Potter, D., *People of Plenty* (Chicago: University of Chicago Press, 1954).

—, *The Impending Crisis, 1848–1861* (New York: Harper Row, 1976).

Rakove, J. N., *The Beginnings of National Politics: An Interpretative History of the Continental Congress* (New York: Alfred Knopf, 1979).

—, *James Madison and the Creation of the American Republic* (New York: Longman Press, 2002).

Randall, J. G., *Constitutional Problems Under Lincoln* (Urbana, IL: University of Illinois Press, 1951).

Ransom, R. L., *Conflict and Compromise: The Political Economy of Slavery, Emancipation, and the American Civil War* (New York: Cambridge University Press, 1989).

Ransom, R., and R. L. Sutch, *One Kind of Freedom: The Economic Consequences of Emancipation* (New York: Cambridge University Press, 1977).

Ratchford. B. U., *American State Debts* (Durham, NC: Duke University Press, 1941).

Ratner, S., *American Taxation: It's History as a Social Force in Democracy* (New York: W. W. Norton, 1942).

—, *The Tariff in American History* (New York: D. Van Nostrand Co., 1972).

Redlich, F., *The Molding of American Banking: Men and Ideas*, 2 vols (New York: Johnson Reprint Co, 1951).

Rhodes, J. F., *History of the United States from the Compromise of 1850 to the Final Restoration of Home Rule at the South in 1877*, 9 vols (New York: Macmillan Co., 1919).

Richardson. H. C., *The Greatest Nation of the Earth: Republican Economic Policies during the Civil War* (Cambridge, MA: Harvard University Press, 1997).

Rockoff, H., *Free Banking Era: A Re-examination* (New York: Arno Press, 1975).

Say, J. B., *Treatise on Political Economy, or the Production, Distribution and Consumption of Wealth* (Philadelphia, PA: Grigg and Elliot, 1842).

Scheele, C. H., *A Short History of the Mail Service* (Washington, DC: Smithsonian Institution Press, 1970).

Scheiber, H., *American Law and Constitutional Order: Historical Perspectives.* (Cambridge, MA: Harvard University Press, 1978).

Schuckers, J. W., *The Life and Public Services of Salmon Portland Chase* (1874; New York: Dacapo Press, 1970).

Schultz W. J., *Financial Development of the United States* (New York: Prentice-Hall, 1937).

Schwartz, B., *Confederation to Nation: The American Constitution, 1835–1877* (Baltimore, MD: Johns Hopkins University Press, 1973).

Schwoerer, L. G., *The Declaration of Rights, 1689* (Baltimore, MD: Johns Hopkins University Press, 1981).

Scott, W. A., *The Repudiation of State Debts* (New York: Greenwood Press, 1969).

Sears, D. O., and J. Citrin, *Tax Revolt: Something for Nothing in California* (Cambridge, MA: Harvard University Press, 1982).

Seip, T. L., *The South Returns to Congress: Men, Economic Measures, and Intersectional Relationships, 1868-1879* (Baton Rouge, LA: Louisiana State University Press, 1983).

Seligman, E. R., *Essays in Taxation*, 8th edn (New York: Macmillan Co., 1913).

—, *The Income Tax: A Study of the History, Theory, and Practice of Income Taxation at Home and Abroad* (New York: Macmillan, Co., 1914).

—, *Shifting and Incidence of Taxation*, 5th edn (New York: Columbia University Press, 1927).

Sexton, J., *Debtor Diplomacy: Finance and American Foreign Relations in the Civil War Era, 1837-1873* (Oxford: Clarendon Press, 2005).

Sharkey, R. P. *Money, Class, and Party: An Economic Study of Civil War and Reconstruction* (Baltimore, MD: Johns Hopkins University Press, 1959).

Shultz, W. J., and M. R. Caine, *Financial Development of the United States* (New York: Prentice Hall, Inc., 1937).

Silbey, J. H., *A Respectable Minority: The Democratic Party in the Civil War Era, 1860–1868* (New York: W. W. Norton, Co, 1977).

Skocpol, T., *Protecting Soldiers and Mothers: The Political Origins of Social Policy in the United States* (Cambridge, MA: Harvard University Press, 1992).

Slaughter, T. P., *The Whiskey Rebellion: Frontier Epilogue to the American Revolution* (New York: Oxford University Press, 1986).

Smith, A., *An Inquiry into the Nature and Causes of the Wealth of Nations* 5th edn (1776; New York: Modern Library, 1937).

Smith, G. W., *Henry C. Carey and the American Sectional Conflict* (Albuquerque, NM: University of New Mexico Press, 1951).

Smith, H. E., *The United States Federal Tax History from 1861 to 1871* (Boston, MA: Houghton Mifflin Co., 1914).

Spaulding, E. G., *A Resource of War – the Credit of the Government Made Immediately Available: A History of the Legal Tender* (Buffalo, NY: Express Printing Co., 1869).

Stabile, D. R., and J. A. Cantor. *The Public Debt of the United States: An Historical Perspective, 1775–1990* (New York: Praeger, 1991).

Stanley, R., *Dimensions of Law in the Service of Order: Origins of the Federal Income Tax, 1861-1913* (New York: Oxford University Press, 1993).

Stanwood, E., *American Tariff Controversies in the Nineteenth Century*, 2 vols (New York: Russell and Russell, 1967).

Story, J., *Commentaries on the Constitution* (1833;Durham: Carolina Academic Press, 1987).

Studenski, P., and H. E. Krooss, *Financial History of the Untied States: Fiscal, Monetary, Banking, and Tariff including Financial Administration and State and Local Finances* (New York: McGraw-Hill, 1952).

Summers, M. W., *The Plundering Generation: Corruption and the Crisis of the Union, 1849–1861* (New York: Oxford University Press, 1987).

—, *The Era of Good Stealings* (New York: Oxford University Press, 1993).

Swisher, C. B., *American Constitutional Development* (Boston, MA: Houghton Mifflin, Co., 1943).

I. M. Tarbell, *The Tariff in Our Times* (New York: Macmillan Co., 1912).

Taussig, F. W., *The Tariff History of the United States* (New York: G. P. Putnam's Sons, 1888).

Taylor, W., *The History of the Taxation of England* (London: Hope and Co., 1853).

Temin, P., *The Jacksonian Economy* (New York: W.W. Norton, 1969).

Thomas, B. P., and H. M. Hyman. *Stanton: The Life and Times of Lincoln's Secretary of War* (New York: Alfred A. Knopf, 1962).

Thompson, E. L., *The Reconstruction of Southern Debtors: Bankruptcy after the Civil War* (Athens, GA: University of Georgia Press, 2004).

Thompson, M. S., *The Spider Web: Congress and Lobbying in the Age of Grant* (Ithaca, NY: Cornell University Press, 1985).

Thornton, M. and R. B. Ekelund, *Tariffs, Blockades, and Inflation: The Economics of the Civil War* (Wilmington: SR Books, 2004).

Trefousse, H. L., *Andrew Jackson, A Biography* (New York: W.W. Norton, 1989).

—, *Thaddeus Stevens: Nineteenth Century Egalitarian* (Chapel Hill, NC: University of North Carolina Press, 1997).

Trescott, P., *Financing American Enterprise: The Story of Commercial Banking* (New York: Harper Row, 1963).

Tucker, D. M. *Mugwumps: Public Moralists of the Gilded* Age (Columbia, MO: University of Missouri Press, 1998).

Unger, I., *The Greenback Era: A Social and Political History of American Finance, 1865–1879* (Princeton, NJ: Princeton University Press, 1964).

Ver Steeg, C. L., *Robert Morris: Revolutionary Financier* (Philadelphia, PA: University of Pennsylvania Press, 1954).

Vidal, E., *The History and Methods of the Paris Bourse* (Washington, DC: GPO, 1918).

Wallenstein, P., *From Slave South to New South: Public Policy in Nineteenth Century Georgia* (Chapel Hill, NC: University of North Carolina Press, 1987).

Waltham, J. L., *Copying Other Nation's Policies: Two American Case Studies* (Cambridge, MA: Schenkman Publishing Co., 1980).

Walvin, J., Fruits of Empire: Exotic Produce and British Taste, 1660–1800 (New York: New York University Press, 1997).

Watson, Harry L. *Liberty and Power: The Politics of Jacksonian America* (New York: Hill and Wang, 1990).

Wayland, F., *The Elements of Political Economy* (New York: Leavitt, Lord, and Co., 1837).

Webber, C., and A. Wildavsky, *A History of Taxation and Expenditure in the Western World* (New York: Simon and Schuster, 1986).

Weigley, Russell F. *History of the United States Army* (New York: Macmillan Co., 1967).

Wells, D. A., *Theory and Practice of Taxation* (New York: D. Appleton, 1900).

Wheen, F., *Karl Marx: A Life* (New York: W. W. Norton, 1999).

White, L. D., *The Jacksonians: A Study in Administrative History, 1829–1861* (New York: MacMillan Co., 1954).

Wilhite, V. G., *Founders of American Economic Thought and Policy* (New York: Bookman Associated, 1958).

Williamson, J., 'Watersheds and Turning Points; Conjectures on the Long Term Impact of Civil War Financing', *Journal of Economic History*, 34 (1974), pp. 631–61.

Wilson, M. R., *The Business of Civil War: Military Mobilization and the State, 1861–1865* (Baltimore, MD: Johns Hopkins University Press, 2006).

Winik, J., *April 1865: The Month That Saved America* (New York: Harper Perennial, 2001).

Winters, J. D., *The Civil War in Louisiana* (Baton Rouge, LA: Louisiana State University Press, 1963).

Wright, G., *The Political Economy of the Cotton South: Households, Markets, and Wealth in the Nineteenth Century* (New York: W.W. Norton, 1978).

Wright, R. E., *Born in Debt: America's First National Debt and Its Lessons for Today* 2007.

Wood, Gordon S., *The Creation of the American Republic, 1776-1787* (Chapel Hill, NC: University of North Carolina Press, 1969).

Yearley, C. K., *The Money Machines: The Breakdown and Reform of Governmental and Party Finance in the North, 1860–1920* (Albany, NY: State University of New York Press, 1970).

Articles and Book Chapters

Ackerman, B., 'Taxation and the Constitution', *Columbia Law Review*, 99 (January 1999), pp. 1–58.

Adams, H. C., 'Taxation in the United States', *Johns Hopkins University Studies in Historical and Political Science,* 2nd series, (May–June 1884), pp. 1–79.

Atherton, L. E., 'The Services of the Frontier Merchant', *Mississippi Valley Historical Review*, 24 (September, 1937), pp. 153–70.

Barber, W. D., 'Among the Most Techy Articles of Civil Police: Federal Taxation and the Adoption of the Whiskey Excise', *William and Mary Quarterly,* 3 (January, 1968), pp. 58–84.

Beckett, J. V., 'Land Tax or Excise: The Levying of Taxation in Seventeenth- and Eighteenth-Century England', *English Historical Review*, 395 (April 1985), pp. 285–308.

Benson, S., 'A History of the General Property Tax', in *American Property Tax: Its History, Administration, and Economic Impact* (Claremont, CA: Claremont Men's College Press, 1965).

Bertolet, J. L., 'Justin S. Morrill', in D. Heilder and J. Heilder (eds), *Encyclopedia of the American Civil War*, 5 vols (Santa Barbara, CA: ABC–CLIO, 2000), vol. 3, pp.1364–5.

Blakey, G. R., 'State Conducted Lotteries: History, Problems, and Promises', *Journal of Social Issues*, 35 (September 1979), pp. 62–86.

Bowers, D. E., 'From Logrolling to Corruption: The Development of Lobbying in Pennsylvania, 1815–1861', *Journal of the Early Republic*, 3 (Winter 1983), pp. 439–4.

Boyer, P. S. 'Borrowed Rhetoric: The Massachusetts Excise Controversy of 1754', *William and Mary Quarterly*, 3:21 (July 1964), pp. 328–51.

Brooks, C., 'Public Finance and Political Stability: The Administration of the Land Tax, 1688-1720', *The Historical Journal*, 17 (June 1974), pp. 281–300.

Brough, Charles H., 'Taxation in Mississippi', in *Studies in State Taxation with Particular Reference to the Southern States*. (Baltimore, MD:Johns Hopkins University Press, 1900): 177-215.

Bullock, C. J. 'Direct and Indirect Taxes in Economic Literature', *Political Science Quarterly*, 12 (September 1898), pp. 442–76.

—, 'The Origin, Purpose, and Effect of the Direct Tax Clause of the Constitution', *Political Science Quarterly*, 15 (September 1900), pp. 217–39.

Callender, G. S. 'The Early Transportation and Banking Enterprises of the States in

Relation to the Growth of Corporations', *Quarterly Journal of Economics*, 17 (November 1902), pp. 111–162.

Calomiris, C. W., and Larry Schweikart, 'The Panic of 1857: Origins, Transmissions, and Containment', *Journal of Economic History,* 51 (December 1991), pp. 807–34.

Cochran, T., 'Did the Civil War Retard Industrialization?', *Mississippi Valley Historical Review,* 48 (September 1961), pp. 197–210.

Commons, J. R., 'Tariff Revision and Protection for American Labor', *Annals of the American Academy of Political and Social Science*, 32 (September 1908), pp. 51–6.

Cook, Robert. 'The Grave of All My Comforts: William Pitt Fessenden as Secretary of the Treasury, 1864-1865', *Civil War History*, 61 (Autumn 1995), pp. 208–26.

Cooper, R., 'William Pitt, Taxation, and the Needs of War', *Journal of British Studies*, 22 (Autumn, 1982), pp. 94–103.

Current, Richard N., 'God and the Strongest Battalions', in D. Donald (ed.) *Why the North Won the Civil War* (New York: Collier Books, 1962), pp. 52–64.

Dawson, J. G., 'The First of the Modern Wars', in S. M. Grant and B. H. Reid (eds), *The American Civil War: Explorations and Reconsiderations* (New York: Longman, Green, Co., 2000), pp. 126–37.

Dunbar, C., 'The Direct Tax of 1861', *Quarterly Journal of Economics*, 3 (July 1889): 436–61.

Egnal, M., 'The Beards were Right: Parties in the North, 1840–1860', *Civil War History*, 47 (March 2001), pp. 30–56.

Einhorn, R. L. 'Slavery and the Politics of Taxation in the Early United States', *Studies in American Political Development*, 14 (Autumn 2000), pp. 156–83.

—, 'Species of Property: The American Property Tax Uniformity Clauses Reconsidered', *Journal of Economic History*, 61 (December 2001), pp. 974–1008.

Ellis, E., 'Public Opinion and the Income Tax, 1860-1890', *Mississippi Valley Historical Review*, 27 (September 1940), pp. 225–42.

Elton, G. R. "Taxation for War and Peace in Early Tudor England," in J. M. Winter (ed.), *War and Economic Development: Essays in Memory of David Coslin* (Cambridge: Cambridge University Press, 1975), pp. 76–103.

Engerman, S. J. and J. Matthew Gallman, 'The Civil War Economy: A Modern View', in S. Forster and J. Nagler (eds), *On the Road to Total War: The American Civil War and the German Wars of Unification, 1861-1871* (New York: Cambridge University Press, 1997).

Eyal, Y., 'Trade and Improvements: Young America and the Transformation of the Democratic Party', *Civil War History*, 51 (September 2005), pp. 245–68.

Farnham, W. D., 'The Weakened Spring of Government: A Study in Nineteenth Century American History', *American Historical Review*, 68 (April 1963), pp. 662–80.

Ferguson, E. J., 'Currency Financing: An Interpretation of Colonial Monetary Practices', *William and Mary Quarterly*, 3:10 (April 1853), 153–80.

Flaherty, J., 'Incidental Protection: An Examination of the Morrill Tariff', *Essays in Economic and Business History*, 19 (2001), pp. 103–18.

Friedman, M., 'Price, Income, and Monetary Changes in Three Wartime Periods', *American Economic Review*, 42 (May 1985), pp. 612–25.

Gates, P. W., 'Charts of Public Land Sales and Entries', *Journal of Economic History*, 24 (March 1964), pp. 22–38.

Gische, D. M. 'The New York City Banks and the Development of the National Banking System, 1860-1870', *American Journal of Legal History*, 23 (January 1979), pp. 31–4.

Gjerde, J., 'Roots of Maladjustment in Land: Paul Wallace Gates', *Reviews in American History*, 19 (March 1991), pp. 142–53.

Goodrich, Carter., 'The Revulsion Against Internal Improvements', *Journal of Economic History*, 10 (November 1950), pp. 145–69.

Grampp, W. D., 'Adam Smith and the American Revolutionists', *History of Political Economy*, 11 (Summer 1979), pp. 179–91.

Greene, J. P., 'Political Mimesis: A Consideration of the Historical and Cultural Roots of Legislative Behavior in the British Colonies in the Eighteenth Century', *American Historical Review*, 75 (December 1969), pp. 337–60.

Grimsley, M., 'Conciliation and Its Failure, 1861–1862', *Civil War History*, 39 (December 1993), pp. 317–35.

Guelzo, A. G., 'Houses Divided: Lincoln, Douglas, and the Political Landscape of 1858', *Journal of American History,* 94 (September 2007), p. 411.

Gutzman, K. R., 'James Madison and the Principles of '98', *Journal of the Early Republic,* 15 (Winter 1995), pp. 569–89.

Hammond, B., 'The North's Empty Purse, 1861-1862', *American Historical Review,* 67 (October 1961), pp. 1–18.

Hofstadter, R., 'The Tariff Issue on the Eve of the Civil War', *American Historical Review,* 44 (October 1938), 50–5.

Hoyle, R. W., 'Crown, Parliament and Taxation in Sixteenth Century England', *The English Historical Review,* 109 (November 1994), pp. 1174–96.

Huston, J. L., 'The American Revolutionaries, the Political Economy of Aristocracy, and the American Concept of the Distribution of Wealth, 1765-1900', *American Historical Review,* 90 (October 1993), pp. 1079–105.

—, 'A Political Response to Industrialism: the Republican Embrace of Protectionist Labor Doctrines', *Journal of American History* , 70 (June 1983), pp. 35–57.

Irwin, D. A., 'Changes in US Tariffs: The Role of Import Prices and Commercial Policies', *American Economic Review* 88 (September 1998), pp. 1015–26.

Jones, A. H., 'Wealth Estimates for American Middle Colonies, 1774', *Economic Development and Cultural Change,* 18 (1970), pp. 1–172.

Larson, J. L., 'Bind the Republic Together: The National Union and the Struggle for a System of Internal Improvements', *Journal of American History,* 74 (September 1987), pp. 363–87.

Lenner, A., 'A Tale of Two Constitutions: Nationalism in the Federalist Era', *American Journal of Legal History,* 40 (January 1996), pp. 72–105.

—, 'Separate Spheres: Republican Constitutionalism in the Federalist Era', *American Journal of Legal History,* 41 (April 1997), pp. 250–81.

Linden, G. M., 'Radicals and Economic Policies: The Senate, 1861–1873', *Journal of Southern History,* 32 (May 1966), pp. 188–199.

—, 'Radicals and Economic Policies: The House of Representatives, 1861–1873', *Civil War History,* 13 (March 1967), pp. 51–65.

Lively, R. A., 'The American System: A Review Article', *Business History Review,* 29 (March 1955), pp. 81–96.

Luthin, R. H., 'Salmon P. Chase's Political Career Before the Civil War', *Mississippi Valley Historical Review,* 29 (March 1943), pp. 517–40.

—, 'Abraham Lincoln and the Tariff', *American Historical Review,* 49 (July 1944), pp. 609–29

Majewski, J., 'The Political Impact of Great Commercial Cities: State Investment in Antebellum Pennsylvania and Virginia', *Journal of Interdisciplinary History,* 28 (Summer 1997), pp. 1–26.

Marshall, L. M., 'The Levying of the Hearth Tax', *English Historical Review,* 51 (October 1936), pp. 628–46.

Maltz, E. M., 'The Idea of the Proslavery Constitution', *Journal of the Early Republic*, 17 (Spring, 1997), pp. 37–59.

Mathias, P and P. K. O'Brien, 'Taxation in England and France, 1715-1810', *Journal of European Economic History*, 5 (1976), pp. 601–50.

Miller, W. K, 'The Revenue: Federal Law Enforcement in the Mountain South, 1870–1900', *Journal of Southern History*, 55 (May 1989), pp. 195–216.

Morris R. B., 'The Confederation Period and the American Historian', *William and Mary Quarterly*, 3:13 (April 1956), pp. 139–56.

Nichols, R. F., 'Federalism versus Democracy', in *Federalism as a Democratic Process* (New Brunswick, NJ: Rutgers University Press, 1942), pp. 49–75.

Noll, F., 'The United States Public Debt, 1861–1975', *EH.NET Encyclopedia*,

R. Whaples (ed.) http://eh.net/encyclopedia/article/noll.publicdebt.

O'Brien, P. K., 'The Political Economy of British Taxation, 1660-1815', *Economic History Review*, 2:41 (February 1988), pp. 1–32.

O'Brien, P. K., and P. A. Hunt, 'The Rise of the Fiscal State in England, 1485–1815', *Historical Research: The Bulletin of the Institute of Historical Research*, 66 (June 1993), pp. 129–76.

Ohline, H. A., 'Republicanism and Slavery: Origins of the Three-Fifths Clause in the United States Constitution', *William and Mary Quarterly*, 3:28 (October 1971), pp. 563–84.

Paludan, P. S., 'What Did the Winners Win? The Social and Economic History of the North During the Civil War', in J. M. McPherson and W. J. Cooper, Jr (eds), *Writing the Civil War: The Quest to Understand* (Columbia, SC: University of South Carolina Press, 1998).

Patterson, R. T. 'Government Finance on the Eve of the Civil War', *Journal of Economic History*, 12 (Winter 1952), pp. 35–44.

Pessen, E., 'Wealth in America before 1865', in W. D. Rubinstein (ed.) *Wealth and the Wealthy in the Modern World* (London: Croom Helm, 1980), pp. 167–88.

Phillips, J. B., 'Methods of Keeping the Public Money of the United States', *Publications of the Michigan Political Science Association*, 4 (1900–2), pp. 1–159.

Pincus, J. J., 'Pressure Groups and the Pattern of Tariffs', *Journal of Political Economy*, 83 (August 1975), 757–78.

Poll, R. A., and R. W. Hansen, 'Buchanan's Blunder: The Utah War, 1857–1858', *Military Affairs*, 25 (Autumn 1961), pp. 121–31.

Rakove, J., 'The Articles of Confederation', in J. P. Greene and J. R. Pole (eds) *The Blackwell Encyclopedia of the American Revolution* (Cambridge, MA: Basil Blackwell, Inc., 1991), pp. 289–95.

—, 'The Origins of Judicial Review: A Place for New Contexts', *Stanford Law Review*, 49 (May 1997), pp. 1031–64.

Ransom, R., 'Fact and Counterfact: the Second American Revolution Revisited', *Civil War History*, 45 (March 1999), pp. 28–60.

Rezneck, S., 'The Social History of an American Depression, 1837-1843', *American Historical Review*, 40 (July 1935), pp. 662–87.

—, 'The Influence of the Depression upon American Opinion, 1857–1859', *Journal of Economic History*, 11 (May 1942), pp. 1–23.

Richardson, H. C., 'A Marshall Plan for the South? The Failure of Republican and Democratic Ideology During the Reconstruction', *Civil War History,* 51 (December 2005), pp. 378–87.

Robertson, D. B., 'The Return to History and the New Institutionalism in American Political Science', *Social Science History*, 17 (Spring 1993), pp. 1–36.

Rolnick, A. J., and W. E. Weber, 'The Causes of Free Bank Failures: A Detailed Examination', *Journal of Monetary Economics*, 14 (1984), pp. 267–91.

Rousseau, P. L., 'A Common Currency: Early US Monetary Policy and the Transition to the Dollar', *Financial History Review*, 13:1 (2006), pp. 97–8.

Rousseau, P. L. and R.Sylla, 'Emerging Financial Markets and Early US Growth', *Explorations in Economic History*, 42 (January, 2005), pp. 1–26.

Scheiber, H. N., 'The Pet Banks in Jacksonian Politics and Finance, 1833-1841', *Journal of Economic History*, 23 (June 1963), pp. 196–214.

—, 'Federalism and Legal Process: Historical and Contemporary Analysis of the American System', *Law and Society Review*, 14 (Spring 1980), pp. 663–722.

Schweitzer, M., 'State-Issued Currency and the Ratification of the US Constitution', *Journal of Economic History*, 49 (June 1989), p. 315.

Seligman, E. R. A., "Remarks on the General Problem of Tax Reform," *Publications of the Michigan Political Science Association*, IV (1900-1902): 279-284.

Skeen, C. E., 'Vox Populi, Voc Dei: The Compensation Act of 1816 and the Rise of Popular Politics', *Journal of the Early Republic*, 6 (Autumn 1986), pp. 253–74.

Slaughter, T. P., 'The Tax Man Cometh: Ideological Opposition to Internal Taxes, 1760–1790', *William and Mary Quarterly*, 3:41(October 1984), pp. 566–91.

Smith, D. V., 'Chase and Civil War Politics', *Ohio Archaeological and Historical Quarterly*, 3 (July–October, 1930), pp. 51–63.

Stegmaier, M. J., 'Intensifying the Sectional Conflict', *Civil War History*, 31 (September 1985), pp. 197–221.

Stevens, E. J., 'Composition of the Money Stock Prior to the Civil War', *Journal of Money, Credit, and Banking*, 3 (February 1971), pp. 84–101.

Sylla, R., 'The United States, 1863–1913', in *Banking and Economic Development: Some Lessons of History* (New York: Oxford University Press, 1972), pp. 232–62.

—, 'Political Economy and Financial Development: Canada and the United States in the Mirror of the Other, 1790–1840', *Enterprise and Society*, 7 (December 2006), p. 657.

Sylla, R., J. B. Legler and J. J. Wallis, 'Banks and State Finance in the New Republic: The United States, 1790–1860', *Journal of Economic History*, 47 (June 1987), pp. 391–403.

Terrill, T. E., 'David A. Wells, the Democracy, and Tariff Reduction, 1877–1894', *Journal of American History*, 56 (December 1969), pp. 540–55.

Timberlake, R. H., Jr 'The Independent Treasury and Monetary Policy Before the Civil War', *Southern Economic Journal*, 27 (October 1960), p. 95.

Van Riper, P. P. and K. A. Sutherland, 'The Northern Civil Service: 1861–1865', *Civil War History*, 11 (December 1965), p. 351–69.

Venable, R. M., 'Partition of Powers Between the Federal and State Governments', *Report of the Annual Meeting of the American Bar Association*, 8 (August 1885), pp. 235–59.

Wallis, J. J., 'Constitutions, Corporations, and Corruption: American States and Constitutional Change, 1842-1852' *Journal of Economic History*, 65 (March 2005), pp. 211–56.

Weiman, D. F., 'Introduction to the special issue on the Formation of an American Monetary Union', *Financial History Review*, 13 (April 2006), pp. 11–17.

Weir, D. R., 'Tontines, Public Finance, and the Revolution in France and England, 1688–1789', *Journal of Economic History*, 49 (March 1989), p. 95–124.

Wells, D. A., 'An Income Tax: Is It Desirable?', *The Forum* (March 1894), pp. 1–13.

Willard, K. L., T. W. Guinnanc, and H. S. Rosen. 'Turning Point in the Civil War: Views from the Greenback Market', *American Economic Review*, 86 (September 1996), pp. 1001–18.

Unpublished Material

Cooper, R. A., *British Government Finance, 1793-1807: The Development of a Policy Based on War Taxes* (PhD thesis, University of North Carolina, Chapel Hill, 1976).

Cummings, J W., 'Financing the Mexican American War '(PhD thesis, Oklahoma State University, 2003).

Flaherty, J., 'The Revenue Imperative' (MA thesis, Texas A&M University, August, 2000).

—, 'The Perceived Power: Government and Taxation during the Civil War' (PhD dissertation, Texas A&M University, 2005).

Joseph, A. M., 'The Cheerful Taxpayer: An Early Modern Political Idiom in the Early American Republic' (Paper read at SHEAR Annual Conference, October, 2000, Buffalo, NY).

Lee, Arthur M. 'The Development of an Economic Policy in the Early Republican Party' (PhD dissertation, Syracuse University, 1953).

Noll, F., 'The Start of a Government Monopoly: Civil War Finance, the Rise of the Bureau of Engraving and Printing, and the Decline of Bank Note Companies, 1863' (Paper read at the 2004 Economic and Business Historical Society Conference, April 2005, Anaheim, CA).

Weidenmeir, M. D., 'Financial Aspects of the American Civil War: War News, Price Risk, and the Processing of Information' (PhD dissertation, University of Illinois, Urbana, 1999).

Wright, R. E., 'Born in Debt: American First National Debt and Its Lessons for Today' (Preprint draft, 2007).

INDEX

For Product Safety Concerns and Information please contact our EU
representative GPSR@taylorandfrancis.com Taylor & Francis Verlag GmbH,
Kaufingerstraße 24, 80331 München, Germany

Printed and bound by CPI Group (UK) Ltd, Croydon, CR0 4YY
08/05/2025
01864509-0001